GW00836741

The
Flying Sheikh

The Flying Sheikh

Najib Alamuddin

Quartet Books
London

First published by Quartet Books Limited 1987
A member of the Namara Group
27/29 Goodge Street, London W1P 1FD

British Library Cataloguing in Publication Data
Alamuddin, Najib
    The flying sheikh.
    1. Middle East Airlines—History
    I. Title
    387.7'095692   HE9868.2.M5

ISBN 0 7043 2640 X

Typeset by M.C. Typeset Limited, Chatham, Kent
Printed and bound in Great Britain
by the Camelot Press, Southampton

Contents

The
Flying Sheikh

Introduction

I set out to write this autobiography, partly for the benefit of my family and friends and partly, it must be admitted, for the pleasures and chagrin of recalling times past with all their triumphs and disappointments. But, as I proceeded, it became clear that, if I was to write a faithful account, I needed also to outline and comment upon the recent history of my beloved Lebanon. I was also concerned to record for posterity the rise of an amazing phenomenon in the history of civil aviation, Middle East Airlines, whose path to success has taken up so much of my life. This is therefore not just an autobiography, the story of a man, but also the story of an airline and a country.

It has been ready for publication for some time, but the insane war of hatred, greed and factional prejudice in Lebanon, with all the twisted logic and denials of truth it involves, has held me back until now. But recognizing that, for me, time is getting short, I have decided to go ahead now and publish. I have kept a great number of secrets, the divulgence of which could hurt many and even destroy some. Aside from sensationalism and the personal satisfaction of revenge – human failings I have always abhorred – there would be no benefits to be gained from their disclosure. I mention only those actions which have, in my opinion, been partly responsible for the present misery of Lebanon, and from which I hope a lesson may be learnt for the future so that any recurrence of the terrible orgies of killings and destruction of the past years may be avoided. Even these truths may well be resented by some, but that matters little to me. An autobiography that shied away from truth would be better left unwritten.

Acknowledgements

I have been greatly encouraged by my wife Ida, who, as has become her second nature, urged me to do what I believed was right. She has read and reread what I have written, giving valuable observations and constructive suggestions. To her goes my heartfelt gratitude and deepest love.

Frank O'Shanohun, my life-long friend, who lived my MEA life with me as the company's public-relations consultant, dedicated supporter and loyal friend, pitched in with my wife Ida in a joint final push to persuade me to publish this autobiography. His help was invaluable.

To Christopher Dobson and Ronald Payne, I want to record my appreciation and sincere thanks for their valuable contribution in editing my work.

Lilo Weigel, my private secretary, typed and retyped the manuscript with tenacious enthusiasm and genuine pleasure. To her, too, go my grateful thanks.

When I hesitated to publish this autobiography, my children, I am happy to say, not only encouraged me to go ahead, but insisted I should write the story of my life in MEA and place on record what I knew of the reasons for why Lebanon has been plunged into its present tragedy.

1
The Druzes

I am a Lebanese Druze, born on 9 March 1909 in Lebanon, before it became a cockpit of violence for quarrelling man. Today the Druzes in Lebanon number about 250,000 – only 10 per cent of the Lebanese population. This is, at best, an inspired guess, for, since 1932, no census has been permitted by successive Lebanese governments. The Druzes, although always a minority, have played an important and, at times, a leading role in the political and social life of the Middle East and in its economic and cultural affairs. For the benefit of those who are not acquainted with the Druze religion – and there cannot be many who are – let me give a short résumé of the Druze faith and its history.

The Druze faith came into being in the eleventh century AD, during the reign of the sixth Caliph of the Fatimid dynasty, Al-Hakim bi-Amrillah (Ruler by God's command). Its headquarters were in Cairo, but the faith thrived in Mount Lebanon and the Anti-Lebanon range, in northern and south-western Syria, in and around Damascus and in northern Palestine. As a result of internal feuds in the early eighteenth century, a substantial secessionist group of Druzes migrated from Lebanon into Hauran in southern Syria and settled as a powerful community in what is known now as Jabal-ad-Duruz (the mountain of the Druzes).

During the second half of the sixteenth century and the first half of the seventeenth, the Druze Emir of the Ma'nid dynasty, Fakhruddin II, was the first to establish in the Lebanon a state practically independent of Ottoman rule. He may be regarded as the founder of modern Lebanon. At one time, this state extended almost as far as Anatolia in the north; in the east, it included Palmyra in Syria, and in the south reached Sinai. During the seventeenth and eighteenth centuries, the Druzes were divided into two feuding clans – Qaysis and Yamanis. Their division and their feuds were a legacy of the two early Arabian

1

parties: the Qaysites, emigrants from north Arabia, and the Yamanites, earlier emigrants from southern Arabia.

The Qaysi and Yamani conflict was not confined to the Druzes. It spread across the Moslem world from Iran to Spain. Among the Druzes, the Qaysi and Yamani clans perpetuated themselves later into Yazbakis (Yamanis) and Jumblattis (Qaysis), and the Druzes are still so divided. They are headed, in their clannish division, by two feudal families: the Jumblattis by the Jumblatt family and the Yazbakis by the Arslan family. These two families have shared equal power and authority over the Druze community until recently, when the Jumblatts took the lead. Of contemporary international fame, there was the late leader Kamal Jumblatt; and today there is his son Walid, who succeeded to the leadership after his father's assassination in 1977.

The rift between the clans was utilized to 'divide and rule'. It was encouraged and spurred on first by the Turks, then by the French, and finally by various successive Lebanese governments which have ruled since independence in 1943. Despite internal political differences, however, the Druzes will quickly close ranks and emerge as a formidable fighting force to confront anyone who attempts to threaten their survival, rights, land or well-being as a community.

President Reagan discovered this in 1983–4 when he committed a powerful United States armada – thirty warships, including two aircraft carriers with 300 fighter bomber aircraft, the battleship *New Jersey*, with its immense guns assisted by a sprinkling of warships from Nato countries – in an attempt to convince the Druzes, Reagan style, by bombing and shelling their homes and villages with thousands of tons of explosives, that they should surrender their ancestral lands and Lebanese rights. This misguided, ill-conceived venture failed miserably and the Americans withdrew, covered with an embarrassment and shame like that felt by the followers of Goliath after his confrontation with David – the difference being that Goliath was not doing it to win elections at home.

Of course, it may not have been the Druzes but the presence of advanced Russian missiles and their technicians, planted in Lebanon and Syria and capable of striking at the heart of Israel, that was the true objective of the mighty armada. But of this there are only political rumours and hearsay and it was, in any case, the Druzes not the Russians who paid the price.

In our family, as children, we grew up as true Lebanese – Druze Lebanese. We were oblivious to the Yazbaki–Jumblatti politics. I was not even conscious that the Alamuddins are Yazbakis until the day when the late Kamal Jumblatt invited me to join his list of candidates for the Lebanese Parliament. Because of my conviction that Middle East Airlines, of which I was then chairman, should not become involved in politics, I declined the invitation with thanks. He then said to me, with a smile: 'You must appreciate the fact that I, Kamal Jumblatt, am asking a Yazbaki to join my list of candidates.' Until then, I had not known or bothered to find out that the Alamuddins are Yazbakis.

Several Druze princes followed Fakhruddin II as rulers of Lebanon, the first among these being the Alamuddins. The Alamuddins were the Yamani standard bearers, the name in Arabic meaning 'the flag of religion'. Some historians state that the Alamuddins were wiped out in 1711, together with several of their closest supporters, in the Yamani massacre by the Qaysis in Ayn Dara, a village in the mountains east of Beirut. Others claim that at least one boy escaped and kept the Alamuddin line going, hence the family's existence today. These historians substantiate their claim by referring to the Druze rule of war, which decreed that only males between the ages of seven and seventy were to be killed in battle, and reason that there must have been Alamuddin males under the age of seven who escaped the massacre. Whatever the truth may be, the princely title was too expensive to keep up after the Alamuddins' assets were plundered by the victors in the battle of Ayn Dara, and a wise ancestor changed it to the more modest sheikh. I personally enjoyed the prestige of bearing the hereditary title of an ancient sheikhdom, especially when I was doing my post-graduate work in England. I confess I exploited its Rudolph Valentino overtones to the maximum. Alas, for all those pleasurable advantages in the 1930s, I have had to pay heavily in the 1970s and 1980s.

The Druzes have always been noted for their resistance to foreign rule. They were, as a minority group, involved in the wars against Turkish and later French domination. In these campaigns, they showed distinguished military ability. Earlier battles against Crusaders and Mongols likewise won the Druzes a reputation for courage and chivalry in which they still take great pride.

The French traveller, C. F. Volney, described them in the eighteenth century:

> . . . daring even to temerity, and sometimes ferocious, they possess, above all, two qualities essential to the excellency of any troops; they strictly obey their leaders, and are endowed with a temperance and vigour of health unknown to most civilized nations . . . Had they among them a few persons versed in military science, they would

readily acquire its principles and become a formidable soldiery . . . There are no Druzes in the cities or on the coast . . . No people are more nice than they with respect to the point of honour . . . [There is] in their manner and discourse a reserve, or if you will, a politeness which one is astonished to discover among peasants . . . The Druzes have another point of honour: that of hospitality . . . Like the Bedouins they pay great respect to the antiquity of families. [Their] proper and distinguishing characteristic is a sort of republican spirit . . . and an indifference to religion.

The Druzes are fatalists and strongly believe that what is written is written and that, at birth, a Druze's age on this earth is recorded in the book of destiny. Nothing in the world can prolong or shorten it. 'He who is destined for nine will never die at ten. Every bullet has an address, and will find it no matter what you do.' These are universally popular sayings among the Druzes. Their belief in an age fixed at birth goes some way to explain their extraordinary courage and lion-hearted bravery in battle. Incredible feats of daring and heroism abound in Druze folklore.

From its inception, the Druze faith demanded the abolition of slavery and polygamy — courageous and revolutionary measures at a time when both those practices were an accepted way of life. During their early history, however, the Druzes suffered a seven-year campaign of persecution and terror such as few communities have ever had the misfortune to experience. Thousands upon thousands were massacred, burnt alive, drowned at sea, crucified and subjected to torture in its vilest forms. Infants were slain in their mothers' arms and men were slaughtered and had their heads impaled on warriors' spears or suspended from the necks of their wives and daughters. Others were dragged by their feet through the streets.

The bloodbath was ordered by the Fatimid Prince Ali, the successor to Caliph Al-Hakim bin-Amrillah, who had disappeared on the night of 12/13 February 1021 and was never seen again. However, before his disappearance, Al-Hakim had summoned Prince Ali and made him solemnly promise to protect his followers, the Druzes, and not maltreat them. It was said Al-Hakim had made the prince take forty oaths to that effect. But as soon as Ali was officially proclaimed Caliph, he went back on his forty oaths and claimed they had expired, at the rate of one a day, forty days after Al-Hakim's disappearance. He was therefore free to inflict on the Druzes any persecution he wished, and this he promptly ordered.

4

From Antioch to Alexandria the Druzes thus suffered their seven-year nightmare of horror and terror in the Caliph's determination to annihilate them. Secrecy therefore became essential for survival, and the Druze religion was forced underground; and so it has remained until the present day. Where a secret has been kept closely guarded for over eight hundred years, it becomes a self-perpetuating, integral part of the life of the community which shares it.

Yet there is really nothing to hide. It is a religion chiselled out of Islam, based on the strict, uncompromising belief in the unity of God and on a direct communion between the individual and the Almighty. There are no intermediaries. Prayer meeting-places are simple structures, indistinguishable from the houses around them. There are no calls or reminders for prayer, no bells or muezzins, and attendance is absolutely voluntary. The religion is not taught in schools. The 'secret' religious books and studies are the preserve of those who ask to be initiated into the religion and are kept secret from all others. The initiated are few and live truly monastic lives which they spend working, praying, doing good and walking humbly in the Faith. They distance themselves from the weaknesses of the flesh and are called the *Uqqal* (the Wise). The uninitiated make up the majority of the Druzes and are known as the *Juhhal* (the Ignorant). They are not allowed to read or even to see the books. I have never myself been privileged to see them. In our household, my mother guarded them, and I believe my eldest sister Nabiha has them now.

The first time I arrived in New York, an immigration officer, for reasons of his own, asked about my religion. 'Druze,' I replied.

'Jews,' he stated.

'No, no, Druze,' I repeated.

'What sort of religion is this?' he asked.

'It is a secret religion,' I replied.

He looked at me sternly, thinking I was making fun of him, and said: 'Come, come, now. There are no secret religions. Tell me something about it.'

'Friend,' I replied, 'it is so secret that I know nothing about it myself.'

Luckily, at this moment, his superior arrived to find what was keeping us so long at the head of a long queue steadily getting longer. My passport was quickly stamped and I was glad to move out of the immigration hall into the land of opportunity.

The Druzes strongly believe in reincarnation. All souls were, according to Druze belief, created at the same time. Upon death, a soul

5

is instantly reborn in another human body. The body serves on this earth as a temporary home for the soul, all souls being created with an equal capacity for good and evil, free to choose between right and wrong and responsible for the consequences of their choice. The soul experiences in its repeated reincarnations all conditions of life, such as fortune and misfortune, riches and poverty, health and illness. Souls are thus granted repeated opportunities to redeem themselves and face an equitable sentence on the Day of Judgement.

It is in their homes that Druze children learn from their mothers and grandmothers what is right and what is wrong, and it is there, in their early years, that their character is shaped for life. The Druze community has the highest ethical behaviour. Truthfulness heads the list. They do not break their word. Hospitality is inbred and earns blessing, for, to them, the most blessed food is that around which many hands gather. Charity is commanded, and it is the responsibility of a person of means, when he makes his will, to leave one twelfth of what he possesses to the poor, the needy and the pious. They respect their elders and treat them with utmost courtesy. They keep faith with all who live in their midst, whatever their religious beliefs. Gentleness and humility are qualities of the Druzes, except when the community is in danger, and then they spring like tigers to its defence.

The call to the Faith was ended very early in the Druze history, and the door to join the religion was sealed for all time. A Druze is born and never converted from another religion. Likewise, he will not himself accept a conversion and missionaries have spent years in futile attempts to persuade Druzes to change their religion.

When a British Anglican mission moved to Baaqline, the village of my birth in Lebanon, they built a prestigious and prominent compound with many substantial buildings, the first to have a tiled roof in the village. They set out to help the needy under the efficient leadership of a Miss Kitchen, head of the mission. After a couple of years of dedicated mission work and appreciable help and assistance to the local population, Miss Kitchen succeeded in convincing Abou Qasim, the mission's gardener, he should convert to Christianity. There was jubilation in the mission and at its headquarters in England, and hopes soared that the Druzes, following Abou Qasim's example, could at last be made to see the light. Things went well for Abou Qasim, who had a large family and much need for his newly increased salary and privileges. However, no other Druzes followed in his footsteps, and as time went by, old age took its toll of Abou Qasim. He fell ill and sent for Miss Kitchen, who hurried to his bedside. He told her how much he

6

enjoyed being a Christian and thanked her profusely for all she had done for him. But he had one last request before he passed on. 'Anything you wish, dear Abou Qasim,' replied Miss Kitchen. After a long sigh, Abou Qasim uttered his deathbed wish. 'I was honoured and dearly loved being a Christian,' he said, 'but I want to die a Druze.'

Baaqline is the largest Druze village in the Shuf district of Lebanon. It is built on a range of hills and faces Dayr Al-Qammar, its Maronite Christian counterpart, across a beautiful valley at the head of which rises the palace of Beit-Eddine, the seat of the Shihabis who succeeded the Ma'ns as rulers of Lebanon.

It was in 1120 that the founder of the house of Ma'n chose Baaqline for his headquarters. In 1613, nearly 500 years later, the Ma'ni seat moved to neighbouring Dayr Al-Qammar, which was, like Baaqline, inhabited jointly by Maronite Christians and Druzes, as were most of the villages of the Shuf district. For over 250 years, Dayr Al-Qammar continued with its mixed population of Druzes and Maronites living in peace and friendship, until the troubles of the mid-nineteenth century culminated in the massacres of 1860. Afterwards, a process of voluntary rehabilitation made Dayr Al-Qammar a Maronite Christian village and Baaqline overwhelmingly Druze. For a long time, Christian families continued to live in Baaqline. I vividly remember Said Haddad, the last male member of the remarkable Haddad Christian family, who was and felt more Baaqlini than I. Despite the recent factional hostilities, Said continued to live in Baaqline until 1981, when he died of old age. His coffin and the crosses in his funeral procession were carried by the Baaqline Druzes — his fellow villagers and friends. The church bells were tolled by Young Druze men and the church continues to stand intact, respected and well cared for.

The Alamuddins have lived in Baaqline since time immemorial. During the last quarter of the nineteenth century, my grandfather built himself a more modern house with very thick walls and vaulted ceilings. He then left the ancestral home, where, it is said, Fakhruddin II was born, with its historical relics and engraved inscriptions, and moved into his new architectural pride. The ancestral home, with all its Alamuddin mementoes, was eventually destroyed in the earthquake of 1956, to be replaced by an enlarged road and shops that were constructed on what remained. Unfortunately, not only had our grandfather been guilty of neglect for the ancestral relics, but so had his children and grandchildren, for none had shown any desire to study, copy or photograph or read the family historical engravings before they were irretrievably destroyed.

7

My father, Sheikh Salim, son of Sheikh Sulayman, married Sitt Wadad of the Takieddines, who were another notable Druze family of Baaqline. The bride was, by Druze tradition, chosen by the groom's mother, but my father was a rebel and stubbornly insisted on at least seeing his future partner. A compromise was finally reached. The bride-to-be was invited, with her mother and aunts, to visit my grandmother. On that occasion, my father was secretly allowed to see his future bride through a keyhole. Despite this novel process of telescopic bride selection, the marriage lasted sixty-six years in an atmosphere of peace and happiness and exemplary family life. My father died on 10 May 1966 at the age of eighty-three, and my mother on 22 January 1973 at the age of eighty-seven.

The keyhole-chosen wife blessed my father with five children – my three sisters, my brother and me. We were all born in Baaqline and grew up in the various Lebanese towns and villages where my father's duties as a judge took him. My sisters and brother all married Druzes, while I, another rebel, married a Christian. My sisters were destined to contribute in their own right to the social and cultural life of Lebanon and of the Druze community.

Nabiha, the eldest, organized and chaired a woman's charitable society in Baaqline which provided medical aid, social and financial relief and practical advice to the menfolk and government administrators – not only in Baaqline affairs, but for those of neighbouring villages as well.

My second sister, Jamal, is a born leader, known affectionately in the family as the 'Field Marshal'. She founded the Shuf Artisanat for embroidery and other works of art, which she developed into a most successful village industry, providing work for scores of women who might otherwise have remained idle, bored and totally dependent on the men in their families even for pocket money. The Artisanat, under her leadership, holds a yearly charity bazaar, the proceeds of which go to the poor and the distressed. During the fighting which plagued the Shuf district following the Israeli invasion in the summer of 1982, she organized, with the help of other Druze women, an efficient refugee relief operation, so easing the misery of thousands displaced by the battles.

My younger sister, Souad, is a founder member of the Association of the Baalbeck International Festival and continues to serve as vice-president of the executive committee. She was especially involved in developing and promoting the Lebanese theatre, which was, prior to her initiative, non-existent. She was appointed Member of the National

Council of Tourism and served on it as the only female member between 1970 and 1981.

All my sisters have followed the path of our mother's love for helping the needy and, like her, do much of that work discreetly and without sectarian discrimination.

My brother Sulayman graduated from the American University of Beirut, joined Near East Resources (NER), a company I formed, and took over its management when I was persuaded to join the management of Middle East Airlines. NER prospered under his leadership, most of his business being with the United Kingdom and so producing hundreds of millions of pounds sterling of British exports to the Lebanon and the Arab world. He was awarded the British CBE (Commander of the British Empire) a few years after I had received that honour myself. The *Daily Telegraph*, with typical English wit, mentioned the honour bestowed on us under a news item headed 'A Brace of Sheikhs', stating: 'When Sheikh Sulayman Alamuddin was invested with the CBE at the British Embassy in Beirut the other day he became the second brother in this distinguished Druze family so honoured.' I am told that we qualify for an entry in the *Guinness Book of Records*, for not only are we the only two Druze brothers to be honoured with the CBE, but we are also the only two Arab brothers to have merited this distinction.

My father was a benevolent tyrant, and my mother an angel who firmly ruled the tyrant and us, the children, with kindness and love. While we feared and respected our father and obeyed his orders, sometimes under silent protest, we adored our mother and would do nothing to displease her. She was quiet, efficient, kind and generous, in a humble and discreet way. She imposed a firm discipline through understanding and love, was soft spoken, and I never heard her speak in a loud voice or with excitement. She taught us our religion, our faith in God and in ourselves, and the standards of behaviour towards our fellow beings.

My mother, as the ruling matriarch of our family, was not unique among the Druzes, for our religion preached from its early birth equality between the sexes. It rejected the entrenched belief that woman was inferior to man and established women's right to share privileges as well as responsibilities equally with men. Druze women, in the past, attended councils of war, were consulted and had their opinions respected. Today, they are always treated as equal partners, not only in the family but in the community. George Sandys, an English traveller who visited Lebanon in 1610, wrote in his book *A Relation of a Journey*

9

(London, 1621) about the great Druze, Fakhreddin II, that he 'never commenced battal, nor executed any notable design without the consent of his mother Al-Sitt [lady] Nasibah [Nasab]'.

The respected and equal role of Druze women was acknowledged and practised soon after the birth of the Druze faith. When, in 1034–5, a dissident movement arose within the followers of the faith in the far regions of Wadi et-Taym, in the Anti-Lebanon mountains, Baheddin Al-Muqtana, the chief aide to Hamza ibn Ali, the proclaimed Imam of the Druze Movement, chose a young woman, Sitt Sarah, to head an all-male delegation to proceed from Cairo to quell the dissidence in turbulent and hostile Wadi et-Taym. It was a most delicate and dangerous mission. A previous male messenger, one of his close aides, had been assassinated upon arrival.

Sarah's mission was a success because the dissidents were captivated by her wisdom, knowledge and sincerity. What was most remarkable, apart from her leadership as a woman in charge of what, in those times, was definitely a man's job, was the fact that in the delegation she headed was her father, the brother of Baheddin Al-Muqtana. He did not mind serving under his daughter and was not concerned that his brother had not entrusted him with this important mission. Both reactions were an early example of the Druze belief in the equality of men and women. It is hard to find a more dramatic example of disciplined acceptance of women's leadership and authority. Sitt Sarah was the first of many women who earned their place in the gallery of fame in Druze history.

From my father, I also learned to be Lebanese and not only Druze, for he was a great believer in Lebanese unity, irrespective of sectarian considerations. His most intimate friends, who were like brothers to him, were Rashid Nakhleh, the famous Maronite poet, Dr Habib Nassif, a Maronite from Jezzine, Bishara Haddad, another Maronite from Jezzine, and Mohammed Jalloul, a Shi'ite Moslem from Bourj el-Barajneh, the scene of the recent and much publicized Shi'ite confrontations with the Lebanese army and the multi-national Peace Keeping Force. To us children, they were all uncles, being a part of our family and we a part of theirs. It was as natural as the Lebanese air we breathed.

After retiring from the courts in 1926, where he was Counsellor at the Court of Appeal, my father partnered two eminent lawyers, a Moslem and a Christian, and established a joint Lebanese legal firm, the first of its kind in those days. Alas, it failed, like so many ventures which aim to convince the Lebanese they are first and foremost Lebanese and not just members of one or other of the many religious communities living in the country. Up to the present day, I could not say whether the Christian partner in the firm was Maronite, Greek Orthodox, Catholic or Protestant. After that painful experience, my father retired to live quietly but in perfect peace on our ancestral farm in southern Lebanon.

I was educated at the American University of Beirut and graduated in 1928–9 with a degree in engineering and mathematics. I played football in the varsity team and was joint captain of the team – a typical Lebanese compromise and probably the only example of two captains for one team in the history of football.

During the summer preceding my senior year at the university, I fell ill with typhoid, which cost me the first academic half of my senior year. I rejoined the classes at mid-term, when the university proposed I take a part-time teaching job and graduate the following year. The part-time job led to my teaching mathematics at the university for four years. I was nineteen years old when I took up teaching, and many of my students were of my own age or even older. They came from all parts of the Arab world, and were not only my students but my friends.

The American University of Beirut was, at the time, the only university in the Middle East where the sons of rulers, sheikhs, important government officials and wealthy merchants could go for their higher education. Most of them were destined to hold important government and business positions. At one time in later years I could count seven prime ministers and scores of ministers in the Arab world who had been either my university mates or my students.

The American University in Beirut was founded in 1866 as the Syrian Protestant College by American missionaries, whose sole objective was to give spiritual guidance and genuine help to the people of Lebanon and the Middle East. Those missionaries were dedicated and taught us, among other important things, that justice is the sacred right of every human being. Their teachings were the basic principles of human rights. In later life, I saw human rights being interpreted not only in political terms but blatantly manipulated and exploited.

How different is the behaviour of the world today from the honest and sincere Christian teachings of the early missionaries at the American University of Beirut. Unfortunately, even in that university, a change set in as the sources of dedicated missionaries dried up. Different types of Americans replaced the missionaries, ones who were not religiously dedicated but who were attracted by the salaries and a desire to see the world. The change was marked. Mine was the first generation of graduates to feel and perhaps resent the impact of this change.

11

I have always been a rebel — not politically, but a rebel against injustice and discrimination in any shape or form, and especially against social injustice. It must come from my Druze heritage. The Druze have always been a minority, and minorities are especially sensitive over their rights, for they have to fight injustice in order to survive.

When I joined the university as a teacher, I disliked the discriminations practised against Lebanese teachers that set them apart from the Americans. Lebanese teachers were not permitted to have corner bedrooms — which, having two windows, were reserved for Americans and Europeans — but were allotted secondary rooms with only one window. This may sound petty, but two windows made a tremendous difference in the hot seasons in Beirut before the introduction of air conditioning. After my first year as a boarding teacher, I created a sensation by moving into a corner room on the same floor which became vacant after an American teacher went home. When I told the Principal that, if he tried to move me, I would resign and make public my reasons, he reluctantly agreed to overlook my trespassing. There was no further discrimination in accommodation.

I was also surprised to discover that American teachers ate together at their own tables in the dining-room while Lebanese teachers ate at others, an imaginery iron curtain hanging between them. I decided to breach the curtain by coming in early one day and going to the American tables for breakfast. The American teachers arrived and there were some angry looks, but nothing else happened. From that time on, all the teachers ate together and there was harmony among us.

Lebanese teachers were not permitted to date American girls. There was no written rule about it, but a ban was clearly maintained against such fraternization. When a visiting American girl wanted me to show her the sights of Beirut, she and I were told gently but firmly that this was not done. I regarded it as a silly infringement of our rights and said it was up to the girl to decide. She refused to be intimidated and we spent a highly enjoyable evening together. We ate a delicious dinner at Ajami's restaurant, which specialized in Lebanese cooking, and still does, and called at the fashionable Kit Kat cabaret to dance. We ended the evening with a drive by the seashore, under a beautiful Beirut full moon, before driving back to her host's house, making sure to arrive at a decent hour to disarm any criticism. It was a normal evening out for two young people, but one made especially enjoyable by the knowledge we were engaged in an act of defiance against bigotry.

The university was basically a charitable institution. The fees charged were never adequate to cover expenses, and only a yearly subsidy from donations and contributions from the United States kept it going. When recession hit the United States in the early 1930s, the university faculty were forced to take drastic measures, one of them being to reduce the salaries of the teaching staff by 25 per cent. The salaries were in dollars, and had been low in any case, and with the cut and the reduced value of the dollar, their value in Lebanese pounds reached an extremely low level. The teaching staff met to consider the cut and formed a committee, of which I was a member, to appeal to the president of the university against what the teachers saw as a harsh decision. The appeal was rejected and the teachers were tactlessly, even rudely, told that, if any of them was dissatisfied, he would be released from his contract to take a job elsewhere, if he was able to find one. I resigned immediately and learnt, from one of my students, of an opening for an Inspector of Education (Mathematics and English) in the government of what was then known as the Emirate of Transjordan. I applied for the post and was accepted immediately.

I never, however, completely severed my relations with the university. In 1964, I was elected as a member of its Board of Trustees, and when I resigned in 1972, was unanimously elected a trustee for life.

2
The Jordan Years and Palestine

When I arrived in Amman in 1933 to take up my new appointment, the city was a very different place from the bustling capital it is today. In the sea of troubles and poverty in the Middle East of that time, Transjordan was an island of tranquillity and peace. Its people were strong-willed and friendly, enthusiastically developing their new country, for Transjordan was still only eleven years old.

The country had been established in the aftermath of the First World War and the break-up of the Turkish empire, when the British and French had cynically divided the spoils of war between them on the lines set out in the Sykes–Picot agreement. This document had been signed in 1916 by Sir Mark Sykes, Foreign Office adviser on Near Eastern Affairs, and by the French representative, François Picot. It was later described by George Antonius in his book *The Arab Awakening* as a 'shocking document'. 'It is not only the product of greed at its worst . . . It also stands out as a startling piece of double-dealing.' Its very existence was revealed, to the embarrassment of the British, only when the Bolsheviks later ransacked the archives of the Tsarist Ministry of Foreign Affairs in St Petersburg. The British government had promised independence to the Arabs in return for their support against the Turks during the war. The promises were not honoured, and the Arabs felt betrayed as the British and French carved up the Middle East between them.

To compensate for the betrayal, and no doubt to ease their conscience, the British installed the two sons of Sharif Hussein of Mecca as monarchs of the two newly defined countries. Faisal became King of Iraq and Abdallah the Emir of Transjordan, until, later, he assumed the title of King. Abdallah, grandfather of the present King Hussein, ruled, under British tutelage, a territory that embraced desert country on the east bank of the Jordan and a chunk of what had once been, under the Turks, southern Syria.

Abdallah enjoyed a measure of independence in choosing a prime minister and appointing ministers to a cabinet responsible to him, but the new state remained dependent upon an annual subsidy from London, and British administrators were in charge of all government departments. The Arab Legion, Transjordan's army, was itself under the command of British officers. And ruling firmly but discreetly was the British Resident, who had the final word in everything. Yet, despite a resentment of English officials as colonial rulers, it was acknowledged that their system of administration was efficient and just. At the time when I arrived, Transjordan seemed one of the happiest small countries in the world.

As an inspector of education, I had to visit every village in Transjordan, each tour taking three to four months since there were no adequate roads, most trips being undertaken on horseback. One particularly agreeable visit was to the desert schools for the Bedouins' children. These were conducted in tents and followed the tribes about on their nomadic travels. The teachers were sons of the tribal sheikhs, selected earlier and sent by the government to high schools and then on to training-college. The tent pupils were brilliant, full of life and a delight to watch.

I also remember with pleasure the introduction of school gardens in the village schools. When a school was built, a plot of land of two and a half acres was attached to it as its garden. Village school teachers, having been trained in the Agricultural College of Tulkarm in Palestine, were thus all qualified to teach the village pupils the basic principals of agriculture. The three R's, geography, history and Qur'an were taught in the mornings, theoretical and practical agriculture in the afternoons. Experiments with selected seeds, fertilizers, irrigation and modern farming methods were carried out. The schools were a great success and popular with both parents and pupils.

My journeys to the north and to the south of Jordan needed to be planned carefully so that half the schools were inspected on the way out, the other half on the way back. This was to give me the chance of a bath, in a Tiberius hotel at the turning-point in the north, and a swim, in lieu of a bath, in the delightful bay of Aqaba in the south. There were no hotels or rest-houses in the villages, and I usually stayed in the teacher's house, or with the *mokhtar* (head of the village). It was unthinkable that an inspector of education should be seen standing naked in a shallow tub in the kitchen, pouring a bowl of hot water over himself — the method of bathing universally used by villagers. Village houses had no toilet facilities. As I look out of the window of my apartment in London, overlooking Green Park, and watch the dogs being taken out for their daily walks, I am reminded of my own experience in the villages of Jordan. It was a common sight, then, to see the school teacher taking the Inspector of Education to the outskirts of the village for his daily walk!

Then, in 1937, the Department of Education received a British Council scholarship for one student from Transjordan to be sent to England for a year of study. The Department and Sir Henry Cox, the British Resident, chose to send me to assess the value of such scholarships, and so, in the summer of that year, I joined the University College of the South-West at Exeter in Devon.

An amusing incident marked my arrival in England. A small residential hotel had been chosen for my stay in London before moving on to Exeter. The morning after I disembarked, I walked into the sitting-room and was pleasantly surprised to find Dan Dennett, an American friend from my teaching years at the American University in Beirut. Dan had the American love of loudly criticizing everything which differed from the American way of life. Naturally, he saw much to criticize in England, and was quite vociferous about it, especially during mealtimes. Many of the residents at the hotel were retired colonial government officers and their ladies, and there was no doubting their failure to appreciate Dan's views, but generally nothing was said. Then, one morning at breakfast, an old lady at the next table said to her companion in a voice to be heard by all: 'What do you expect from the Americans, my dear, they are nothing but white natives.'

It was typical of Dan Dennett that he greatly enjoyed the old ladies' wit. But afterwards he became far more circumspect in his criticism. Dan returned to Beirut during the Second World War, as a special official of the United States government. Sadly, he was killed in an air crash in the mountains of Ethiopia. His death was a loss to his government and country, and also to the Arabs, for he was a true friend.

I spent a year at Exeter University, during which I studied the English educational system, political economy, the English way of life, and, what proved most useful to me later, English newspapers and how they functioned. Like all Arabs of my generation, I resented foreign domination and came to the United Kingdom, the land of British colonialists, full of animosity. But when I saw the English in their own country, it was a revelation. Kind, courteous and generous, they were so different from the English we had met with in the Middle East. At

17

weekends, foreign students would be invited out in small groups to English homes. They would be driven to and from the university by their hosts, and shown every kindness. We were taken through the beautiful countryside of Devon and Cornwall, introduced to that famous institution, the English pub, and fed healthy meals while our hosts enjoyed listening to what we told them about our own countries and people. After such a weekend, it was unlikely that they and we would ever meet again. We Arabs pride ourselves on our hospitality, but that enjoyed during those weekends surpassed our own by far.

At the university I had the good fortune to meet students of twenty-five nationalities, to study with them and to compete with them on the playing-fields of Exeter. It was an experience which served as my first lesson in international understanding and helped me greatly in dealing with foreigners.

After my year at Exeter, I returned to Transjordan in the summer of 1938. Shortly after my return I was asked to accompany the Prime Minister, Toufic Pasha Abul Huda, to London as one of the two-member Jordanian delegation to the Round Table Conference on Palestine in February 1939. I was sure I had been chosen only for my knowledge of the language, because Toufic Pasha's English was not adequate for the occasion. However, as the conference progressed, I came to admire his patriotic honesty and he appreciated the help I was able to give him, and in that way a mutual friendship and respect developed.

We arrived in London six weeks before the conference started so as to negotiate modifications of the Anglo-Jordanian Treaty with the Secretary of State for the Colonies, Mr Malcolm MacDonald. The talks centred on the need to increase the annual financial subsidy. This provided my first lesson in how to negotiate from weakness and yet obtain results with dignity. Toufic Pasha handled the negotiations in a masterful manner, general agreement was soon reached and we were then left in the care of Colonial Office experts for the drafting of documents. It was a unique opportunity to learn the art of treaty drafting. Documents, it seems, are composed by experts to leave as many loopholes as possible, so giving their principals the maximum scope for different interpretations later on. I would never have believed that sentences, phrases and even words could carry so many different shades of meaning but I learned quickly, shuttling frequently between the Dorchester Hotel, where we were staying, and the Colonial Office. Sir John Shuckburgh, the Deputy Under-Secretary of State at the Colonial Office, who was my senior in position and age, seemed to take pleasure teaching me the art of drafting. Later in my career, when I had to scrutinize commercial contracts, I was grateful for the skills acquired from him.

The conference convened in February 1939 as war clouds gathered ominously in Europe. It was a last effort to find a diplomatic solution to the Palestine problem at a time when the British could spare neither troops nor money to control the conflict between Jews and Arabs. Obviously the attitude of the Arabs and the Moslem world was of great strategic importance to the British government at that time. The moving spirit behind the conference was the Colonial Secretary, Malcolm MacDonald, who had warned the House of Commons that, in Palestine, 'a strong policy could restore order, but not peace'. By chance I had already met Malcolm MacDonald in 1938, through Philip Smithels, my tutor at Exeter, who had been at school with him. He wrote to the Colonial Secretary after hearing my views on Palestine. I should like to think that my fervent presentation of the Arab viewpoint helped him to understand the depth of Arab feeling on the subject.

Ironically, Syria and Lebanon, the two countries which later became most deeply involved in the problem, were not invited. Being at the time under a French Mandate, they were not considered independent. Yet there was a Jewish delegation and squabbles began immediately, even before the official opening. The Arabs, for once displaying complete unanimity, categorically refused to meet with the Jewish delegation. The British government compromised by holding simultaneous but separate talks with both sides.

The delegations included prominent leaders from Palestine and from all the participating Arab countries, the most illustrious among them being Emir Faysal, head of the Saudi delegation, later King Faisal of Saudi Arabia. I met him frequently and was impressed by his wisdom and serenity. He was a man of few words, but those that he did speak were concise and to the point.

At the preliminary meetings, it soon became apparent that the Arabs could not agree on a unified policy. All they could do was present a front behind which they had agreed to disagree. When I think about it now, with the knowledge of what has happened in the half-century since, I feel certain that the Arabs were *never allowed* to agree on a unified policy, especially on their relations with Israel. Powerful interests who are past masters in the art of 'divide and rule' have been behind most Arab disagreement and discord.

The Jordan delegation was shunned from the start by other Arab delegations, and practically excommunicated. As representatives of

Emir Abdallah, we were accused of being there only to advance a plan for a union between Palestine and Jordan under His Highness's rule. There were meetings to which we were not invited, and many discussions froze immediately upon our arrival. The delegates, however, reversed their position once we had presented our statement to the conference. It was the strongest and toughest statement of all, and credit for it must go to Toufic Pasha Abul Huda, who was a Palestinian in origin, who loved Palestine and was one of the most honest and sincere of Arab nationalists. Unfortunately, because of protocol, our statement came at the tail end of the proceedings. Nevertheless, its enthusiastic reception by nearly all the delegates compensated, to some extent, for their earlier hostility.

There were many amusing incidents during the conference, the most memorable being the late arrival at the opening session of His Highness Saif El-Islam Hussein, head of the Yemen delegation. The Arab delegates were gathered in the imposing conference room at St James's Palace, and Mr Neville Chamberlain, the British Prime Minister, was there to deliver the opening speech. Lord Halifax, the Foreign Secretary, Malcolm MacDonald, the Colonial Secretary, and a number of other ministers and officials were also present. All the Arab delegates, except for Saif El-Islam Hussein, had arrived on time. We waited and waited. Officials telephoned his hotel only to be told he had left forty-five minutes earlier.

Protocol made the British wait for nearly fifteen minutes before they decided to proceed without him. Ten minutes later, at the close of the Prime Minister's opening speech, in he walked, magnificent in his flowing robes and using his beautifully jewelled sword as a walking-stick. In startling contrast, there trailed behind him a shabbily dressed dragoman in a civilian suit, which looked as if it had never been pressed, and with a week's stubble on his dark jowls. All eyes were on His Highness and on his extraordinary follower. Then, in mid-stride, the dragoman announced in a penetrating, high-pitched voice, 'His Highness saw zee sun and enjoyed her.' There was stunned silence. Only the good manners of the British and the embarrassment of the Arab delegates prevented a gale of laughter. We found out later that, oblivious to time, he had sat on a bench in the park, enjoying the sun, which had surprised everyone by showing itself in London in February.

A second incident occurred during the ball given by the Egyptian Embassy to celebrate the birthday of King Farouk. All the delegates were invited, as well as the upper crust of London society. We gathered in the vast ballroom, where I happened, by chance, to be standing near one of the Yemeni delegates, named Qadi Ali. At that time it was the fashion for women to wear low-cut strapless dresses, and as Qadi Ali took a look at the ladies, his beard started trembling, his eyes grew brighter and bigger and he started mumbling in Arabic, 'God save us, God forgive us, God chase the Devil.' His low-voiced supplications to Allah went on with increased intensity as more ladies arrived, and when the music started and men took women in their arms to dance, the rate of oscillation of Qadi Ali's beard increased dramatically and his eyes nearly bulged out of his head. With a wild look he turned to me and exclaimed, 'These are not men, they hold naked women in their arms and nothing happens.' It was useless to try to explain the conventions of Western dancing to a man outside Yemen for the first time in his life. Quick to defend my manhood, I nodded in agreement.

After the seventh meeting of the conference on 16 February 1939, we once again lost His Highness, Saif El-Islam Hussein, when he deserted and left for Paris. He claimed to have been insulted at a dinner given by an Arab embassy in London, where, in his opinion, Emir Faysal had been seated higher at the table than himself. Neither telephone calls nor emissaries who travelled specially to Paris could persuade him to return. Arab unity and the Palestine cause were invoked, but His Highness's personal honour and prestige were far more important, and he remained in Paris. It was only after much persuasion by the British government and some of the Arab delegations that he returned to London for the last two sessions.

In spite of His Highness's regrettable absence, the conference had gone to work, propelled by the dynamic Malcolm MacDonald. Alas, an incredible amount of time was wasted in debate on the constitutional significance of letters exchanged between Sharif Hussein of Mecca and Sir Henry MacMahon, the British High Commissioner in Cairo in 1915. Such studies were sterile and academic in 1939, especially when the Balfour Declaration of 1917, which promised a 'National Home' in Palestine to the Jews, had been implemented by the British government and been in operation for over twenty-two years. This communication to Lord Rothschild from Mr Balfour, the Foreign Secretary, on 2 November 1917 had declared:

His Majesty's government view with favour the establishment in Palestine of a national home for the Jewish people, and will use their best endeavours to facilitate the achievement of this object, it being clearly understood that nothing shall be done which may prejudice the civil and religious rights of the existing non-Jewish communities in Palestine, or the rights and political status enjoyed by the Jews in any other country.

It was fascinating to learn from an article in *The Times* in 1977 that the man who drafted this formula, which has been at the root of the Palestine drama ever since, was in fact the British Conservative politician, Leo Amery, a civil servant at the time. In an interview shortly before his death, Mr Amery revealed that the text was scribbled, in a moment of inspiration, on the back of an old memo.

This account remains controversial, for, according to British Foreign Office papers, Mr Balfour had asked Lord Rothschild and Professor Weizmann, the leading Zionists, to submit the formula. The British government, however, modified that formula, toning down words and phrases and rejecting the proposed inclusion of south Lebanon, Transjordan, Hawran and Hermon in the prospective 'National Home'. What is abundantly clear is that the declaration was the work of Zionists, for even Leo Amery admitted that he, too, was a Zionist supporter.

Nevertheless, those who believe that Great Britain alone was responsible for providing the Zionists with their 'National Home' are mistaken. The Four Great Powers of the time, the United States of America, Tsarist Russia, France and Great Britain, were jointly responsible. The British came under pressure from the others to make a statement of sympathy to the Zionist cause so as to ensure Jewish support in the war. And Balfour made his declaration only after consultation with Washington, Moscow and Paris.

I remain convinced that, apart from the Zionists, who knew what they were after, not one of the powers nor any of the non-Zionist politicians involved in the Balfour Declaration knew for certain what was really implied by it, nor did it ever occur to them that, by approving it, they would bring chaos, war and misery to the Middle East. They never imagined how this text, only sixty-nine words long, could one day threaten the whole world with a war of annihilation.

The Arabs were late, very late, to fight collectively as governments against the rape of Palestine. They waited twenty-two long years and, even then, it was only because the British invited them to the Round Table Conference that they at last came forward to defend the legal and human rights of the Palestinians and take the British government to task for the betrayal of the promises given to all the Arabs through Sharif Hussein. Had the British interpretation of the Hussein–

McMahon correspondence, the Balfour Declaration, the Sykes–Picot Agreement and the various political statements that followed been challenged collectively by all Arab governments at the earliest possible date, then the results could have been very different.

As the conference discussions became shrouded in confusion, it was obvious that the Arabs and British were in complete disagreement as to the actual objective of the conference. The British wanted a solution to the problem of Palestine and its future development. They were on the brink of a war with Hitler, and their ultimate need for American assistance, which would depend on Zionist influence in the United States, doomed the talks to failure before they started. The Arabs approached the conference with a great deal of caution, with little faith in British government promises and discord in their ranks. They hoped to persuade the British to reverse their position on the Balfour Declaration, and at long last made it plain that they unanimously rejected a 'National Home' for the Zionists in Palestine. The British government, having heard the views of the interested parties, produced a set of proposals which the Arab delegations turned down.

Yet, despite their rejection by the Arabs, the British government issued the MacDonald White Paper, 'a policy statement' in which those proposals were embodied. The Arab reaction was one of dismay, but the Zionist reaction was one of violence. They mounted terrorist attacks against the British and the Arabs. The White Paper marked the beginning of 'Gun Zionism'. Then came the Second World War, which offered Zionism more opportunities internationally, diplomatically and even militarily. The White Paper, the only positive result of the Round Table Conference, lay dead and buried shortly after its birth.

The 1939 conference was a disaster for the Arabs. But we have only ourselves to blame for what transpired. Collectively, as governments, we did not even face up to the problem of Palestine until the British summoned us to the conference. And once we were there, as usual divided, we were concerned more with individual interests than with the fate of Palestine and the whole Arab nation.

This event in London was my initiation into politics and gave me my first glimpse of its ugly face. Nevertheless, it was an invaluable experience, affording an opportunity to learn some of the facts of political life. On my return to Amman, fresh from the excitements and disappointments of high diplomacy, I found myself plunged into the world of commerce by my promotion to the post of Inspector General of Customs, Trade and Industry. As a reward for the success of the London mission in obtaining a bigger subsidy for Transjordan from the British, the Emir awarded Toufic Pasha and me the 'Nahda', the country's highest decoration.

At that time, the customs department and the inspectorate were kept pretty busy. The Second World War had broken out and the export to Europe of luxury goods such as carpets and rugs was halted. Shipping priorities could be granted only to goods needed for the war effort. As the low customs tariffs in Jordan attracted large quantities of all kinds of commodities from Near Eastern countries which did not qualify for shipping priorities for export to Europe and the Far East, it was only natural that there should have developed a large-scale smuggling spree of all types of goods to neighbouring countries. This was not confined to commodities destined for the needs of neighbours, and much of it found its way further north to Europe through Turkey. Quantities of castor oil, for example, poured into Jordan – enough to keep the local population on the run for years. It was discovered, however, that the castor oil was meant not for the Jordanians' insides, but found its way north to the Germans for the lubrication of aero-engines.

My personal war on the smugglers brought me into contact with some pretty nasty examples of human behaviour, for uncovering serious smuggling depended heavily upon informers. There was a ruling in the department that an informer was to be rewarded with a substantial percentage of the value of the seized goods, his identity being known only to the British Director General and to myself. The reward was to be paid secretly in cash, with no receipt required. It was while dealing with informers that I realized how rotten the human character can be. Friends informed on friends, relatives on relatives, brothers on brothers, and even wives on husbands. I was amazed to find how such behaviour seemed to be a universal characteristic of human nature.

Then I was appointed Chief Censor. Assisted by scores of civil servants who did the routine work, I dealt only with correspondence of the highest in rank, in the government and outside. To censor the correspondence of the English community, a British assistant was appointed. He reported to me and I, in turn, reported to the Prime Minister. Carrying out the duties of Chief Censor also added greatly to my education in human nature.

The fact that censorship was being imposed was kept secret for as long as possible. The censors were carefully chosen from among senior government officials of impeccable integrity, and British experts conducted training-courses. When word eventually got out that the mail was being opened, correspondents became cautious and the censors had to start looking for coded messages.

One day a letter written by a well-known merchant was brought to my attention. It contained an unusual message, and our British experts had insisted that any strange message should be given special attention. Addressed to his brother in Damascus, it told him that a certain merchant was sending a truck load of pomegranates, combs and quarrying materials to be smuggled from Transjordan to Syria. The date and point of entry into Syria was given, so that the writer's brother could inform the Syrian authorities. There were also instructions to make certain that both brothers should get their share of the Syrian reward.

At first glance, it seemed a normal informer's letter. What attracted further attention was the composition of the cargo to be carried by truck. It looked like a very odd mixture, the more so since Transjordan did not produce pomegranates in quantity for export. The identity of the informing merchant and his relationship with the man he was betraying was also revealing. These two men were life-long friends who had fought side by side in the Syrian Revolt against the French in 1925. One had been seriously wounded in battle, and there was a famous story that he had been saved by the faithful comrade who carried him for five kilometres to the nearest medical aid. It was the wounded man himself who told me the story. The two friends had taken refuge in Transjordan after the collapse of the Syrian Revolt and started separate businesses. They remained very close and their relationship was cited as an example of sincere friendship.

When the letter was referred to the experts, they quickly deciphered the code message. Pomegranates meant hand-grenades; combs meant rifle and revolver ammunition, for the word in Arabic means a haircomb, and also a rifle or a pistol magazine; while quarrying materials were obviously explosives. It emerged that the informer was the one whose life had been saved in 1925 by the friend he was now treacherously exposing.

Working in Jordan, I was fortunate enough to meet people who made the history of the Jordan we know today. At the top of the list are King Abdallah, his son Prince Talal, and the youngster who is now King Hussein of Jordan. I also met the Bedouin chiefs, Mithqal El-Feyez, Haditha El-Khrisha and Mohammed Abou Tayih — unforgettable personalities, true men of the desert. There were also the merchants who laid the foundation of Jordan's economy and who were the real creators of its present prosperity. And there were the scores of young students who later became important in the government of their country and its economy.

25

The two most outstanding British personalities with whom I worked were the legendary Glubb Pasha, Commander of the Arab Legion, and Sir Henry Cox, the Resident. Glubb had served earlier in Iraq after resigning his British commission in 1926. Between 1926 and 1930, Glubb Pasha did such a successful job in stopping tribal warfare in the Iraqi desert that the government of Transjordan was greatly impressed. In 1930, he was invited to perform the same miracle in the deserts of Transjordan. Again he succeeded in spectacular fashion, and the last Bedouin raid in the desert took place in 1932.

Glubb succeeded because of his personality and his love for the tribes, which they greatly appreciated. Speaking and writing Arabic fluently, he mastered the Bedouin dialects. He lived with the Bedouins, dressed like them, ate with them, discussed their problems with sympathy and gained their respect. Among the Bedouins he was affectionately known as Abu-Hnayk (the man with the jaw), for a part of his lower jaw had been shot away.

Underlying Glubb Pasha's success was his policy of employing the Bedouins to police their own deserts. His ingenious method of enlisting the sons of the sheikhs of the tribes in his Desert Force greatly assisted his mission. A spirit of pride in belonging to the Desert Force and in wearing its magnificently colourful uniform, cleverly designed to appeal to the Bedouins, went a long way in attracting all the recruits the force required.

Sir Henry Cox was the quiet and discreet British Resident who had overall say in the management of the affairs of Transjordan. He maintained excellent relations with Emir Abdullah and with each one of his Prime Ministers. He was one of the nicest people to work with, but most exacting when British interests or the interests of Transjordan were at stake.

The most important event in my life took place during this period in Jordan – my marriage to Ida. Ida is the daughter of two well-known Swiss who worked for the German Medical Mission at Urfa, southern Turkey. They were there at the time of the Armenian massacres and were recruited after the First World War by the American Near East Relief Organization to collect Armenian widows and orphans and to transport them to safety in Lebanon. Some of them had to be smuggled across the border. Books have been written about their great work and both were fondly known to the Armenians as 'Papa and Mama Kuenzler'.

Ida and I had met at the American University in Beirut, where we became very good friends. But we both thought that our university friendship had ended when she went to Europe for her post-graduate medical education and I left for Jordan. Fate, in its infinite wisdom, decreed differently. Ida was asked to take the position of doctor-in-charge of the Anglican missionary hospital in Amman, and so we met again. The friendship was soon kindled into a blazing fire of love, and we married in 1940. She has been my wife, friend, supporter and our family builder. Without her unflinching support, her patience and many sacrifices, I would have never been able to devote so much of my time to my work, and without hard work, success would have been impossible.

Hardly had I settled in to my new and important functions in Jordan before I was appointed to one of the highest positions in government service as Chief Secretary to the Prime Minister, which office was still held by Toufic Pasha, who knew me well from the time I had served with him at the Round Table Conference in London. By tradition, the chief secretary, who was in fact secretary to the government, was the man chosen to succeed as Prime Minister should a government fall, and all three of my immediate predecessors had been so honoured. Naturally, I felt proud and happy at being considered for such an important position. At the same time, I began to have doubts about the wisdom of having accepted it. Although the work was both significant and exciting, its disadvantage was that the post was highly political and, in the nature of things, involved me deeply with politicians. To be frank, I have never very much liked either politics or the people involved in them.

In fact, the last thing I really wanted was a political career, and it was this feeling of unease which began to spoil the pleasure and fascination of working in Jordan. Ida was soon aware of my unhappiness. We were both conscious of the fact that life in Jordan had lost its lustre and agreed that the time had come to move on. In 1942 I therefore resigned and, leaving behind many friends among the sturdy, independent and loyal people of Jordan, we returned to Beirut. Our stay in Jordan had been an experience which we had both enjoyed and have always remembered with great affection.

To step ahead in my narrative at this point, and give the reader our personal family chronicle, our marriage was blessed with four children: two girls, Rima and Ida, and two boys, Makram and Karim. Ida was named after her mother, but called by the pet-name Idali so as not to have the two Idas mixed up. We were destined to lose our Rima in 1963, but she lives forever in our hearts.

Makram, born in 1944, in due course graduated from the American

University in Beirut in business administration. He joined Intra Bank a few months before it collapsed, and then moved on to our Near East Resources. He formed an associated company, Near East Telecommunication Installation Company (NETICO), of which he is chairman and president. From 1970, he was vice-president of the Lebanese Stock Exchange. His greatest feat was the laying down, during the civil war, of an underground cable between Beirut and Tripoli in the north of Lebanon. It is due to his NETICO team of technicians and workers that the telephones of Lebanon have kept functioning during eleven years of civil war. He is a sportsman who excelled in show jumping and tennis. He married Laila Faris, a Christian, the daughter of the late Dr Nabih Faris, who was a well-known professor of Arab history at the American University of Beirut and of an American mother. Laila and Makram have given us our two eldest grandsons Sari and Tamer, aged eighteen and fifteen respectively at the time of writing.

Karim and Ida are twins, and were born in 1947. Ida married, before graduating from the university, Salim Diab, a Shi'ite businessman from a well-known Lebanese family originally from Syria. The outcome of the marriage was a divorce and two grandsons, Aboudi and Karim, aged thirteen and eleven respectively. Ida left after her divorce to finish her education in San Francisco, and graduated with distinction in fine arts. She is a splendid sportswoman, excelling in show jumping and swimming, who now resides in London and works as an artist.

Karim also graduated in business administration from the American University, and did post-graduate work in agriculture at Reading University in England. He then took over the management of our ancestral farm in the south of Lebanon, managing to look after the farm during the first eight years of the civil war, dodging the shells and bombs directed at the farm for no reason whatsoever except to cause damage and destruction. He was unable to reach the farm after the Israeli invasion of 1982, because the roads were cut off by the Israeli forces. He married Randa, daughter of two Druze relatives, Fouad and Lilly Moukaddem. Karim is also a fine sportsman, a first-class shot and tennis player. Randa and Karim gave us two further grandchildren, a girl, Leena, and a boy, Jad. Leena is naturally the queen of the brood, the only girl among five grandsons.

All grandchildren stuck it out in schools in Lebanon for nine years, despite the shelling, the bombing, the Israeli invasions and the schools' frequent opening and shutting. With the endless war heading into its tenth year, they moved out, the Alamuddins to schools in Villars-sur-

Ollon, Switzerland, and the Diabs, believe it or not, to an outstanding Lebanese school at Bath, England. Their fathers, like all the Lebanese, are still hoping to survive in a country that seems to be stubbornly refusing to do so.

3
Lebanon Again, and Middle East Airlines

Back home in Lebanon from Jordan, I was happy to abandon the world of government service and to move into business. Together with two friends, the late Charles Sa'd and Abdallah Salaam, I founded Near East Resources (NER), the company with which the family was to become so closely associated. Charles, who had other heavy responsibilities and thought success slow in coming, decided to leave, and Abdallah Salaam and I remained. It was tough going, but I always enjoyed hard work.

Our first success was a wartime contract to supply timber to the British Army. When the war in Europe ended, we began trading in practically every commodity for which a market could be found in Lebanon. Within ten years, we had built a sound business and became regional representatives for some of the most important British and American firms: Rolls-Royce, Vickers, Standard Telephones and Cables (STC), its mother firm, the International Telephone and Telegraph Corporation (ITT) and many others. Near East Resources successfully negotiated for STC with the Syrian Department of Posts, Telegraph and Telephones, what was considered at the time the biggest telephone and radio supply contract in the Middle East. We also supplied ITT navigational aids and lighting-equipment for Beirut International Airport. Near East Resources soon became well known and made its mark on the Lebanese scene.

Early in 1951, I was appointed to the Superior Economic Council of Lebanon. The council did very little, despite its prestigious title, which impressed foreigners. But the appointment did produce an invitation for me to represent Lebanon at the International Conference on Land Tenure and Related Problems in World Agriculture, held in October 1951 at Madison, Wisconsin. This conference was sponsored jointly by the US government and the University of Wisconsin. High-ranking US government officials with scores of assistants, professors from seventeen

31

American universities and fifty-one American experts, all of international fame in their subjects, attended.

Thirty-five countries from all over the world were represented. Land tenure and the related problems in world agriculture were thoroughly discussed and analysed — a land-tenure wailing-wall being in full operation during the whole conference. The misery of farmers, their low standards of living, their deficient productivity, the tyranny of landlords and the suffering of the farming community appeared to be identical in most countries, especially those in the underdeveloped world.

Lebanon was the smallest country represented, and it naturally followed that I was the last of the foreign speakers. There seemed to be no point in just moaning, so I decided to deviate from the common style and ventured to offer a few constructive suggestions, the most important of which was to make the fullest use of the promises made to the conference by the representatives of the US government, which were no doubt sincere and motivated by a desire to help. I appealed to the conference to accept the challenge and announced that Lebanon would be submitting a request to the US government for farmers to be granted credit facilities at reasonable rates of interest, coupled with an appropriate extension programme.

It was no use, I said, attempting to solve land-tenure problems without such credit. There was no point in simply seizing large estates from feudal landlords, dividing them up and distributing them to the farmers, for, within five years, small units so created would have reverted to the money-lenders. Merchant money-lenders would then simply take over, and on the whole I preferred the possibly more merciful feudal landlords. I also warned against government-to-government aid, against grants in the form of charity, and against imposing aid in a manner which would offend national dignity, integrity, religious laws and long-established traditions.

The speech was well received, especially by the American representatives, who recommended me to waste no more time in Madison but to explain my project to Washington. On my rounds there, I was delighted to find that many government officers dealing with the problems of the Middle East were old colleagues from the American University in Beirut. What I tried to get over to them were the dangers of government-to-government aid in developing countries. Corrupt governments are further corrupted when financial aid is given to them to spend in the same way they have been spending their own resources. The best way to handle aid is to encourage joint ventures, based on private enterprise, to set up banks and financial institutions with the object of helping the country by providing much-needed credit facilities at reasonable interest rates.

My ideas were enthusiastically received, and I was asked to return to Lebanon without delay. The Americans were going to send representatives immediately to discuss my suggestions on the spot. Full of faith and hope, I returned home. Nothing was heard from Washington for more than a year, by which time I was working with Middle East Airlines. Then, one day, I received the long-awaited visitor, a man unknown to me and on his first visit to Lebanon. He telephoned from the Ministry of Agriculture and introduced himself. I asked when had he arrived in Lebanon, and was stunned to hear him say, 'Six months ago.' Without apology, he went on to inform me that he intended to call on me the following day at 11 a.m. An angry reply flashed across my mind, but I controlled my Druze temper and told him he was welcome.

Within half an hour, an irate executive from the ministry phoned to tell me that the American had told him that I had, in Washington, suggested keeping aid away from the Lebanese government, especially the Ministry of Agriculture, and had recommended aid through private enterprise because, he claimed, I had no confidence in the government and the ministry and had therefore suggested channelling it by way of private enterprise.

The following day, the American arrived in my MEA office at 11 a.m. on the dot. After the usual but brief exchange of courtesies, he proceeded to lecture me on how he thought aid to underdeveloped countries should be administered. Needless to say, his thoughts were diametrically opposed to mine and to the project I proposed, which was never, as it happened, mentioned in his forthright, one-sided address. Government-to-government aid was the only policy to follow, he said, because it enabled the United States to control the governments who got it, the funds themselves and the way these should be spent. It was the only policy which worked. He cited a few examples, and then came the revelation. The American government had decided on a big aid programme for Lebanon — it was to be called Point Four and would soon be officially announced. All Lebanese problems, including those of the farmers, would soon be solved. With Point Four, Lebanon would prosper in no time at all.

I was dumbfounded, but had no quarrel with him. It was his superiors in Washington who had changed their minds. 'I wish you the best of luck, and it was most revealing meeting you,' was my only comment. We shook hands and he departed, exuding superiority and confidence. For a while, I could not believe what I heard. What had happened to the conference in Madison and to the enthusiastic lobbying in Washington? Why this change of mind? Why were the Americans so attached to the policy of government-to-government aid? In trying too hard to 'sell' democracy by giving aid, the Americans seem to ignore a basic flaw in human character. As the old saying has it: 'Whenever you give somebody something for nothing, the first person he comes to dislike will be you.'

The Point Four Programme was introduced into Lebanon with a great fanfare. Soon afterwards, scores of American technicians arrived, and the Lebanese were asked to submit any project they believed beneficial to the country. Point Four officials also planned their own surveys. Great excitement was generated as the Lebanese put forward projects galore. Yet after all the surveys and studies, nothing much happened. The farmers received no real help and continued their tough hand-to-mouth existence. The Point Four Administration was then dismantled and the Americans returned home, having spent substantial amounts of American taxpayers' money on themselves.

Saddened as I was by the failure of my efforts to secure sensible American aid for Lebanon, events in this field had been overshadowed by developments which had come about after my return from Washington and were to have an effect on the rest of my life. Early one January day in 1952, when the sun was shining and the sky was blue after a couple of days of rain, I had been in my office in Near East Resources, which overlooked the sparkling sea on St George's Bay, with Sanin Mountain with its white cap of snow and the beautiful Lebanese hills and villages in the background. It was a day when the spirits were lifted and problems seemed to disappear, promoting thoughts only of good things and of life in the future and all it had to offer. At this point Saeb Salaam walked into my office for a morning coffee, accompanied by his brother Abdallah, my business partner in Near East Resources.

Saeb Salaam, a Sunni Moslem who was chairman of the newly formed Middle East Airlines (MEA) and also deeply involved in Lebanese politics, had some news for us. Sheikh Bishara El-Khoury, Lebanon's first President after winning independence, had provoked a political crisis at the end of his six-year period of office by contriving to revise the constitution so he might serve a second term of six years. Although the move was thoroughly unpopular, the opposition had been unable to block the constitutional change within Parliament and had therefore launched an extra-parliamentary campaign of vilifying the government with charges of general mismanagement, corruption and nepotism.

The news from Saeb Salaam was that the President had appealed to him to come to the rescue by forming a new cabinet. Naturally, his brother and myself were anxious to know what Saeb's response had been, and we were both disappointed to learn he had rejected this opportunity to serve his country at a critical moment. His grounds for rejection were that he could not possibly abandon his position as chairman of Middle East Airlines, especially since there had just been a serious rift in management, as a result of which he had kicked out Fawzi El-Hoss, his partner, joint founder of the airline and its technical director.

It seemed to me at the time a great pity that Saeb should feel unable to deploy his considerable political talents to resolve the nation's political crisis simply because of his business responsibilities. In a moment of patriotism, personal friendship, impetuosity and, it must be admitted, extreme ignorance of the aviation business, I boldly offered to look after Middle East Airlines in his absence if he consented to become Prime Minister. Knowing the nature of Lebanese politics and the precarious position of governments in Beirut, I assumed that the helpful gesture would involve me in absence from my own company only for six months, or twelve at the most. Once convinced that I really meant what I said, Saeb was delighted.

Two days later, Saeb telephoned to say he had informed the President about his change of mind and that he would shortly be forming a new cabinet. To ready myself for my new task, he asked me to take up the position of general manager before he was officially asked to form the cabinet. So it came about that I joined Middle East Airlines in February 1952 and was introduced to senior members of the staff, most of whom were members of Saeb's family, relatives of relatives, or members of his political constituency. I also met regional executives of Pan American, with whom MEA was at the time associated. As soon as Saeb was formally asked to form a new government, I was promptly left on my own, in control of an airline and totally ignorant of the difficulties and problems of aviation management.

As it happened, Saeb Salaam's first term of office was short-lived. He made a brisk start upon what was known as 'Operation Nettoyage' by announcing plans to eradicate corruption and reform government. He dismissed officials, including several who were closely connected with the President. Nevertheless the opposition's extra-parliamentary campaign continued, backed by a general strike in the face of which Saeb Salaam joined forces with the opposition in demanding the resignation of the President. Finally Sheikh Bishara El-Khoury, reluctant to use security forces to break the strike, gave in to opposition demands and was replaced by Camille Chamoun as the new President. Saeb's term of office had been short indeed, lasting only a few days. He returned to MEA with a promise that he would be called upon to form a government once the new President had settled in office. He asked me to stay on to help him out at MEA, and I did so. Meanwhile, the presidential promise was kept and Saeb formed a government. This time, his absence from the airline was much longer than the first. I had by then become so completely immersed in Middle East Airlines and its unending stream of crises that I was continually being asked to stay on for 'just a little longer' until some fresh difficulty was resolved. That 'little longer' finally lasted for twenty-six years.

My previous experience in education, business, government and diplomacy helped, in the early stages, to compensate for my lack of aviation expertise. Also invaluable in coping with the complex tasks of managing an airline was the skill, acquired in all these fields, in handling human relations. It was a formidable challenge, however, for I knew I had to learn quickly how to master the intricate problems then facing the airline. My first discovery was the extent to which the organization over which I now had control had been paralysed at management level by the fierce personal battle between its two founders, Saeb Salaam and Fawzi El-Hoss, who were at each other's throats in a complicated series of legal battles. The resulting recrimination divided the staff into rival camps which harmed the work of the company. To explain how that came about, it is necessary to understand something of the history of the airline.

Middle East Airlines was formed and registered in Beirut on 31 May 1945 with a capital of £L1 million. Its president/general manager was Saeb Salaam, and its technical manager Fawzi El-Hoss. Saeb was a member of a leading Moslem family and a notable political figure. He later served several times as Prime Minister, and today, in his late seventies, remains an influential figure in Lebanese politics. Fawzi, who was to die in a riding accident in April 1966 at the early age of fifty-five, was also a Moslem of powerful personality who had, exceptionally for an Arab at that time, a technical training in aviation. He provided the driving force which brought the dream of a Lebanese airline to reality. Sadly, Fawzi was to die exiled by Saeb from the airline he had helped to create and promote during its early years.

A first step towards giving Lebanon an airline of its own had been taken some time before the foundation of Middle East Airlines, and it

36

happened, strangely enough, in Chicago. During the early months of 1944, the United States had initiated a series of exploratory discussions with other governments that were particularly interested in the post-war development of international civil aviation. It had become clear that rules for the conduct of civil aviation needed to be worked out. These talks culminated in the Chicago Conference when, on 1 November 1944, fifty-five neutral and allied states met to establish an internationally agreed civil air system.

Lebanon sent two delegates, Camille Chamoun, then Minister for Lebanon in London, and later to be President of the Lebanese Republic; and Fawzi El-Hoss, who acted as his technical adviser. Chamoun, chairman of the delegation, encouraged Fawzi and assisted him in making contacts with British delegates who were later instrumental in providing Middle East Airlines with its fleet of De Havilland Rapides.

The presence of two representatives from tiny Lebanon at this historic aeronautical occasion was especially noteworthy. It was the start of continuing Lebanese influence in international aviation affairs. That gathering of delegates from all over the world was to exercise a formative influence on the whole pattern of post-war flying. At the conference, the foundations of the next decade of civil aviation were laid.

It is interesting to note that the proceedings of the Chicago Conference recorded the Lebanese suggestion for the inclusion of Arabic as an official language in the International Civil Aviation Conference. The Lebanese have always been active in defending the Arab cause and have contributed much towards its international presentation and advancement. They have also contributed greatly to the promotion of both Arab culture and business.

One of the British advisers at the Chicago Conference, Major Robert McCrindle, then deputy director-general of BOAC, recalled that Fawzi El-Hoss was, at the time, assumed to be director-general of Lebanese civil aviation. And why not, when Lebanon still had no civil aviation, no department of civil aviation, no director-general of civil aviation? It had only Fawzi El-Hoss.

Following the conference, Fawzi went to see George Cribett, then assistant under-secretary at the British Air Ministry, who had also been in Chicago. Both he and McCrindle had talks with El-Hoss and discussed with him the formation of Middle East Airlines. The result was an agreement with BOAC, dated 28 August 1945. It was to run from 15 September 1945 until terminated by twelve months' notice in writing. Under the agreement, BOAC was to advise on technical matters, to second staff, to give reasonable facilities for training officials and to act on behalf of MEA in ordering equipment and spares. For its part, MEA undertook to reimburse BOAC for seconded staff, to pay BOAC for the cost of training together with other fees agreed upon. The technical advice offered by BOAC was not mandatory. It could only be offered and not enforced. As a result of the agreement, the British Ministry of Aircraft Production leased three Rapides. This was the fleet with which MEA proudly started operations. With its cedar-tree emblem, it was soon to become known as the 'Christmas Tree Airline'.

Shortly after MEA, another Lebanese airline company was registered, the Compagnie Générale de Transport (CGT), the predecessor of Air Liban. In line with the true political tradition of Lebanon, where MEA was founded by Moslems, CGT was founded by Christians. MEA was associated with the British (BOAC); CGT was associated with the French (Air France). The new arrival on the airline scene had an immediate effect on MEA. Traffic rights needed to be shared at a time when air traffic to Lebanon was in its infancy and its slow growth did not really justify the presence of two competitors on any of the routes.

The immediate consequence was that a price-cutting war began. Neither airline was a member of the International Air Transport Association (IATA), not that it would have made any real difference if they had been. CGT conducted the war aggressively, and MEA had to follow suit if it was to survive. The true explanation for the lavishness with which CGT cut its prices became known to me only in 1963, in the course of negotiations for the purchase of Air Liban when Air France disclosed that, in its association with the Lebanese shareholders in CGT, it had to guarantee them against all losses, and also guarantee an annual dividend of 9 per cent on their shareholding. Air France had been falsely informed that this was what BOAC had offered the shareholders of MEA. No wonder Air Liban was so generous with Air France's money. In the long term the prodigality was to turn out to be a blessing. The excessive losses in Air Liban eventually induced Air France to sell it to MEA.

Middle East Airlnes' people were always suspicious of Air Liban. One never-forgotten incident occurred when a Junkers 52, used as a civil transport by CGT, swung off the runway for no apparent reason and ran into MEA's first two DC–3s. The Junkers wedged itself between the two newly acquired aircraft, which were parked side by side on the tarmac. The wings of both DC–3s were heavily damaged and one of them was a write-off and had to be replaced. Perhaps it *was* an accident, but such was the atmosphere of suspicion that many people in MEA were convinced their splendid new aircraft had been deliberately sabotaged by their competitors.

Nevertheless, despite the competitive war with CGT and a fair share of teething troubles and growing pains, MEA had its successes and services went well and became profitable. Before long, the Rapides were found to be too small to serve MEA needs and ambitions. This led to an argument with BOAC, who insisted that MEA was not technically capable of operating aircraft bigger than Rapides. In their opinion, the child aspired to fly too high. Middle East Airlines thought differently and wished to soar ever higher. As a result, MEA severed relations with BOAC and Fawzi El-Hoss immediately flew to Washington, DC. There he was successful in obtaining a letter from the US government, giving him priority for the purchase of war-surplus aircraft and equipment abroad.

In the autumn of 1945, Fawzi went to Payne Field, the US Air Transport Command air base at Cairo, in search of surplus DC–3 aircraft. He succeeded in buying two of the best available and had them flown to Beirut. It seemed that Middle East Airlines would soar after all, but before long, fresh difficulties emerged. Spare parts and engines were not available and the slender financial resources of the airline could not sustain the requirements of a bigger and more expensive fleet. Help was needed.

Hoss looked to the United States this time and negotiated an agreement with Pan American Airways based on the American company's contribution of three more DC–3s, with spare engines and other parts, in return for 36 per cent of the shareholding of Middle East Airlines, which was transformed from a partnership into a shareholding company with a registered capital of £L1,250,000. With a fleet of four DC–3s, MEA was immediately able to extend its scheduled services along the Arabian Gulf, where it pioneered air transport. By the end of the year, its staff had grown to 166. Pan American's policy was to encourage its new partner to expand in directions especially chosen by Pan American for feeder traffic so as to compete in that part of the world with its rival, Trans-World Airlines. Under the American Civil Aeronautical Board's policy of division of traffic rights, TWA had been assigned the whole of the Arab world, except for Baghdad and Beirut, which were allotted to Pan-Am.

It was while Middle East Airlines' operations continued to expand in the new partnership that relations deteriorated between Saeb and Fawzi, the founders. It is strange how disputes between friends or relatives may so rapidly develop into bitter enmity. The more intimate the friendship and the closer the relationship, the more virulent the quarrel is likely to be. Their disputes came to a head in 1951, when Saeb dismissed Hoss as technical manager, so heralding an avalanche of lawsuits in the Lebanese courts and the long, abusive quarrel.

Hoss had originally owned 4⅓ per cent of Middle East Airlines. When MEA was changed to a shareholding company, he was given an option for a further 17⅔ per cent to be paid out of his share of future profits. But, before a formal contract for the option could be signed, the partners quarrelled. The question of who actually owned the option shares formed the basis for a feud that became a company legend. Hoss's claim to the shareholding continued to give him a seat on the board, making it inevitable that meetings should develop into arenas for acrimonious argument. The effect of the internal tussle would, however, have been minimal had it not been that the regional management of Pan-Am supported Hoss.

It was against this background of internal strife, of which I was blissfully ignorant at the time, that I assumed responsibilities as general manager of Middle East Airlines for what I was sure would only be a temporary period. It soon became apparent to me that Pan American was far more heavily involved in the airline's affairs than seemed warranted by its 36 per cent shareholding. The offices of its regional executives were on the same floor as the management of MEA, and its regional director was a frequent visitor to Saeb's office and to mine. Also to my surprise, I found that the MEA district sales manager in Beirut was an American seconded from Pan-Am. And so were the district sales managers of Dhahran (Saudi Arabia) and Cairo. Although all three were, in theory, employees of MEA, they rarely followed MEA's instructions or sales policies where these were not approved by Pan-Am.

My entry into Middle East Airlines' management coincided with the arrival in Beirut of Norman Blake, the new regional director of Pan-Am, a charming man and one of the best-mannered Americans I have ever met. From the start, he made me feel at ease where, by contrast, his American aides in Beirut missed no opportunity to express their astonishment at the appointment of a novice such as myself to be general manager. Norman Blake's co-operative attitude helped greatly in overcoming my apprehensions as I began to realize the enormity of the responsibilities I had undertaken and the many problems that faced me.

My first task was to find elbow room within which I could effectively manage the airline. This, I realized, could be achieved only by trying to create a conciliatory atmosphere between Saeb and Fawzi, the quarrelling partners. Originally I had thought that the tension between them would not be too difficult to relax, and I proceeded to do everything in my power to improve things. I discovered that the quarrel was chronic, however, and had reached a point of no reconciliation. What I did manage to achieve was to establish good relations with nearly all the Pan-Am regional executives as well as with the district sales managers seconded to MEA. I kept them informed of everything they had the right to know through improved channels of communication.

While worrying over the Salaam—Hoss quarrels and the tension between Salaam and Pan-Am, I still had to manage the airline with its day-to-day operations, its organizational problems and, most important, the establishment of a correct employer—employee relationship. There was a conspicuous lack of text-books on airlines and their management, and so I had to make do with articles from trade magazines, which were informative if not very instructive. To fill the gaps, I sought out practical advice from people working in MEA, visiting every department to get the benefit of their experience. In the process, I found out a good deal about the staff, their difficulties and their aspirations.

Our Pan American associates were also enormously helpful on technical matters and offered the services of Robert Bell, a former officer in the US Marines and one of the best men I have ever worked with. He became assistant general manager, and his professional expertise soon had its effect on company efficiency. With him came Horst Penzel, an efficient German financial controller who not only took charge of the accounts but was also able to reassure the Americans about the state of MEA's economy. Woodward, another Pan-Am executive, was temporarily seconded from their industrial relations and personnel department to help with that side of the business. With the benefit of such expert advice, we set out to build up an airline with high standards that would bear comparison with any company with a world-wide reputation. The process involved a complete programme of intensive training, carried out both in Beirut and abroad.

For the rest, I made use of my own experience, and also benefited from the invaluable help of the airline's staff, especially the 'old timers' who had received me with mixed feelings at first but who soon came round to offering full co-operation. Throughout my time with the airline I remained constantly grateful for the assistance and understanding offered by every member of the staff, from baggage loaders to company vice-presidents.

In February 1953, a year after taking over as general manager, I submitted a detailed report to the Board of Directors on what had been achieved so far and outlined a charter for the future of Middle East Airlines and its workforce. Although some modifications were needed later to cope with events, the document remained as a blueprint for the airline until my retirement at the end of 1977. The basic principle was the establishment of non-factional social justice within a partnership of employees and shareholders. It guaranteed that jobs and promotion would go to men and women best qualified for the task, regardless of religious persuasion or political influence. We had to try to keep the company out of politics and to persuade the staff to act as a family, inspired by a patriotic belief in a united Lebanon. On a more practical level, it was necessary to reorganize the salary structure, modelling it on that of more experienced progressive airlines. Intensive training, locally and abroad, in aviation skills and techniques was to be carried out at all levels in the company and be given top priority. Manuals were to be produced and every necessary aid was to be obtained with the aim of implanting in MEA all the accepted standards of the civil aviation industry.

To improve staff morale, I initiated a programme of industrial relations reform, granting a five-day week and offering family allowances. What was considered even more revolutionary in Lebanon – indeed, I believe it was unique in the Arab world at the time – was the provision of free medical and dental treatment for the staff. A cafeteria offered healthy meals at reduced prices, and a social and sports club was established.

Following this pattern of enlightened staff treatment, I later set up a relief fund financed by the company and administered by the employees from which they could obtain interest-free loans to cope with family emergencies. Scholarships were arranged for the children of the employees. A co-operative store, financed by the company but administered by the employees, was opened. There were marriage and childbirth bonuses and travel concessions. And, most revolutionary of all, I introduced a profit-sharing scheme through which employees would be able to buy shares in the company on advantageous terms. In addition, they were also offered a bonus of 20 per cent of the company's profits. It was a most ambitious programme, and it needed some audacity even to propose it, but it was all achieved.

I have always firmly believed in the merits of benevolent employer–

42

employee policy, and the realization of my programme was certainly the keystone to success in building Middle East Airlines. It is ironic to recall how, because of it, the Lebanese business community saw me as a dangerous socialist revolutionary whereas, had I proposed such measures in Europe, I would have been considered a mild socialist reformer.

From the start, I told the staff that MEA was *their* airline and that they had a say in their own future. This was not mere propaganda, and over the years I made them feel it and believe it by constantly reminding them of the importance of human capital and of the fact that the shareholders, too, were equal partners in Middle East Airlines. My personal philosophy was to be a jump ahead of employees in granting their due rights even before they thought of making demands, far less of resorting to industrial action. I repeatedly pointed out that the salaries and benefits they derived from the airline not only equalled, but actually exceeded, the benefits of the shareholders. The message was that a real partner in an organization which assures his own and his family's livelihood would be foolish not to work hard for its growth and prosperity, and would be completely mad to do anything to harm it. That is why, during my time at Middle East Airlines, we never had a strike except for one in 1952 which had greeted my joining the company.

All the airline's radio operators except one, radio operator Chehab, had gone on strike just before Christmas, during our busiest period when we were carrying seasonable supplies to the oil companies in Saudi Arabia and the Arabian Gulf. They struck because they were getting a monthly salary of £L285 as compared with the salary of £L1,020 being paid for the same job by the rival Air Liban; and, even though Middle East Airlines could justifiably argue that salaries in Air Liban were tied to Air France rates, the difference was so great as to cause me concern. Nevertheless, I resented the timing of the strike and the fact that it was being carried out without any attempt to discuss the problem with the management. It was also illegal, because it contravened Article 342 of the Lebanese Penal Code which prohibited strikes in communication services. I therefore took immediate steps to end the strike by dismissing all the strikers by telegram. With the help of Chehab and radio operators from the Lebanese Air Force and from civil aviation, I temporarily replaced the strikers and MEA fulfilled all its Christmas commitments.

We were at home in Shimlan, celebrating the New Year, when the door opened and a huge bouquet of beautiful Lebanese flowers advanced

43

into the house. Behind it came a delegation of the strikers, who were received and treated as guests in my home. I did not mention the strike, but they did, expressing their regrets and asking to be allowed to return to work. After a reasonable time, their salaries, as well as those of other employees in similar straits, were fairly adjusted.

4
The Pan-Am Affair

Despite my efforts to ease the growing tension between Pan American and MEA, relations were deteriorating fast. In the first half of 1952, an argument had developed between Saeb and Norman Blake about the use of profits from the previous year. Saeb wanted these to be distributed to the shareholders. The regional director strongly opposed this on the grounds that MEA needed to save all its profits to finance the purchase of more modern and bigger aircraft. It was valid reasoning, but Saeb argued that the sum represented by the profits was insignificant and would make no real difference to the purchase of aircraft. Both sides were intransigent. Saeb proposed that they should ask the President of Pan American, Mr Juan Trippe, to arbitrate, and the regional director had to accept. A meeting was arranged in London when Mr Trippe was planning to visit the United Kingdom. The meeting was short and decisive. Mr Trippe arbitrated in favour of Saeb's request.

The matter was trivial compared with the real mission Mr Trippe wished Saeb to undertake. He was anxious for Saeb to contact Moussadiq, the Prime Minister of Iran at the time, with a proposal to form an American consortium to negotiate a new oil deal with Iran. Saeb readily agreed, but, as it turned out, Trippe believed that Saeb had failed him by being unduly slow in contacting Moussadiq and the deal fell through. MEA thus lost the sympathy and support of Juan Trippe, a factor which may have played a decisive role later.

Saeb and the regional director returned to Beirut, one buoyant and happy, the other angry, not only for having been let down by his president and so easily losing his argument, but because he was firmly convinced it was wrong for under-capitalized Middle East Airlines to distribute all profits without leaving any provisions for the purchase of much-needed new equipment. He was sympathetic to Salaam's pressing need for funds, but felt his loyalty was to the success of the

45

Pan-Am—MEA joint venture. Life in Middle East Airlines went on, but in an atmosphere charged with suspicion and growing friction among the shareholders.

In the late summer of 1952 in the midst of many other worries, I was faced for the first time with the problems of the Hajj (pilgrimage to Mecca) season. An unexpected mass of *hajjis* descended on Beirut, mostly from Turkey. The Hajj hotels were overflowing, with pilgrims sleeping in halls and corridors, and they began to despair. So thousands marched on Beirut International Airport, where they camped patiently and prayed five times a day to Allah to provide them with transport to Mecca. MEA and the other airlines with regular flights to Saudi Arabia were fully booked and had no additional capacity to offer. A doctor leaked to the media his fear of an epidemic of plague or cholera as a result of this unusual influx. Whereupon the Lebanese Prime Minister panicked and ordered that the pilgrims be transported at all costs. He even threatened to requisition international aircraft flying into Beirut, and use them to carry the pilgrims to save the country from catastrophe. There was no possibility of accommodating them on airlines operating normal Hajj flights, and the Prime Minister's threat to international airlines was unrealistic. He knew, we knew and the international airlines knew that there could be no question of requisitioning aircraft and crews, but the pilgrims and the Moslem public did not know. His Excellency gained undeserved popularity and we were left to handle a real crisis.

I took my problem back with me to Shimlan, the village where we had been living since 1949. Shimlan is a gem of a Lebanese village, rightly called 'The Balcony of Lebanon'. Perched high in the mountains, it seems to hang over Beirut, and it is possible from there to see most of the coast. My daily morning drive from Shimlan down to the airport, through the glorious beauty of the Lebanese hills and forests, often helped me to think clearly, and the next day was no exception. An idea came to me which seemed to offer a solution to the Hajj crisis. We would ask the American Ambassador for help. The Americans had military transport planes based in Libya and West Germany and, if they agreed, not only could they solve the crisis but would also earn the gratitude of Moslems everywhere.

Saeb Salaam accepted the suggestion and telephoned the American Ambassador, who was sick in bed but who at once agreed to pass on our request. Three days later to our surprise and delight, American transport planes of the Military Air Transport Services (MATS) began landing in Beirut. It was a demonstration of the renowned efficiency of

46

the Americans, the transport fleet coming under the command of a Colonel Rush.

I never believed there could be a connection between name and character until I saw the colonel in action. He arrived on the Thursday afternoon and wanted to start embarking passengers exactly an hour after he touched down. But no one was ready for such a rush, for we had never expected such an immediate response. The staff were overworked with routine operations and with calming the impatient, at times angry, Turkish pilgrims. I persuaded Colonel Rush that his operation, which he named 'Pilgrimlift', should begin at the crack of dawn on Friday. No one slept that night and MEA employees showed themselves to be wonderful, untiring and efficient. They assembled the pilgrims, who spoke only Turkish, in plane-load groups – and what a task it was. We had to call on Armenian employees who spoke the language but who hated the Turks because of the massacres of 1915. Then came the task of convincing pilgrims afraid of being left behind that they could not all travel on the first plane. Whenever we called for 'Mohammad Hassan', more than sixty would rush forward claiming the name. Then we had to draft in Turkish speakers to accompany the pilgrims on their flight to Jeddah. Experience of Hajj flights made it imperative for safety's sake to have the *hajjis* accompanied. It was a common event for certain of them to try to start lighting primus stoves inside the aircraft to brew up tea.

Operation 'Pilgrimlift' was completed without a hitch. The MATS crews, under the formidable Colonel Rush, were highly efficient, and their planes flew round the clock with the precision of the best Swiss timepiece. MEA employees were outstanding in handling the operation on top of their own work.

Colonel Rush was not only a symbol of high-powered American efficiency, but also a friendly man with a remarkable sense of humour. During his brief time in Beirut he made many friends. I asked him one morning if our Transport Department was giving him satisfaction, and whether our drivers, like all Lebanese, were not driving too fast. 'Buddy,' he replied, 'those red devils of yours don't drive too fast, they fly too low!' Our cars were painted red, hence the 'red devil' nickname.

Operation 'Pilgrimlift' was a one-way operation from Beirut to Jeddah. Pilgrims love to overstay their welcome in Saudi Arabia and the *hajjis* gradually filtered back on normal commercial flights. The one-way fares they should have paid MATS were collected and deposited in a local bank in the name of the American Ambassador, 'Harold B. Minor in Trust'. It amounted to £L707,400, and a cheque for that

47

amount was later handed over in a well-publicized ceremony to Saeb Salaam, president of the hastily formed 'Moslem Charities Fund Society'.

At the end of 1952, MEA submitted a claim for £L49,112 to the American Embassy for such services as traffic handling of aircraft, transport from town to airports and back, lunch boxes and so on, all provided on written requests from MATS. The claim was fully documented and accompanied by receipts from Beirut and Jeddah. The embassy replied, in January 1953, that it did not consider the claim as chargeable to the Military Air Transport Service. We were referred instead to the Moslem Charities Fund Society, which declared an inability to pay, claiming that the total sum of the generous American contribution had been publicly announced and already allocated to Moslem charities.

Subsequent approaches to the embassy were referred to Washington. Three and a half years later, on 1 May 1955, the American Ambassador, Donald Heath, who had replaced Mr Minor, wrote and told me that, 'in the opinion of the United States Air Force any charges due to MEA for services rendered in connection with the airlift should be defrayed from the proceeds of the airlift fund'. We pressed our claim and, six years after 'Pilgrimlift', the American air attaché at the embassy wrote, telling me he had been instructed by the department of the US Air Force, Washington, that there were no 'appropriate funds to the Air Force for reimbursement of Middle East Airlines for supplies and services furnished to MATS during the "Pilgrimlift" of 1952', and that he had been further instructed that, if we wished to pursue the matter, we might wish to bring an action in the US Court of Claims. When we tried to find out how to bring such an action, an American diplomat sternly informed us it would be inadvisable. Later I was given to understand that persistence on my part might be interpreted as anti-American. The case was therefore diplomatically closed, the board of MEA agreeing to the debt being written off our books. As a result of 'Pilgrimlift', Ambassador Harold B. Minor had been voted 'American Ambassador of the Year' and Saeb Bey hailed by the Moslems for the donation of £L707,400 to Moslem charities. I, for my efforts, was accused of being anti-American.

MEA and the US Air Force had co-operated happily enough in speeding the *hajjis* on their way to Mecca, but commercial relations between the airline and its transatlantic associate, Pan American, were a great deal less satisfactory that year. All signs were that the partnership was bound to fail sooner or later. Mutual trust had vanished and the partners' interests were diverging. Pan American was getting fed up with the Salaam–Hoss squabble, the under-capitalization of the airline, the desire of the Salaams to draw out all profits and their consequent refusal to build up the necessary financial provisions for new equipment. Pan-Am considered the ambition to grow and expand without financial contribution from the majority shareholders to be unrealistic, and they did not wish to play Father Christmas and supply the required funds to the quarrelling shareholders. They were beginning to question the value to Pan-Am of their association with MEA under the Salaam–Hoss feud, and greatly doubted the ability of the airline to survive in such acrimonious circumstances. Something had to be done.

Pan-Am, who had always favoured Hoss, went into action to force the Salaams out of MEA and bring back Hoss, who was anxious to repay Saeb in kind by ousting him and his family in turn. The squeeze was on, and Saeb thought of asking BOAC to step into Pan-Am's shoes. He asked me to go to London and gave me two letters, one to Sir Miles Thomas, the other to Basil Smallpeice (later Sir Basil), then respectively chairman and deputy chief executive to BOAC. I had never met them, but Saeb knew them well and was on good terms with them. Upon arrival in London a meeting was arranged with them by a mutual friend, Sir Francis Brake of Standard Telephones, who was also on the board of BOAC.

I first met Sir Francis in the days before I joined MEA, when I stopped in London to see him on ITT business when my wife and I were on our way to New York. After the business discussions were over, Sir Francis started to chat. He asked how we were travelling on to the States. 'By air, on Pan-Am,' I replied. 'Why don't you travel by sea on one of the Queens?' asked Sir Francis. I told him I had tried, but all cabins were full. 'Wait a minute,' he said. 'The managing director of Cunard is a friend of mine. Let me see what I can do.' Someone had cancelled a reservation that morning on the *Queen Elizabeth*. The sailing date was a few days later than the day we planned to fly, but that was of no consequence.

One morning, at the Athenaeum Court Hotel where we were staying, the morning paper arrived with breakfast as usual. The front page carried dreadful news: '*Empress of the Skies* crashes at Shannon with only one survivor'. That was the day we had planned to leave by air for New York and the *Empress of the Skies* was the Pan-Am flight on which we had been booked. If it had not been for Sir Francis, we would not have been alive. One could easily say it was coincidence, but I am convinced it was not. It was fate, and we, the Druzes, are born fatalists. My Swiss wife used to believe in a Swiss form of fatalism, but her faith was greatly strengthened after fate changed our destiny on the *Empress of the Skies*. When she published her own account of our family life, she used the title *Maktoob* — Arabic for 'it is written'.

There is another, less dramatic story about the same voyage that I love to tell my English friends. Shortly after we went aboard, the steward came to our stateroom to offer assistance. He must have read the title 'Sheikh' on the passenger list, because a look of bewilderment came over his face when he opened the door and found no flowing robes, no olive skin, not even a hooked nose. He asked my wife, who was reading an English novel, whether she needed any assistance. She declined his offer in faultless English — naturally enough, having studied at a Scottish school and taken her medical degree at the American University. Then he turned to me and, in deliberately slow and clear English, asked whether I needed any assistance myself. I replied, 'No, thank you. Actually, I prefer to do my unpacking myself.' He backed out of the room, and I heard him tell the maid, waiting outside: 'He's nothing but a bloody Englishman.'

Saeb's letters were courteously received, but BOAC was most reluctant to re-establish any relationship with MEA. They were still angry with the way the previous relationship had ended. Furthermore, in contrast with Pan American, BOAC had no need for MEA as a feeder for its services. BOAC already served every point in the Arab world and had all traffic rights from Beirut. Most important of all, BOAC flatly refused to make any move which might be interpreted as a wish on its part to oust Pan-Am from MEA. Apparently an official understanding between the United States and the United Kingdom to prevent poaching on one another's preserves in the Middle East had existed since 1948. Indeed, I was told, even if BOAC finally agreed to take over Pan-Am's interests in Middle East Airlines, it would have to secure the full approval of the US government.

The situation was most discouraging, especially since it was impossible to fault the reasons for BOAC's reluctance to become involved again in Middle East Airlines. However, apart from my desire to help Saeb and our own airline, I could see, in an association between BOAC and MEA, hope for the possible realization of a dream I had of uniting all the Arab airlines. As a start, you could turn MEA and all the airlines associated at the time with BOAC in Aden, Kuwait, Iraq, the Gulf and Jordan into one united Arab airline, with BOAC providing the technical expertise. The dream fired my imagination and doubled my enthusiasm. I refused to give up and searched hard for arguments to convince BOAC they should change their negative attitude.

I had a feeling that the three knights – Sir Miles, Sir Francis and Sir Basil – saw their role as a greater one than simply safeguarding BOAC's interests. The 'Three Wise Men' were keen to encourage British exports and promote the technical progress of British aviation. Like several of their European counterparts, they were concerned at the increasing American stranglehold over the civil aircraft manufacturing industry. I therefore did my best to advance the theory that an association with MEA would lead naturally to the airline being equipped with British aircraft. This could encourage similar sales to airlines throughout the Middle East, an argument they had the foresight to appreciate. To this I added my second argument, that, while BOAC currently enjoyed traffic rights throughout the Middle East, such a privilege could not last long without an association with MEA.

My two arguments won the day with BOAC, and I obtained their agreement, in principle, to buy the shares of Pan-Am, provided Pan-Am drew out of MEA of its own free will. I was also anxious to obtain assurance that, if BOAC joined MEA, we should get modern, bigger aircraft. This was given without hesitation.

Assured of BOAC's albeit conditional interest, Saeb called a meeting with the regional director of Pan-Am at which the problems facing the partnership were frankly discussed. It was evident that the existing situation, with its misunderstandings, recriminations and suspicions, was doing nobody any good, especially not the fledgling Middle East Airlines. The situation could not be allowed to continue. Either the partners must agree to mend their fences and reorganize the company in such a way as to guarantee its future, or else a friendly divorce was inevitable. The regional director stressed that Pan-Am had no intention of withdrawing or of disposing of its holding in Middle East Airlines. He suggested, however, that, in the absence of any plan for expansion under the present corporate structure of the company, the Salaams should give Pan-Am an option to sell the Salaam shares to other interested parties. Saeb agreed to sell at a price to be determined by chartered accountants and bankers chosen by both parties. The regional director then referred this proposal to Pan-Am's headquarters, and after a few months the reply arrived.

Pan-Am still had no desire to withdraw from MEA, but would purchase 40 per cent of the Salaam shareholding, subject to certain conditions and at a price fixed by Pan-Am. These were practically all the Salaam shares, but excluded the 22 per cent under the Salaam–Hoss dispute. Intra Bank then, on behalf of Pan-Am, made a formal offer to the Salaams, who objected that the price was too low and proposed arbitration by bankers or a Dutch auction. Pan-Am rejected both proposals and, insisting it was not prepared to pay more than the price offered, told the Salaams to take it or leave it.

Saeb tried hard to persuade Pan-Am to modify its rigid stand, but got no response whatsoever. He then, after consultation with BOAC, counter-bid, offering to buy the Pan-Am shares at a price of 50 per cent higher than that offered by Pan-Am, or to sell all the Salaam shares to Pan-Am at his new price. To everyone's surprise, Pan American agreed to sell its shareholding to Saeb at the price offered.

Saeb was, at this stage, bargaining discreetly with BOAC. Scores of letters were exchanged and, in the process, I made several trips to London. General agreement with BOAC presented no difficulties on most points, and trouble arose only when the Salaams tried determinedly to persuade BOAC to buy all their shares in MEA.

Originally BOAC had it in mind to purchase only the Pan American holdings of 36 per cent. Under pressure from Saeb, however, they agreed to buy up to the maximum 49 per cent permitted by the Lebanese government to a foreign investor in an airline. Even this did not satisfy the Salaams. They insisted on selling all their shares, arguing that, if BOAC wanted management control, it had to buy the majority shareholding. It was a new twist, since it had been understood throughout all the early negotiations that any BOAC participation in MEA shareholding was subject to its having management control.

BOAC negotiators argued that for them, as foreigners, to acquire a large majority holding was neither in their own interests nor in the best interests of the airline. I was able to talk them round, however, once I had obtained approval for the arrangement from the President of Lebanon and had persuaded Yousif Bedas, chairman of Intra, to agree that his bank would front for the surplus shares. The presidential agreement was conditional on an assurance that it would be a temporary arrangement, and that the surplus shares would eventually be sold to Lebanese nationals.

In this manner, the Salaams had their way, and BOAC advanced Saeb the funds he needed to buy the Pan-Am shares. Once that was done, he sold these shares to BOAC, together with all the Salaam shares, thus forcing on the British a total holding of 78 per cent. In fact, the only part of MEA's capital BOAC did not hold was the 22 per cent whose ownership remained in dispute between the Salaams and Hoss — all this, of course, being a closely guarded secret at the time.

Saeb was then invited by BOAC to continue as chairman, and I agreed to resume my work as general manager, but on a temporary basis. I was anxious to return to my own company, NER, but BOAC made me promise to help in finding and training a suitable replacement general manager of Lebanese nationality before I left.

The Pan-Am–MEA relationship therefore ended on 21 December 1954 with the sale of its shareholding, but friendly relations none the less continued. MEA owed a great deal to Pan-Am for its existence and early progress. Training-courses, technical assistance and the help of people like Robert Bell had a permanent influence in setting MEA on the path to expansion and prosperity. I made lasting friendships with many of the Pan-Am executives I worked with, and have remained grateful to them for their contribution to my early tutelage in aviation. I also cherish the memory and kindness of one of the greatest pioneers in civil aviation, Juan Trippe, then chairman and chief executive of Pan-Am, whom I had the privilege of meeting on several occasions.

During the protracted negotiations with BOAC, a plan was conceived by Sir Miles, Sir Basil, Sir Francis and myself to form an aviation leasing and maintenance company in Beirut, the name Mideast Aircraft Service Company (Masco) being coined. The aim of this company was to encourage the sale of British aircraft to airlines in the Middle East, and possibly, at a later date, to east and north Africa. Sales were to be through a hire-purchase scheme allied to maintenance contracts with Masco. At the same time, companies associated with BOAC in the Middle East would come to Masco for engineering work and would benefit from cheaper and more efficient aircraft maintenance in the area. The idea was received enthusiastically, and the President of Lebanon, under a new law to encourage investments, promised that Masco would qualify for a six-year exemption from taxes.

Masco was officially formed in August 1955; its founding and objectives were announced by Sir Miles Thomas at a special Middle East conference attended by the chairmen of all airlines associated with BOAC as well as Lebanese dignitaries, BOAC representatives in the Middle East, a large number of British executives and the usual crowd of journalists and other media representatives. The news was hailed locally as a constructive project with far-reaching potential benefits to the Lebanese economy and Lebanese technical training. But it was viewed with suspicion by non-British aircraft manufacturers. Strangely enough, the British aircraft manufacturers, for whose benefit it was conceived, failed to show the slightest interest.

Meanwhile, our shareholding troubles continued to plague us. Fawzi

El-Hoss blamed Saeb and the Salaams for selling Middle East Airlines to the British, complaining that, as a result, the shareholding of the Lebanese airline was no longer Lebanese. He spelt out the dangers to Lebanese civil aviation and to national aspirations, and presented his arguments to the President of the Republic, the Prime Minister, other ministers and members of parliament. He also took court action against MEA and Pan-Am, claiming conspiracy to defraud him of his rights.

Of course, he was right in saying Middle East Airlines had been sold to the British, but I had, fortunately, kept the President of the Republic informed of all that was happening. The political storm passed without doing the airline serious harm. The court case, however, dangled over the two airlines pending a final settlement of the Hoss–Salaam affair.

5
BOAC and Politics

Despite its local difficulties, Middle East Airlines was a hive of activity and was riding high in 1955. Masco had been formed, and our first three Viscounts, on lease from Hunting Clan, arrived. Expansion of the operation was well on the way, and so, to cope with the rapid growth, I started recruiting new staff to help the old timers. One of our new recruits was Asad Nasr, who was born in Palestine in 1927, emigrated to Lebanon and obtained Lebanese nationality. He had graduated from Cambridge University in 1950 in mathematics and law.

Before joining MEA, Asad Nasr was working at the American University in Beirut, and had also done a part-time job in statistics at the Ministry of National Economy. I appointed him, in 1955, to the newly born statistics section in MEA, and later selected him to head the airline's first department of planning and economics. Nine years later, in October 1964, I was to promote him to general manager, a post he would head until his election as chairman at the end of 1977, when I retired.

To mould the new recruits, we looked to BOAC for support, which was generously given. Our people attended training-courses in London and BOAC experts were sent to Beirut to help MEA to grow from a local DC–3 operation into an international one flying Viscounts. One early request I made to BOAC was for a financial controller and a treasurer, not only to help in organizing MEA's accounts department but also to put their minds at rest as to how the money was being spent. My growing experience told me that, in any partnership, where partners are not actively participating in the day-to-day operation, then money and how it is spent soon becomes the first seed of contention.

Partnership between a nationalized giant such as BOAC and a small private company like MEA was bound to have inherent problems, but these we had anticipated and were prepared to live with. Even so, we underestimated a number of previously unsuspected difficulties, which began to snowball, especially after the 'Three Wise Men' departed from the scene of the BOAC–MEA–Masco association in May 1956. Their replacement by people who were not only ignorant of the Anglo-Arab objectives of the association but also downright hostile to it and its development hardly helped matters. Nevertheless, we were patient and soon learnt that decisions in our new association with BOAC were bound to take an abnormally long time. Every proposal, before it could be agreed, had to pass through two boards and two British ministries – the board of MEA or Masco, the BOAC board, the Ministry of Transport and the formidable British Treasury. In 1955, ABAMEL (Associated British Airlines Middle East Ltd) was created to look after the associated companies of BOAC in the Middle East, and this automatically added yet another board to the list.

Despite the complexities of working with such a mixture of authorities, MEA and Masco progressed and grew. But, because of delays and the meddling of so many masters, the cost remained high.

The year 1955 had been a most important one in the history of MEA, when our ambitious airline put into service the most modern aircraft at its time, the four-engined turboprop Viscount. MEA was proud to be the first airline in the Arab world to fly such an aircraft. As I had predicted at the start of the negotiations with BOAC, it did not take long for other airlines to follow in MEA's footsteps and equip themselves with Viscounts.

MEA began its Viscount operation with services to Cairo, Dhahran and Baghdad. There followed services to Athens and Rome, heralding our expansion from a regional into an international operation. We also joined IATA (the International Air Transport Association) to gain international prestige and to demonstrate our serious intention of joining the international aviation club.

When it came to our inaugural flight to Rome, our sales and public-relations departments jointly prepared a list of Lebanese dignitaries from the government, the business community and the media who were to be invited. The list could be no more than forty-eight, because that was the total passenger capacity of the Viscount. Our legal adviser, the late Jamil Mekawi, then Minister of Public Works, shepherded the flock, assisted by a senior executive from MEA. Technically, the flight was a great success. The Viscount was the fastest of all aircraft operating to Rome, and also the most comfortable, since it flew above the weather. For MEA, however, it turned out to be a public-relations disaster. Having invited forty-six dignitaries we

56

made, as a consequence, more than five thousand enemies: those 'friends' who were furious at not being invited. Even Lebanese ambassadors stationed in neighbouring Arab countries were offended at having been left out. Had we forgotten all the help they had given, they asked.

A storm of Lebanese indignation broke, which lasted several years. Unfortunately, we fared no better with the dignitaries who did go on the trip to Rome. Some were annoyed because their hotel rooms were on floors lower than the rooms reserved for others. The sizes of rooms were also taken as intended discrimination. But the most unforgivable sin was our failure to get them all invited to the official dinner given by the Italian Minister of Public Works. Middle East Airlines, in the opinion of those omitted, should have informed the Italian authorities of their importance. I vowed, after this revealing experience, never to have another inaugural flight out of Beirut.

To give Masco an early start, MEA transferred to the new company its engineering installations and facilities as well as its engineers, technicians and the rest of its engineering labour force. Masco commenced its operation by contracting to carry out the servicing of MEA's fleet. Plans for Masco hangars, workshops, stores and offices were put in hand on a large area of airport land alongside the aprons and taxiways. I had managed to purchase this land from the Civil Aviation Authorities, and its acquisition established Masco as an integral part of Beirut Airport, so enjoying the facilities without having to pay airport charges. To this was added more land, bought from a private owner. The purchase of government land at the airport had been a miracle, and to buy additional land was a fortunate foresight and the soundest of business investments.

Masco's elected board represented BOAC, Field Aircraft Services on behalf of Hunting Clan, Skyways, MEA and the required number of Lebanese nationals. I was elected chairman in addition to my duties as chairman and chief executive of MEA.

In June 1955, BOAC ordered ten Viscounts, some to replace MEA's leased Viscounts, the balance for Masco to lease to airlines in the area. MEA's Viscount operation then expanded further to cover the whole of the Middle East and most of western Europe. Our service to London was inaugurated on 18 June 1956, the first flight which arrived at London Airport carrying a three-year-old sapling cedar to mark the occasion. The sapling was presented by the Lebanese Minister of Agriculture to plant at London Airport as a token of Anglo-Lebanese friendship. In a ceremony attended by the Minister of Aviation, then Harold

Watkinson, and a number of top BOAC executives, the cedar tree was planted at Heathrow by Air Marshal Sir John d'Albiac, commandant of the airport. Initially, Sir John had been concerned lest the growth of the tree might later interfere with air traffic. I had replied that it would take a Lebanese cedar hundreds of years before it could reach the height of the lowest building at London Airport. With my assurance accepted, the Lebanese cedar was granted official permission to grow in British soil.

In 1967, the tree was transplanted to a new location to make way for the building of an airport church. With its commemoration plaque, it is still at London Airport, and after thirty years has grown to a little more than four feet high — hardly a hazard to air traffic. Nevertheless, as an extra precaution, it must have had the effective attention of a pruning expert for it now grows sideways. For me, it remains the most beautiful of all cedars, symbolizing MEA's lasting gratitude for the assistance BOAC gave our airline and my hopes for MEA to live as long as the tree.

While MEA forged ahead, there continued to be internal troubles, the most harmful to future plans being the Salaam–Hoss disagreements. By this stage, it would have needed a magician to disentangle the accusations and counter-accusations, the claims and counter-claims and dozens of lawsuits pending in the courts of Lebanon. As time went on, it became abundantly clear to me that a solution must be found to clear the way for MEA's long-term plans and enable me to continue in my endeavours to improve labour relations. The split in loyalty among employees augured badly in this. Once again, it was contemplation of the beauty of the mountains and valleys of Lebanon as I drove to Beirut from my home in Shimlan that provided the inspiration.

My plan was complex, and it took time and diplomacy to persuade BOAC to go along with it, although the Salaams and Hoss needed little convincing. By then, even they were anxious to end their quarrels and get paid for shares they were not absolutely sure they really owned. The solution I proposed was for BOAC to double-purchase these shares from the Salaams and from Hoss — in fact, to pay twice over for them. This would have been no easy pill to swallow, except that BOAC was to pay for the shares from refunds I had managed to obtain on fuel tax they had overpaid on flights operating in and out of Beirut International Airport. BOAC had abandoned hope of ever recovering the overpayment and had, in fact, written it off in the accounts.

On 10 August 1956, the Salaams and Hoss, flanked by their respective lawyers, appeared in my office to set things straight. With the Notary Public present, both parties agreed, at a single session, to drop more than twenty court cases against each other, both penal and civil. So ended a legal feud that had become a legend in Lebanon. No one was happier than I, for at last MEA was free of the shareholders' squabbles. Acquiring the disputed shares meant that, for a while, BOAC owned 100 per cent of MEA's shareholding, a situation that could not be allowed to become permanent since it had come about through expediency and not through policy.

These were not, however, the only changes to be experienced in 1956. On 1 May, Sir Miles Thomas was replaced by Sir Gerard d'Erlanger as chairman of BOAC, with Sir George Cribbett appointed deputy chairman. Meanwhile, Saeb had joined the Lebanese cabinet in 1956 as Minister of Petroleum Affairs, in which role he clashed with the Iraq Petroleum Company over a retroactive tax law he wanted to introduce. The news had adverse publicity in London, causing BOAC to take the view that Saeb was no longer a suitable chairman for their wholly owned MEA. Saeb himself, because of his friendship with Jamal Abdel Nasser, had no wish to work for the British. When he resigned from the chairmanship, I was appointed temporarily in his place – a temporary election that became permanent and lasted twenty-two years.

In Middle East Airlines, an atmosphere of excitement and optimism prevailed. Alas, fate would not allow it to last. Ominous clouds were gathering and during the next two years, political storms spread all over the Middle East, including troubles in Jordan, the nationalization of the Suez Canal, the collusion of the British, French and Israelis over the ill-fated invasion of Egypt, rigged elections in Lebanon and plots and intrigues by all the parties interested in the Middle East and its oil. In May 1958, fighting broke out in Beirut, and within a few days, Lebanon was in a state of civil war which paralysed the country. The rebels, armed and financed by Abdel Nasser through Syria, aimed to overthrow President Camille Chamoun and to incorporate Lebanon within the United Arab Republic. Saeb Salaam headed the rebel forces within the capital, Kamal Jumblatt was in command in the mountains, and other feudal lords led their armed men in their own fiefs.

Meanwhile, even more trouble was brewing in the area. In June, King Hussein of Jordan foiled yet another attempted *coup* in Amman. His relative on the throne of Iraq, King Faisal, was less fortunate. Caught completely by surprise, he and his family fell victims to a revolutionary *coup* in Baghdad on 14 July. The Prime Minister, Nouri Said, and many of his cabinet were assassinated, and it was generally assumed that Nasser was responsible. For the Western powers, it seemed the last straw, and immediate counter-action followed. After President Chamoun appealed to the United States for help, American marines landed on the beaches of Beirut. Simultaneously, the British joined in by flying troops of the Parachute Regiment to Amman in support of King Hussein.

In Lebanon, there seemed something rather absurd at the time about the dramatic arrival of American marines on the crowded midsummer beaches of Beirut, where they were greeted by bikini-clad beauties and offered ice-cream. Many stories were told about the naïve Americans. One reported that a marine, arriving ashore near the airport, asked the first Lebanese he met, 'Hi, is this Ayrak?' — as Americans pronounced Iraq.

The marines stayed for three months, without firing a shot on that occasion. But a stalemate soon developed, since American policy was far from clear and divided about what it hoped to achieve by intervention. The stated aim was to go to the aid of President Chamoun, the legally and democratically elected head of state, in response to his appeal. But other Americans favoured a more even-handed approach to maintain links with the feudal lords, then considered as rebels, by aiding them as well.

This played into the hands of the Lebanese, for Lebanon loves a political stalemate and has, over the years, developed a total philosophy based on the slogan, 'no winners, no losers'. After five anxious months, the civil war ended and it seemed that the only losers were the innocent victims of the fighting. The behaviour of the Americans, and their dialogue with the militant rebels, was, however, to have a lasting and damaging effect on Lebanon. It legitimized the use of armed uprising against an elected government as a substitute for democratic political opposition, and once it was established that, by taking up the gun, a faction could obtain political (and commercial) advantage without fear of consequences, then the gun became the most powerful force in Lebanese politics.

The continual political turbulence in the Middle East between 1956 and 1958 played the very devil with the running of MEA. Airports were frequently closed to traffic, services rerouted, aircraft grounded in troubled airports, passengers unable or afraid to go to airports, and employees prevented from getting to work. Inevitably, it led to losses of revenue and increases in expenditure. Air transport is exceedingly sensitive to political disturbances. Human beings, like birds, do not like leaving their nests during storms. The company's cash flow was shot to hell. Credit was restricted, and almost dried up altogether.

60

Those who owed money to the airline delayed payment indefinitely.

MEA and Masco were soon in dire financial straits. Masco did not have enough funds to pay salaries for the month of May 1958. To meet the crisis, Intra Bank allowed an overdraft against my personal guarantee. MEA then had enough, but only just enough. The banks were ready to lend money in normal times, but not during civil wars. Those in need quickly became 'untouchables' and, to the bankers, a friend in need was no friend at all. We could not appeal to the government, which was too busy fighting for survival. Furthermore, how could Saeb's airline, as MEA was then called, hope for government aid when Saeb himself was leading an armed movement to overthrow that government? Our only hope was BOAC.

I travelled to London and literally begged for help. There was sympathy for our plight among friends at BOAC, but no sympathy in the United Kingdom or the British government for Jamal Abdel Nasser and his anti-British activities. His efforts to force Lebanon into the fold of the United Arab Republic were greatly resented. Urgent requests for more British funds to be invested in a Lebanon which might end up in his pocket met with a cool reception. My persistent cap-in-hand pleading, however, with the support of friends in BOAC and the British sense of fair play and sympathy for the underdog — MEA in this case — finally enabled me to obtain financial help, but only on a month-to-month basis. Without it, neither MEA nor Masco could ever have survived.

This outline of political events and upheavals in the Middle East from 1956 to 1958 should not only highlight the spectacular achievements of Middle East Airlines despite the problems, but also help to explain the background to the unfortunate misunderstandings which sowed the seeds for the break-up of the second BOAC–MEA partnership. These events had their origins in the appointment of Sir George Cribbett as chairman of British Associated Companies Ltd, better known as BOAC–AC, a new company incorporated in 1957 to co-ordinate BOAC's interests in seventeen associated companies in widely scattered parts of the world. Sir George had been a member of the British delegation to the Chicago Conference in 1944, and afterwards a senior civil servant in the Ministry of Aviation, and was knowledgeable in the official side of civil aviation. He encouraged and sponsored the first BOAC/MEA association in 1945, and resented tremendously the 'tactics' and abrupt termination of that association by MEA. I therefore expected hostility from him, but not an all-out war.

The subject and timing for BOAC–AC's offensive were shrewdly chosen. The cumulative losses of MEA at the end of 1958, although substantial, had been incurred during a period of costly development amid political upheavals which culminated in a five-month civil war in Lebanon. Without asking for explanations, BOAC–AC went into the attack with aggressive speed. A letter of 29 April 1959 chastised the airline for 'losses which seemed incredible for such a comparatively small company'.

Knowing that letters are never adequate in a sensitive and potentially explosive misunderstanding, I travelled to London, anxious to discuss the question and to give any explanations thought necessary. Sir George listened to me with the cool 'keep-your-bloody-distance' attitude that only the English have mastered. As I soon realized, the chairman was not really interested. He seemed to have made up his mind long before my explanations, although he admitted that MEA had passed through exceptional difficulties arising from the political disturbance in the area. Nevertheless he insisted that an overall loss of £1,350,000 sterling at the end of 1958, even if it embodied losses of previous years, 'was incredible for such a comparatively small airline'.

During informal discussion over lunch, I was made to feel that the political upheavals in the Middle East were the Arabs' own doing and that the civil war in Lebanon need not have happened had some Lebanese not been so anxious to follow Abdel Nasser. 'Saeb's part in the civl war,' Sir George said, 'is surprisingly difficult for the British to understand. Loyalty is expected from partners.' I explained that Saeb was not a partner of BOAC in MEA. He did not own a single share in the airline. He had been asked, by BOAC, to serve as chairman of MEA, and had resigned in 1956, two whole years before the start of the civil war. While Saeb had fought that war, MEA had not. Sir George had hardly done his homework!

Back in the office after an excellent lunch in his favourite restaurant in Jermyn Street, Sir George agreed that, in mitigation of the magnitude of the losses, Middle East Airlines had been operating entirely on loan capital. Even so there was, in his opinion, a considerable loss to be justified. I brought up the fact that Masco had been heavily subsidized by MEA because BOAC had given no instructions to its associated companies in the Middle East area to send their engineering work to Masco. Without that extra work, Masco had become an expensive organization, surviving mainly on the work it did for MEA, which was proving very costly and was the major reason for the losses. Mentioning Masco was like waving the proverbial red rag.

'Masco was a big mistake,' he said. 'Had it been allowed to expand, it would have deprived engineering organizations in the United Kingdom of work normally entrusted to those organizations. This would have caused serious unemployment problems. The whole concept of Masco is pregnant with political complications and is impossible to achieve in a Middle East torn apart by the inability of the Arabs to agree among themselves on any collective project.'

I had the feeling, as one of the original architects of Masco, that I was being held partly responsible for it and its unrealistic objectives. At once I seized on BOAC–AC's attitude to Masco and proposed to take it back into Middle East Airlines, initially on a lease basis. The proposal was quickly agreed to and the arrangement concluded in June 1960.

My visit to London had not been very successful, though, and the discussions had little effect. It had been like talking in a vacuum. The arguments sounded hollow, with no echo or resonance. Sir George had listened courteously and patiently, but his constant response was to emphasize the heavy responsibility BOAC–AC carried in this case as trustees of the British taxpayers' money. There was nothing personal in it, but I should be aware that public money was involved and that Sir George was answerable to the British authorities for the way such money was handled.

'Sir George,' I had said, 'BOAC has not lost a penny in Middle East Airlines, nor has the British taxpayer. All the losses you are so worried about are covered by loans contracted by MEA from BOAC. The interest on these loans is being paid monthly and punctually to BOAC through the IATA clearing-house. There will be no loss to BOAC unless MEA is declared bankrupt and the value of its assets do not meet its liabilities. MEA is not bankrupt, and now that the political troubles are behind us and the development problems ironed out, I look to the future of MEA with great confidence.'

Sir George did not share my confidence and, as I learnt some time later, BOAC had written off the loans to MEA as losses in their own accounts. A strange sort of write-off, since we were never informed and continued to pay interest on these loans to BOAC.

6
The Break with BOAC

I returned to Beirut, sad and angry. Sad, because I sensed our association with BOAC was coming to an end; angry, because I knew my explanations had been given a hearing without actually being heard. I had a feeling that a decision had already been taken, either to wind up MEA or to bring it under direct control from London. A deluge of letters and strange requests by BOAC–AC soon confirmed my suspicions.

In a letter on 8 July 1959, BOAC–AC made the oddest demands. MEA was to increase its capital by converting the loans, which covered the 'losses', to equity capital, and BOAC–AC alone was to receive the complete new share issue. All existing arrangements, ingeniously worked out by BOAC and MEA lawyers to legitimize BOAC's ownership, for a temporary period, of 100 per cent of MEA's shareholding, were to be cancelled and all the shares in question transferred to BOAC–AC. The 12,500 shares (20 per cent) which had been allotted to the employees by a unanimous decision of the board of directors and the shareholders, were to be denied to the employees and appropriated by BOAC–AC. MEA services to Europe were to be withdrawn. Finally, a message arrived from Sir Francis Brake, saying BOAC–AC had decided to appoint a British general manager. The offensive was launched.

To have complied with BOAC–AC's requests would have publicly exposed Middle East Airlines as virtually owned and controlled by the British. The Lebanese government would have cancelled our licence and MEA would have been destroyed, ostensibly not by BOAC–AC, but by its own government. This clever move I foiled by an immediate refusal of all the bizarre demands, but BOAC–AC was incensed with the audacity of my stand. I suppose they had every reason, from their point of view. It was certainly an affront for someone who owned not a single share to challenge those who owned them all. Now I come to think of it, I must have had plenty of nerve.

Following my refusal, the offensive was stepped up. Sir George, as deputy chairman of BOAC, commented publicly that the corporation had sunk £6 million sterling into Middle East Airlines. He used the word 'sunk' rather than 'invested', and naturally his statement was picked up by the English press and provoked a discussion of MEA's affairs in the British Parliament. The Labour Opposition made political capital of the news of BOAC's losses in MEA, and described MEA as 'one big sieve through which public money has been poured'.

On 20 July 1959, Harold Watkinson, the Minister of Civil Aviation, made the following statement in the House of Commons: 'In Middle East Airlines, however, I regard the situation as being extremely grave. Therefore, I have approached the chairman of BOAC and he has appointed Sir George Cribbett to go into the whole matter. He quite agrees that we cannot go on with the dramatic losses in this company and that matters must either be wound up or some other different arrangement come to.' The British press were active in bringing to the attention of the public the 'extremely grave' situation of Middle East Airlines and the sensational description of MEA as 'one big sieve through which public money has been poured'. It was evident that BOAC–AC had briefed the Minister, and had most probably drafted the Minister's statement to the House. I remembered what BOAC–AC had said in their letter of 29 June 1959: 'It is quite clear that neither Parliament nor the British public will accept losses of the magnitude incurred and that we shall be obliged to consider liquidation unless some constructive and drastic change of plan can be brought forward.'

After press cuttings of what was said in the House of Commons were sent to me from London, I wrote to BOAC without mincing my words. I pointed out that the official statement by the Minister of Aviation, that BOAC intended to wind up Middle East Airlines, could have originated only with BOAC–AC and demanded that BOAC–AC come to the defence of MEA and publish the true facts. There was no response, so once more I travelled to London to enter into the lion's den.

I was itching to fight for MEA, for its employees and for Lebanese civil aviation as well as for the interests of BOAC and Anglo-Arab civil aviation in general. I was determined to save the airline, yet seemed a lonely warrior going into battle with the giants in their own arena, armed only with the courage of my convictions and the nerve of one who believes he is fighting for a just cause. The 'Battle of the Sieve' was on.

Fate, in its infinite wisdom, decreed that Yousif Bedas, chairman of

Intra, a member of the MEA board and a personal friend, should also be travelling to London that day on the same aircraft. Yousif noticed I had been taking more than the one or two drinks I usually kept to, and also observed my disquiet. When he asked the reason, I told him of this latest development. He wanted to know what I planned. 'Fight like hell,' I replied. 'Fight as I have never fought before.' He said, 'I'm with you and prepared to back you all the way.' As we made the final approach to London, he turned and exclaimed, 'Why don't we buy out BOAC? The new BOAC management obviously have no faith in MEA or in Lebanon. We have. Keep me informed, and the best of luck in your fight.'

I was used to Bedas's brilliant lightning decisions, and believed in his faith in MEA and his devotion to Lebanon, but I was also a little worried. I knew that Bedas hated flying and always fortified himself against its imagined perils. Perhaps it was Johnny Walker Black Label that prompted his encouraging outburst. Perhaps, when its effect had worn off, he would draw back from going all the way. Nevertheless, I worked out an offer to Sir Gerard d'Erlanger, chairman of BOAC, for buying all the shares and repaying all the loans. When I showed the draft to Bedas, his enthusiasm was unabated, and to my relief, and without prompting, he gave me a letter from Intra Bank guaranteeing all the commitments in my proposal.

Armed with this, I submitted my offer to Sir Gerard d'Erlanger on 29 August 1959. I told Sir Gerard that the reputation and prestige of MEA had suffered considerably in Britain, in the Arab world and throughout the Mediterranean area because of unsubstantiated statements made in the House of Commons and the unwillingness of BOAC to come to MEA's defence. The British public had been told only one side of the story. I stressed that BOAC had not paid a penny of the losses, for these, produced mainly by political troubles, were covered by 6 per cent interest-bearing loans from BOAC. No actual payment of losses in MEA had ever been made by BOAC or the British taxpayer. All that BOAC had invested in MEA was the price they paid for their shareholding. I gratefully acknowledged the loans, which had helped us to overcome our hardships, but said that, to be fair to MEA and BOAC and the objectives that inspired the association, I wished to relieve BOAC and the British taxpayer of the burden of any losses.

Determined to demonstrate to the British public that MEA was not 'one big sieve through which public money has been poured', I therefore offered to buy immediately, and for cash, all of BOAC's shares in MEA at the price paid. I was also prepared to repay, in full, all the loans made to MEA according to an instalment schedule to be agreed, to be guaranteed by Intra Bank or by any bank of BOAC's choice. BOAC, having been paid the cost of their shareholding and all loans, should then refund to MEA all profits made on dealings with MEA – those made on the sale or lease of aircraft to MEA as well as profits arising from the difference between the interest charges MEA had to pay BOAC on loans and those paid by BOAC on its borrowing. I sought no compensation for the feeder business MEA gave BOAC, or for the protection of BOAC's unlimited traffic rights into and out of Lebanon. Neither was anything asked for the substantial subsidy made by MEA to BOAC's Masco.

While I waited for Sir Gerard to reply, I looked for a public-relations organization to help me present our case to the British public. I was informed of Frank O'Shanohun, an English journalist of Irish origin, who was starting his own public-relations company. We met in the Athenaeum Court Hotel, where I was staying, Frank starting the discussion by asking if I had any skeletons in my cupboard. I replied that the only skeletons I wished to accommodate in my cupboard were those of the people who hated Middle East Airlines. Having heard our story in detail, and satisfied himself that my cupboard was free of undesirable bones, Frank pitched in with all his dynamic force. He organized a press conference for 25 September 1959, timed to enable me to discuss Sir Gerard's reply.

Sir Gerard in fact replied on the 22nd, stating: 'Let me say at once that I should be very sorry to think that our association should come to an end but, in view of your letter, we must obviously endeavour to come to some mutually satisfactory arrangement.' He then refused my offer and proposed an agreement which would preserve our association.

At the press conference arranged for the 25th, I delivered a statement outlining our story. As question time began a journalist asked: 'Now, Sheikh, how many wives have you got?' 'When you are running an airline you have no time for more than one,' I replied. The answer appealed to the British sense of humour and got the meeting off to a good start. Numerous questions relating to the issues then followed, and were answered to the journalists' satisfaction.

I had faith in Frank, and in his outstanding ability, but could only fear for the chances of a lonely Lebanese fighting the giant government-owned BOAC. I was, however, pleasantly surprised by the attitude of the British aviation press and the fair stand they took on our side. One journalist referred to me as the 'Flying Sheikh', a title that stuck with me ever after.

The press conference was the start of a life-long friendship between Frank and myself and a very close association between MEA and his public-relations organization. MEA owes much to Frank O'Shanohun and his agency for its prestige and excellent reputation in the United Kingdom and elsewhere. That meeting, moreover, forged many friendships with British aviation writers which I cherish to this day.

The resounding success of the press conference hastened BOAC's desire to reach a satisfactory arrangement. Lengthy meetings produced an agreement on 20 November 1959, which came to be known as the Cribbett–Alamuddin agreement. But our victory looked too good to be true, and so it proved. Hardly four months after its signature, most of its important articles were changed by BOAC–AC, and this is how it came about. When, in accordance with the agreement, MEA requested financial support to buy British Comet 4Cs for its equipment programme, BOAC agreed to give the required support in the form of a guarantee. BOAC–AC insisted, however, that granting the guarantee should be conditional on scrapping nearly all the important clauses of the Cribbett–Alamuddin agreement. As if that was not enough for them, a totally new condition was also introduced. Fifty-one per cent of the shares of MEA must be sold to Lebanese nationals prior to granting the guarantee.

A victory over a superior power is a temporary illusion. Sooner or later you will find yourself cornered on a vital issue and left with a choice of take it or leave it. I had no alternative but to take it. With my faith in *inshallah*, I accepted the new conditions laid down by BOAC–AC so as to make sure we had a chance of the guarantee. Without the superb Comets, our growth would have been stunted and our survival much in doubt.

I promptly went to Bedas and told him of the latest turn of events. He was willing to assist, but needed convincing. After a long discussion and some hard selling by me, he accepted the deal. Intra Bank bought 51½ per cent of the shares of MEA and, as a result, the Comet was secured. But do not make the mistake of thinking that Intra Bank was a charitable organization or Bedas a missionary. Far from it. Intra was an aggressive bank with but a single objective: to make money. Bedas was a brilliant banker with a remarkable nose for a good investment. He believed in MEA and its profitable future. He also sensed that he could impose his terms on BOAC for the purchase of the shares. He got away with paying only their par value, which was a very profitable transaction for the bank.

Discussions with De Havillands on the purchase of Comets had been going, on and off, since the beginning of 1958, and were periodically suspended because of political fighting in Lebanon and the frequent squabbles with BOAC–AC. Once the tug-of-war for the guarantee was over, a contract for four Comet 4Cs was quickly signed and deliveries made in December 1960. The Comets were all in service by mid-April 1961. It was a tremendous challenge to a small airline like MEA to switch from operating Viscounts to flying Comets.

Seasonal changes at the top of BOAC were meanwhile taking place. Sir Gerard d'Erlanger retired in April 1960 as chairman of BOAC, and Sir George Cribbett retired as chairman of BOAC–AC, to be replaced by Keith Granville. During the five years of our second association, BOAC had had three chairmen and BOAC–AC two. It was like a game of political musical chairs.

Granville was a professional commercial airline executive who had risen from the ranks, and who had been stationed in Cairo as manager for the African and Middle East division of BOAC in 1947. It was reported that, in that capacity, he had been much involved in the affairs of the first BOAC–MEA association and its untimely end. Moreover, he harboured a grudge as a result of an unfortunate incident which happened a year or so before he took up his chairmanship of BOAC–AC. Sir George Cribbett had sent me a telex, suggesting Granville be elected to the board of MEA to represent BOAC–AC. As was usual procedure, Terleske, the MEA financial controller seconded from BOAC, was consulted. He came to me and asked whether I knew Granville's name had been Solomon before he changed it by deed poll. I told him I did not. Salim Salaam, nephew of Saeb, followed, saying that Granville had been Mr Solomon when MEA had dealings with him as manager of the African and Middle East division. In the light of the Arab–Israeli tensions in the region, and the effect the election of Granville/Solomon to the board would have on MEA in the Arab world as well as on BOAC itself, I took the first flight to London to discuss the problem with BOAC.

I explained my feelings to the highest powers in BOAC and BOAC–AC, and to Granville himself, and refused to yield to pressure to accept Granville on to my board. My stand was neither appreciated nor completely understood. I had my way, but made no friends, and felt a premonition of serious troubles ahead. These came much sooner than I expected. Granville's appointment as chairman of BOAC–AC brought MEA under his jurisdiction.

The first encounter took place when MEA wanted to increase its capital. MEA had been, since its formation, consistently under-capitalized and operating on borrowed finance. Having finally found Lebanese shareholders ready not only to invest in MEA but also to increase their investment when needed, I heaved a sigh of relief and proposed an increase of capital. The costly preparations for the introduction of our Comet fleet and other important requirements made such an increase imperative.

The reaction of BOAC–AC was, to say the least, odd if not hostile. Granville knew that an increase in capital for MEA was essential and that I was not asking BOAC–AC for funds from the United Kingdom. The Lebanese shareholders were prepared to pay cash for their 51½ per cent share of the increase, and I proposed to BOAC–AC that their 48½ per cent share be covered by converting to capital some of the existing BOAC loans to MEA. To my surprise, BOAC–AC not only rejected the increase of capital but also insisted on maintaining their level of shareholding at 48½ per cent. This insistence was clearly intended to block the increase. We could not have proceeded with an increase of capital without BOAC–AC's 48½ per cent because legally, to increase its capital, a company in Lebanon required the approval of a majority of two thirds of its shareholders.

To compound the blow, BOAC–AC, not content with rejecting our legal and justifiable request, demanded an immediate settlement of all outstanding loans. They knew that, without the increase of capital, which they were blocking, there was not an earthly chance of MEA settling those loans immediately. Evidently the move was meant to provoke the confrontation which I was anxious to avoid. Thus I rejected their demands flatly. To meet our requirements for working capital, we instead borrowed money from local banks in Lebanon. This, of course, increased our interest charges and reduced our profits – which was also possibly what BOAC–AC wanted.

I proceeded to London to discuss our problems and explain the difficulties arising from BOAC–AC's odd reaction to our need for a long-overdue increase of capital. BOAC–AC's attitude continued obstinately negative. In Arabic we use the phrase 'talking to a wall' when arguments and appeals meet a deaf ear. I was talking to a special kind of wall, a wall that did not even produce an echo. I had the distinct feeling that Granville had made up his mind to liquidate our association and that nothing I could say would have the slightest effect on that decision.

Aside from Granville's personal hostility, I could fathom no logical reason for BOAC–AC's attitude. MEA had overcome its difficulties. Our association with them was flourishing. We had been making profits regularly since the end of the fighting in 1958. After our purchase of the British Viscounts, the Middle East skies were buzzing with Viscounts bought by airlines that followed our example. Similarly, after we bought British Comets, many airlines in the area did the same. We had fully protected BOAC's valuable traffic rights, and a paper prepared by BOAC's general manager for eastern routes, dated 25 May 1959, said that the value to BOAC of traffic to and from Beirut was assessed at £1.5 million sterling per annum. In the same paper, the value of feeder business, passengers and freight, carried by MEA from points in the Middle East and fed into BOAC's services at Beirut, was estimated at £300,000 sterling per annum.

Commercially, BOAC was therefore benefiting, as admitted by its manager of eastern routes, by nearly £2 million sterling a year. In addition, we paid BOAC annually over £8 million sterling for the handling of our aircraft at London Airport — catering, overhauling aero-engines and various other services. Moreover, Middle East Airlines had become the predominant airline in the Arab world, exactly as BOAC's 'Three Wise Men' and I had foreseen and planned. It was a joint venture of inestimable value to British–Arab co-operation in civil aviation. Why, therefore, break it up?

Although I was convinced that the break-up was in sight, as a last *acte de sauvetage* I requested Vice-Admiral Sir Matthew Slattery, then chairman of BOAC, for a meeting at which I hoped to solicit his help. On meeting the admiral, I gave him a résumé of the problems in our association with BOAC–AC, strongly requesting that efforts be made to find solutions and establish a clear-cut policy for co-operation. I added that, unless the necessary action was taken soon, I was afraid divorce would be the only option. To my surprise, he swiftly opted for divorce. I accepted the decision, confident in the support of my friend Yousif Bedas.

The alacrity with which the proposal was taken up gave me an edge which I used to advantage. We in the Middle East, and especially in Lebanon, are renowned for our traditional skills in bargaining and our love of the art. It was said that, during the Second World War, an English officer asked a Lebanese urchin how much did two plus two make. 'Are you selling or buying?' was the prompt reply. Because BOAC–AC was so eager to get rid of us, two plus two, in our case, made a most advantageous three when buying.

A series of events swiftly followed. A meeting with Keith Granville produced a letter on 12 June 1961, confirming that BOAC was willing to enter into negotiations for the sale of its shareholding in MEA and that negotiations should include a full arrangement for the settlement of all outstanding financial matters. The matter would be dealt with expeditiously, I was promised, once my offer was received. As I had, in fact, been preparing my offer ever since my meeting with Admiral Slattery, when a break-up was agreed, I was able to send it back by return of post on the same day. On 3 July, a letter came from Granville stating that the BOAC board had approved my offer with some modifications. By 16 August, after a few short bouts of bargaining, all necessary arrangements were signed and sealed.

The BOAC board and Her Majesty's government had certainly given their approval for the break-up of an arrangement designed to promote co-operation between the United Kingdom and the Arab world with record speed. The break-up with MEA was the beginning of the liquidation of BOAC's interests in all Arab airlines. How difficult it is to build, and how easy to destroy. But, as Pope John Paul II said while pleading for peace among nations, 'Passions obscure reality.'

I was not the only person to be puzzled by the break-up and its speedy liquidation. There were many others equally curious, especially in the United Kingdom. A question on the subject was raised in the House of Commons by Mr William Shepherd, MP, on 6 November 1962, to which he received no answer from the Minister of Aviation, Mr Julian Amery, the son of the Leo Amery who claimed he had drafted the Balfour Declaration. Perhaps, one day, the explanation will come to light. *Inshallah!*

The financial settlement, once agreed, was simple and straightforward: the Lebanese shareholders would buy the 48½ per cent shareholding of BOAC at par value, 50 per cent to be paid in cash, the balance to be paid after twelve months with the guarantee of Intra Bank. At Yousif Bedas's suggestion, Abdallah Khoury joined in purchasing the shares, Abdallah being one of the founders of the Contracting and Trading Company (CAT), and a mutual friend. Intra Bank and the two of us therefore bought the 48½ per cent, a loan from Intra Bank enabling me to pay for my shares.

All the loans from BOAC to MEA were to be paid back in five annual instalments, without interest and guranteed by Intra Bank. The purchase agreement of our Viscounts from BOAC would remain valid, and the balance was to be paid over five years, with interest, guaranteed by the mortgage on the aircraft which had been held by BOAC ever since the Viscounts were bought by MEA.

BOAC's guarantee to De Havillands for our purchase of the Comet 4Cs would be maintained, as would the mortgage on these aircraft held by BOAC. BOAC agreed to sell to MEA the Masco installations, equipment and spare parts for the sum of £707,700 sterling. Of this MEA would pay £73,700 sterling in cash and the balance in ten equal annual instalments without interest. A mortgage on the land and buildings would be offered as security.

The sale of Masco brought the only losses sustained by BOAC in all their association with MEA. They were too eager to get rid of Masco, and in doing so practically gave the company away. So far as everything else went, their investments were repaid in full, their loans repaid with interest. Their losses in turbulent 1958 were more than compensated by the profits they made on selling MEA the Viscounts. These they had bought at a much lower price than the one they charged to us, and since they were 100 per cent owners of MEA at the time, no one had a right to object. BOAC also made substantial profits from charging us 6 per cent on loans, while they borrowed at 3 per cent, and continued to do so even after the loans were written out of their accounts.

The purchase of Masco was the most profitable single deal Middle East Airlines had ever entered into. The land on which MEA's administration offices and engineering services are now built was bought at less than £L1.5 million. Masco land, moreover, had its own private source of water, yielding 5,000 gallons an hour, which remains of inestimable value. The hangars, workshops, equipment, spares and other installations were bought for less than £L5 million. These arrangements brought immense profits and unlimited savings to MEA, from cheap water to needing to pay no rental charges to the airport authorities for shops and hangars and incurring no parking charges for aircraft and equipment. The land, buildings, installations, equipment and spares bought with Masco from BOAC would easily fetch over $1,000 million at today's prices. These valuable assets were a major factor in preserving Middle East Airlines despite its colossal losses over the previous nine years.

Cumulative losses and development costs at the end of 1958 (the year of civil fighting in Lebanon) had reached a figure of £L19,164,727. BOAC, as sole shareholder at the time, should have paid these losses at the end of 1958, but decided, instead, to cover them with interest-bearing loans to MEA. We had regularly paid the interest on these, and I was determined, while our association with BOAC survived, that they should be repaid out of future profits. After the break-up and the manner in which it was done, however, I could see no earthly reason for such magnanimity, especially since BOAC had already recouped the losses from profits on the sale of Viscounts to

MEA, excessive interest rates, charges for services and other items. I therefore requested that BOAC should exempt MEA from having to repay these loans as losses for which BOAC had been legally responsible and which had, as such, actually been written off in their accounts. BOAC agreed they would ask for no repayment.

My two friends and partners, Yousif Bedas and Abdallah Khoury, two of the smartest Lebanese businessmen who ever lived, then came up with a suggestion which could have been of substantial personal benefit to each one of us. It was that we should keep the £L19 million in the books of Middle East Airlines as a debt due to the three of us, to be shared equally and repaid from future profits. They argued that we had replaced BOAC when we bought their shares, and that the debt was ours by legal right. They produced opinions from their legal advisers to support their claim.

I objected and argued that such an action, legal as it may have been, would burden the accounts of the company and discourage other Lebanese from buying shares. It would also hinder any possible merger with other Lebanese airlines, and could be very restrictive when we needed bank loans for the purchase of new equipment. They were unconvinced, and so I threatened to quit if they persisted. They did not appreciate my obstinate stand and thought I was being altruistically foolish. Both insisted that, one day, I would regret my idealism. Nevertheless, they finally agreed to write the debt out of the MEA accounts and to consider its annulment a parting gift from BOAC.

Looking back at this incident, and at the behaviour of the shareholders of Middle East Airlines at the time and after my retirement, I think that my late wise friends, Yousif and Abdallah, were possibly right. Perhaps I was a sentimental fool.

7
MEA Becomes Lebanese

The purchase of BOAC's shareholding was acclaimed by the Lebanese media as a victorious achievement. Upon my return to Beirut, after the signature of the severance agreements, I was given a hero's welcome. Telephone calls, telegrams and letters of congratulation poured in, and many called round personally to express their appreciation.

I cannot say, however, that all of Lebanon was jubilant over the deal. A great many Lebanese thought we had made a mistake. Others disliked our success, and certain foreign interests looked on it as a dangerous precedent. By contrast, the airline employees were triumphant over their independence from foreign control. Happy at their loyalty and support, I was nevertheless growing worried about the way in which the affair was becoming politicized and anxious to halt this unwelcome development. The break-up was neither a Lebanese victory over the British nor a defeat for BOAC. It was a regrettable failure of a joint venture which, had it succeeded, could have produced substantial benefits for everybody. The political antagonism to the joint venture and its subsequent failure should have been an early warning of the catastrophes that were to hit Intra Bank, MEA and Lebanon. But mankind has never been endowed with foresight.

I was concerned that, once the euphoria subsided, the employees would begin to worry about the future of the company. BOAC had been a sheet-anchor for MEA. Had we forgotten its rescue operation in our troubles during the fighting of 1958? There was also the prevailing impression, especially in Lebanon, that a local airline could not survive without the support of a major foreign carrier. Air Liban and other airlines in the Middle East had provided ample evidence for this belief.

I moved fast to reassure the employees and the Lebanese public of MEA's potential prospects and to depoliticize the story of the break with BOAC. I called a meeting of all employees in Beirut, and sent a detailed circular to employees at outstations, to tell them we had not severed our relations with BOAC, that we were still friends and hoped to continue our co-operation, both technical and commercial, for a very long time. I said we had made arrangements to continue our engineering handling and traffic handling of BOAC aircraft at Beirut for at least five years. We were also maintaining the commercial pooling agreement.

The new Lebanese shareholders, and their desire to help MEA, were emphasized in all our communications. It was also necessary, however, to emphasize the difference between the expectations of the new shareholders and those of BOAC, for whom dividends, although important, were not the only consideration. The Lebanese shareholders, patriotic as they may have been, were interested in profits and dividends. If MEA wanted to keep their support, it must work hard to provide them regularly with their deserved profits. There was no other source of financial assistance. MEA could not look to the government for help because of the multiplicity of airlines in Lebanon. In any case, government help, even if available, meant interference, and interference would paralyse the airline and almost certainly drive it into loss. The future therefore depended on ourselves, on our hard work and efficiency.

It was also made clear that Middle East Airlines was completely Lebanese and belonged entirely to its employees and its shareholders. But while the shareholders had many other interests, the employees had only Middle East Airlines to guarantee their future and the livelihood of their families. Their future was in their own hands. MEA was their airline. This theme I repeated on every occasion, and it appeared in all my statements, reports and discussions. The employees began to believe that the airline was really theirs. It was this belief, together with the growing conviction that the airline was one great Lebanese family, that again and again enabled MEA to face many crises and somehow manage the miracle of survival.

Having put the whole affair in its true perspective, we braced ourselves to tackle the challenge of total independence. We took the first reassuring decision — and raised the capital threefold, from £L6,250,000 to £L18,750,000, and then proceeded to make the transition to independence as smoothly as possible. We did not intend to part with our foreign technical staff since we were happy to have them. In any case, except for one senior technical executive, all foreign pilots and engineers were employed directly by MEA. They, in their turn, were all happy to stay. Even the one seconded technical executive resigned from BOAC to remain with MEA.

Nevertheless, the foreign employees needed reassuring about the security of their jobs since they were worried that up-and-coming Lebanese would want to replace them. They were therefore guaranteed employment with MEA until they retired, or until they decided to leave of their own free will. MEA would not, however, appoint foreigners to new positions where qualified Lebanese were available to fill them. The foreign pilots and engineers were Britons, Australians, Americans, Germans, Russians, New Zealanders and Rhodesians. In fact, in MEA there existed a mini-United Nations, but one that functioned happily and produced results.

At no time were we in more urgent need of maintaining our established good image than at this stage of development. Our reputation in Europe and in the Arab world had received quite a jolt. 'BOAC Associate' was a magic tag that evoked public confidence in the safety of our operation and provided passenger appeal. How could a Middle Eastern airline of a small country like Lebanon have satisfactory technical standards without help from the West? This doubt was unfortunately shared equally by Arabs, Europeans and even Lebanese.

A great many people, especially those of the older generation, were frightened of flying. Since man is not born with wings, they considered leaving the ground to be unnatural and hazardous. It was logical therefore for them to look, when travelling, for the airline with the highest technical and safety standards, and our BOAC link had given the travelling public added confidence. Several incidents showed that passengers had not all developed unreserved confidence in the Lebanese operation. One Arab ruler in the Gulf, who frequently chartered MEA aircraft for his travels, would insist on having an English pilot. A Lebanese Minister of Public Works, whose ministry controlled civil aviation, refused to take a flight to Europe when informed the pilot was Lebanese. Therefore quick action was needed to allay fears that MEA's technical standards would suffer without BOAC. We could not possibly survive if we lost the confidence of the travelling public. It certainly didn't help that competitors and others anxious to harm MEA began to spread news of an 'impending technical decline'. We had to fight malicious rumours and also prove that our technical standards would not only be maintained but even improved now we were on our own.

A programme of intensive training was organized in Lebanon and abroad. MEA's training-centre in Beirut became by far the best in the Middle East with the help of the best-qualified training experts, both foreign and Lebanese. Employees of other airlines also studied at the training-centre, where they were warmly welcomed. The public were told about it. A public-relations campaign was launched to let everyone know that our foreign pilots and engineers were staying on. MEA was pleased to spread the news that it conformed to the technical standards of BOAC – among the highest in the aviation world. It was moreover emphasized that our Lebanese pilots and engineers were trained at BOAC and other technical training-centres abroad. We made sure everyone realized that we would employ only Lebanese pilots and engineers who attained higher technical standards than the foreigners.

Notwithstanding this concern for the after-effects of the break with BOAC, the good image of Middle East Airlines was well maintained, thanks to the efforts of our public-relations consultants, headed by Frank O'Shanohun, and our PR department, headed by Sami Rababy. Sami had left the position of general sales manager of Coca-Cola in Lebanon to join Middle East Airlines in 1958. Besides his excellent work for MEA, he was destined to make a substantial contribution to tourism in Lebanon and its prestige, nationally and internationally. He represented Lebanon on tourist international bodies and was repeatedly elected and re-elected as chairman of their most important committees – four times as chairman of the Affiliate Members Committee of the World Tourism Organization and twice as chairman of the Académie Internationale du Tourisme. Sadly, as a reward for his efforts, Sami was kidnapped in 1985 and held captive for over five months. In the turmoil of a vicious civil war, such 'appreciation' is not uncommon for those who serve the best interests of their country.

All of that lay in the future, however, and to return to events as they happened, one Monday morning, in August 1961, I received a telephone call from the Jordanian Court Chamberlain with a message that King Hussein wished to see me as soon as possible. Next day, in Amman, His Majesty explained that Transocean, an American airline, had pulled out its subsidiary, Air Jordan, suddenly leaving the country without air communications. King Hussein was asking for urgent help from Middle East Airlines, and we were ready to oblige.

'When will it be possible for MEA to start?' asked the King. 'On Thursday,' I replied. And, on Thursday, Viscounts of Middle East Airlines were duly in Amman on His Majesty's service. The King had also expressed a wish that MEA should form a new Jordanian airline, in partnership with his government and Jordanian nationals. He promised his full support and that of his government, and this was officially confirmed in a letter from the Prime Minister.

MEA undertook to provide the necessary services on a temporary basis while the new airline was being formed. At our request, the government took steps to rationalize the structure of civil aviation in Jordan by revoking the licence of Air Jordan and the licences of four other airlines which were not in fact flying.

The new company, Jordan Airways, was granted a licence and exclusive rights to all the kingdom's domestic and international routes. The government undertook, for a period of ten years, 'not to grant any other airline or any individual or group of individuals, any licence or permission to operate regular or charter services on any internal or international Jordanian air routes'. We reserved the right for MEA to cancel its agreements with Jordan Airways and withdraw from the operation should the government go back on this undertaking.

The company was formed, and the capital distributed: 25 per cent to the Jordanian government and 35 per cent to MEA, with the remaining 40 per cent available to Jordanian investors. Management of the airline was entrusted to MEA, Jordan's painful experiences with other airlines inspiring a demand that MEA should guarantee payment of the airline's losses. In return for this guarantee, and for managing the airline, MEA was to receive 10 per cent of the profits, if any. Jordan Airways started operations on 1 October 1961.

This was MEA's first association with an Arab airline and potentially a stepping-stone towards other partnerships which might eventually, God willing, lead to a united Arab airline. At MEA, we were determined to make a success of it, to give Jordan and the Jordanians the best possible service and prove to King Hussein we were worthy of his confidence. I was particularly anxious to show my gratitude to the country where, between 1933 and 1942, I had spent the happiest ten years of my life, and to the people who had made me feel so much at home there.

No effort was spared to make a success of this joint Arab venture, and I instructed our staff to give priority to the requirements of Jordan Airways. MEA aircraft, including Viscounts, were placed at the disposal of the new airline so that it could introduce services flown by our crews from Amman to Cairo, Beirut, Kuwait, Jeddah, Doha, Damascus and Aqaba. On the Beirut–Jerusalem–Beirut run, we pooled all traffic on a fifty-fifty basis. The MEA training-centre was also placed at the disposal of Jordan Airways staff, and it was there that Jordan's first pilot passed his examinations for a commercial licence. In addition to these services, MEA chartered other aircraft to Jordan Airways for high-season demands, to meet the needs of tourist traffic in the Holy Land at Christmas and Easter, the Hajj flights to Mecca, and the movements of students and teachers between Jordan and the Gulf.

Realizing that tourism was one of the important sectors of the Jordanian national economy, we embarked on extensive advertising to attract visitors. MEA and Jordan Airways jointly invited travel agents from Europe and the United States to visit the places of interest in Jordan and in the Holy Land. We distributed circulars, posters and other items. A coloured film on Jordan was produced by United Artists to be shown throughout the world. We also invited journalists from Europe and the United States to visit Jordan. Middle East Airlines and its European and American public-relations consultants made all the arrangements and MEA shared in all the expenses.

Inclusive tours, organized by MEA for Jordan, produced 50,000 tourist days from European tourists alone during the first half of 1963. Jordan Airways had fulfilled its commitments and more, and the reliability of its operation was excellent. Ninety-one per cent of its flights left on time. During its second year of operation, it carried 40 per cent more passengers than in the first year.

Despite this record, it became obvious that we were being denied the promised government support. Foreign airlines continued to enjoy traffic rights to which they were not entitled under Jordan's air agreements. Jordan Airways was denied the benefits and exemptions usually granted by countries to their national airlines. Although specifically promised by the government, the transportation of government officials and delegations was not given to Jordan Airways. An application to the Department of Civil Aviation for permission to start jet services between Jordan and Europe was turned down with no reason given.

This unco-operative attitude by the Jordanians was accompanied by a campaign of denigration directed at MEA's management of Jordan Airways. We were accused of diverting tourists from Jordan to Lebanon, of stealing passengers from Jordan Airways, of exploiting Jordan Airways through overcharging, and of discouraging Jordanians from qualifying as pilots and engineers. It was also claimed that the Viscounts bought by Jordan Airways on hire purchase from MEA were overpriced, obsolete and not even airworthy. All of these accusations were false, the campaign being led by two highly placed government officials, abetted by two members of the board of Jordan Airways who were not of our choice. King Hussein granted me several meetings at which I explained the situation. He was most understanding and, as a qualified pilot, enjoyed discussing aviation. Alas, none of these meetings improved matters at Jordan Airways. King Hussein must have had many more important problems requiring his attention than those of the airline. The campaign continued and no explanations could deter it.

Early in September 1963, a meeting of the Amman Council of Ministers was called to grant a licence to a new airline in Jordan in which the Jordanian government would participate, and which was authorized to transport passengers and freight on Jordan's internal and international routes. It was a duplicate licence to the one already granted to Jordan Airways. MEA had not even been consulted or informed in advance. The new airline was to be formed in association with Lebanese International Airways (LIA). Clearly, the new licence was in violation of the agreement concluded between MEA and Jordan Airways and approved by the Jordanian government. Even worse, it was a flagrant violation of the formal assurances given me by the Prime Minister of Jordan that the government, with the blessing of His Majesty, would respect their promise that Jordan Airways should be the only airline in Jordan.

There were obviously some very powerful reasons which prompted the Jordanian government to reverse its policy so completely, and I had my own ideas on these. Although I am by nature a fighter, I realized, from what I knew of the background, that opposition would in this case be futile. Besides, my deep affection for Jordan and its people prevented me from causing a public row. If the slightest official criticism of the management of Jordan Airways by MEA had been put forward as a pretext for granting a licence to the new airline, I would not have hesitated to hit back and reveal all that I knew. In an effort to pacify me, a special envoy arrived in Beirut. I contented myself by asking him to remind those who sent him that, because of the happy days I spent in Jordan earlier in my life, and my love for Jordan and the Jordanians, I felt bound by the traditional Druze belief that one should 'not throw stones into a well from which one has drunk'.

Jordan Airways was liquidated by its shareholders on 8 December 1963, exactly two years, two months and thirteen days after its birth. It took little time before Lebanese International Airways was pushed out and Alia became the official airline of Jordan. MEA was rewarded for its sincere but wasted efforts with a loss of £L1 million and a harsh lesson — keep away from associations with Arab airlines. They are doomed to fail. It is so planned, perhaps so written.

8
The Air Liban Merger

For more than sixteen years, Middle East Airlines and Air Liban, the other principal Lebanese airline, had been strong competitors, fighting each other with no holds barred. The battle was more politically than commercially motivated, for the affair involved Lebanese Christians against Lebanese Moslems. There were also international involvements. While MEA had been an associate, first of the Americans and then of the British, Air Liban was firmly in the French camp by way of its association with Air France. For this reason, the French lined up first against the Americans and then against the British. The political in-fighting was especially bitter and the wounds inflicted long remembered.

For as long as the honeymoon lasted between the French state airline and Air Liban, local shareholders in the company enjoyed considerable advantages, including a guaranteed annual dividend on their capital of 9 per cent, even in those years when the company lost money. It was, in fact, Air France which had to absorb the losses from Air Liban operations. Lebanese board members of Air Liban also received generous fees, representation allowances and, what was even more desirable for businessmen who travelled frequently by air, the benefits of unlimited free travel on both Air Liban and Air France flights. In return for these costly concessions, Air France was free to impose its will on the Lebanese airline.

By 1961, it was becoming clear that the costly honeymoon must soon end. Air Liban was registering an annual loss of over £L8 million, the forecast being for losses running at the rate of almost £L1 million a month. When the Lebanese shareholders were asked to help by surrendering some of their luxurious benefits, they reacted violently, claiming that the losses in Air Liban were fictitious and accusing Air France of overcharging the airline for all its services. This untoward show of ingratitude was strongly resented by Air France, whose chairman discreetly contacted Yousif Bedas in Paris to find out whether MEA might be interested in buying Air Liban.

Bedas referred the question to me. Although I was intrigued, I entertained some doubts. Air France wanted the negotiations to be conducted in utmost secrecy, and so clandestine meetings were arranged in Paris at the home of their director-general. After a number of meetings and some intensive bargaining, the elements of a deal were put together. An agreement was initiated on 6 August 1962 that all Air Liban shares were to be sold to MEA since Air France wanted to cut completely free from the partnership.

Naturally, a tense atmosphere dominated the negotiations, which were further complicated by the fact that, although I understand French, I did not speak it well enough to use it in formal talks. I had studied French at the American University where it was added to the curriculum of the Lebanese students as a necessary evil. The French consider speaking their language by foreigners to be a prerequisite of friendship. For a Lebanese not to speak the language is unforgivable. My brother Sulayman once had an exchange with an immigration officer upon arrival at Paris Orly Airport from London when he filled in his entry form in English. 'Vous êtes Libanais?' asked the officer. 'Yes,' replied my brother. 'Alors pourquoi vous écrivez en Anglais?' 'Because I like it,' said Sulayman, producing an explosive reaction. What – a Lebanese preferring English to French! My brother was almost forbidden entry to France for this unspeakable outrage.

The director-general of Air France spoke English well, but was determined not to use it in formal negotiations. A compromise was arrived at. He spoke French and I replied in English. I was branded an anglophile and an americanophile into the bargain. I have to confess that I did not, at that time, very much like the French. In 1925, when I was a highly impressionable sixteen-year-old, the Druzes in Djebel Druze in eastern Syria had risen in revolt against the French. The revolution was a fierce battle, with heavy casualties on both sides. The French lost mostly foreign legionnaires, Senegalese and other recruits from their colonies, but we Druze lost the flower of our young men. The Druze warriors, led by the late Sultan Pasha El-Atrash, were driven out of Djebel Druze and took refuge in English-ruled Jordan, so, no doubt, reinforcing the French conviction that the English were behind the Druze revolt.

When I was in Jordan, I had the pleasure of meeting the exiled Sultan Pasha and most of his fellow warriors. We became good friends, and the story of the revolt was frequently discussed. Their account of what happened, and of the unpleasant side to the fighting, amplified my already hostile feelings towards France and the French; and then the strained relationship between MEA and Air Liban did nothing to improve my attitude. During those six weeks of discussion in Paris, however, a positive change took place in my feelings. This was not caused by my talks with the executives of Air France, but through my daily contacts with ordinary French people. Taxi drivers, who wanted to know where I came from, broke into friendly smiles when they heard, 'Liban'. 'What a beautiful country!' 'My father was there,' or, 'My sister is married to a Lebanese,' or, 'My brother has a Lebanese wife,' were the typical reactions of many ordinary French citizens. I felt that they all liked Lebanon.

I had always known that France was the only Western power that really cared for Lebanon. Great Britain was closer to the Gulf and other countries east of Lebanon. The United States mainly favoured Israel and viewed the Arab Middle East in the light of its ties there. The Eastern Bloc countries were obsessed with political doctrine, and their views on the Arab countries were subjected to their ideology. Western and Communist powers alike cared only for their own interests. France, however, was, in relation to Lebanon, an exception. My feelings towards the French began to change as affection began to replace resentment.

In itself, the Air Liban agreement was brief and simple, though suspicion and politics intruded here and there. The agreement was made, subject to the approval of the French government, and in an intuitive moment I insisted it should also be subject to the approval of the Lebanese government. As a privately owned company, Middle East Airlines did not need government approval, but, knowing my Lebanon, its internal politics and the deep-rooted attachment of a large section of the population to France and to Franco-Lebanese relations, I felt on safer ground with that condition in the text.

I returned to Beirut, happy that we were, at last, on the way to uniting the Lebanese airlines, and went to see General Fouad Chehab, President of the Lebanese Republic, to tell him of our achievement, and of my revived hopes for establishing a single Lebanese airline. He listened to my account of the discussions and received a photocopy of the three-and-a-half-page initialled agreement. He read it and promised to let me know his views later, complimenting me on the wisdom of subjecting the agreement to his approval.

I waited some time, but no news came from the President. I did, however, receive a request from Air France to attend an urgent meeting in Paris. Air France had been asked by their government to suspend further action pending the outcome of official discussions between the French and the Lebanese governments. I was told that Colonel Antoine Sa'd, a high-ranking officer in the Lebanese Army, had brought a personal letter from President Chehab to General de Gaulle requesting that France should not abandon its important role in Lebanese civil aviation. Air France was instructed accordingly to drop the agreed sale of Air Liban to MEA.

To resolve what looked like an impasse, I proposed to the chairman of Air France, who was still smarting under the insult of the Lebanese shareholders of Air Liban, that, instead of an outright sale, we consider a merger between the two airlines whereby Air France would sell the shares of Air Liban to MEA and would purchase 20 per cent of the shares of the combined company. This would guarantee a French 'presence' in Lebanon which, it was thought, would please both governments. It was not what I had hoped for, but there was no alternative. A new agreement was duly hammered out, subject to both governments' approval. The name of the merged airline was to be Middle East Airlines—Air Liban, and it would purchase at least two French-built Caravelles as evidence of goodwill. Middle East Airlines undertook to employ all Air Liban's Lebanese personnel, but none of the French personnel – a refusal that was to cause enormous difficulties and nearly cost us the merger.

On my return to Lebanon, I was summoned to see General Chehab, who said he had been informed of the new agreement but, before making a decision, was anxious to clarify some information he had received from one of his aides. Was it true, he asked, that an overwhelming majority of the employees in Middle East Airlines were Mohammedan and that most of them were Palestinians and Egyptians? I was shocked by these questions, for I had never thought of the employees of MEA in terms of religion. Explaining this to General Chehab, I added that we had never made a census of the religions of our employees. To answer his question correctly I would have to ask for statistics and would then report my findings.

The census was taken, and the results were a surprise. In Lebanon, MEA had, at the time, a total of 2,039 employees, of whom 57 per cent were Christian, 42.9 per cent Mohammedans and 0.1 per cent Bahai or Hindu. The Christians received 69.6 per cent of the salaries, the Mohammedans 30.2 per cent and the Bahai and Hindus 0.2 per cent. We had 139 Lebanese employees of Palestinian origin, and 64 Lebanese employees of Egyptian origin. Of the Lebanese of Palestinian origin, 20 were Mohammedan and 119 Christian. Of the Lebanese of Egyptian origin, one was Mohammedan and 63 Christian. Armed with these significant figures, I went to see General Chehab again.

As he read the neatly tabulated columns, he became very angry – not with the evidence but with the aide who had given him false information. On the question of Palestinians and Egyptians, I explained that we had none in Middle East Airlines. There were simply Lebanese employees of Palestinian and Egyptian origin. It was the government which had granted them Lebanese nationality, and hence they must be treated as ordinary citizens. Surely General Chehab would not permit the creation of second-class citizens? All Lebanese were, by the grace of God, equal regardless of religion or origin. I added, to the President's embarrassment, that it seemed to me that in Lebanon we do not have true Lebanese in the national sense of the word, but people who are either Christian or Mohammedan, living together in a geographical entity called Lebanon. The President reluctantly agreed, but was not amused. I left his office sadly convinced that nothing in Lebanon is Lebanese except its cedars; and some claim that even these are Phoenician.

The President asked for more time for his experts to complete studies of the merger and requested that further action be suspended until the end of 1962. We could only agree. In Paris, meanwhile, the politicians took over. One day I received a visit from M. Robert Vergnaud, then director-general of civil aviation and 'envoy extraordinary' to the French government on 'Mission Merger'. After a three-hour meeting, it became plain that the French government was having second thoughts. Certain government departments in Paris had been unwilling to abandon the use of Air Liban as a political vehicle in the Middle East. Air France's financial losses in Air Liban were, in their view, negligible in comparison with the political advantages. Vergnaud's arrival marked the beginning of months of political negotiation.

There was a flurry of diplomatic activity between Paris and Beirut. The French Embassy in Beirut had played the leading role in telling Paris about local opposition to the merger and had expressed its own objections. Consequently, a new Franco-Lebanese solution was proposed by the French. The Lebanese government was to participate in a merged airline with 30 per cent, Air France would also get 30 per cent and the 'Intra Group' would have the remaining 40 per cent. This was the first time that the Lebanese shareholders in MEA had been referred to as the 'Intra Group'. It was a deliberate and mischievous gesture, since it was common knowledge that General Chehab disliked Intra Bank and its activities.

Jealousy of Intra Bank had motivated many people, especially the banking fraternity, to launch a hostile campaign. It was claimed that Intra Bank was not Lebanese, but Palestinian. Some asserted it was Arab, and, because Bedas had been the manager of Barclay's Bank in Jerusalem before he came to Beirut, others speculated it must be English. Some went so far as to claim that its capital was Jewish. It was also alleged that Intra was a growing danger to Lebanon, gaining control over Lebanon through loans to local industrial and financial enterprises. Such rumours were the work of various of the anti-merger activists. Having failed in their Mohammedan-Palestinian-Egyptian intrigue, they were resorting to scare tactics, whispering about a fictitious threat to Lebanese civil aviation, to the Lebanese economy and even to Lebanon itself, should control of its airlines fall into the hands of the 'Intra Group', the 'hate-name' they coined for the Lebanese shareholders of Middle East Airlines.

The proposed Franco-Lebanese solution was, in fact, a clear reversal of the deal we had negotiated with Air France. Instead of a merger of Middle East Airlines and Air Liban, in which Air France acquired a minority shareholding of 20 per cent mainly as an *acte de présence*, it would now become an acquisition by Air France of the whole merged airline. All that was needed was the purchase of 10 per cent in addition to the 20 per cent already agreed for Air France to hold the reins. The Lebanese government, owner of 30 per cent, would have been only too pleased to place Air France in overall control and management of the merged airline. President Chehab, we were told, had already given his blessing to this solution.

The Lebanese shareholders of Middle East Airlines, who had fought hard to build up their company and to free it from foreign participation, were thus expected to sit back and surrender their company to foreign domination and be content to subsidize 40 per cent of the losses of the politically merged airline. This turn of events left me furious. Although the new plan was totally unacceptable, I decided to tread softly, for it could not be in the long-term interests of Middle East Airlines openly to oppose the participation by the Lebanese government in the merged airline. Ostensibly, therefore, I welcomed the Franco-Lebanese solution. But I carefully planted a powerful mine in its path by making one reservation: Intra Bank, as a result of its faith in the management of MEA and because of its important shareholding, had given substantial guarantees on behalf of MEA, including one for the purchase of

Caravelles. If the 'Intra Group' were to be deprived of control over the airline and of their important shareholding interest, then it was certain that the bank would refuse to continue with these guarantees. These would need to be taken up by the new controlling group – the Lebanese government and Air France. I felt sure that, if the Lebanese government agreed to give such guarantees, then it would be asked for similar ones by LIA and TMA, the other two Lebanese airlines. Furthermore, such guarantees would, of course, require the approval of the Lebanese Parliament.

It worked like magic. The government quickly declared itself unwilling to participate in the shareholding of the merged airline, which brought Vergnaud back with a new proposal which he and the French Ambassador to Lebanon discussed with the President of the Republic. This one was simple and sweet. The Lebanese shareholders of Air Liban would have 30 per cent, Air France would buy 30 per cent and the remaining 40 per cent would be left for the 'Intra Group'. The President approved it in principle and, at Vergnaud's request, promised to assist in urging the Lebanese shareholders of Air Liban to take up the proposed percentage investment in the merged airline.

Vergnaud's definitive proposal took time to arrive. It was set out in the form of a protocol between Air France and Middle East Airlines. It was a one-page document, very precise, very concise, that had clear objectives: to merge the airlines so as to relieve Air France of its financial commitments to Air Liban; to snatch control of the merged airline at minimum cost and hand it over to Air France; and to deliver a kick, where it hurt most, to MEA and its anglophile 'Intra Group' shareholders. So far as the French were concerned, it was the final solution, and we were given forty-eight hours to reach a decision.

Robert Vergnaud and I had frequently locked horns during this affair. He was an astute negotiator, capable of discussing the most controversial issue with a charming manner. He had the extraordinary ability to make you feel pleasure rather than pain even as he cut your throat. Nevertheless, a warm friendship, based on mutual respect, later developed between us. I respected his ardent devotion to French interests, and he appreciated my firm stand on behalf of MEA and the interests of Lebanese civil aviation. As chairman of the Institute of Air Transport (ITA), he kindly invited me in 1963 to join its board which included some most distinguished air-transport personalities. When Vergnaud resigned the chairmanship of ITA early in 1977, he and other board members honoured me by asking me to accept the chairmanship in his place. Regretfully, I had to decline, because of my work in

Middle East Airlines, and in fact I resigned from the board of ITA in December 1977, after my own retirement.

In 1962, however, Vergnaud's one-page protocol looked very like an instruction from a colonial power to an airline in one of its colonies. Lebanon and the Lebanese love France, but Lebanon has long ceased to be a French colony. Civil aviation, however, is considered an exception, for even today Lebanon does not have an air agreement with France. The French still exploit their air traffic rights to Lebanon by divine right and the Lebanese are granted their rights to France by condescending tolerance.

I was sick and tired of these tedious, distasteful and seemingly endless machinations. The delay in receiving the approval of both governments had naturally produced rumours that were beginning to have a destabilizing effect on Middle East Airlines. Nevertheless, I was determined to save the merger if possible. The future of MEA and its employees, and of Lebanese civil aviation, depended largely on merging Middle East Airlines and Air Liban as a first step towards uniting all the Lebanese airlines. Lebanese civil aviation could not possibly survive with five airlines fighting for passengers, freight and traffic rights. I was convinced that President Chehab had been deliberately misinformed and badly advised. Nevertheless, it would have been suicidal for Middle East Airlines to seek a confrontation with the President when the government, through its control of traffic rights, had a stranglehold on the future of any airline in Lebanon.

The new protocol was by far the worst of the proposed solutions because the shareholders of the merged airline were politically grouped. Air France and *les amis de la France*, the Lebanese shareholders of Air Liban, were designated as the first party, the much-resented 'Intra Group' as the second. The voting majority was predetermined and went to the Air France–Air Liban group with their 60 per cent shareholding. Rather than a merger, it amounted to a takeover of Middle East Airlines in which the 'Intra Group' was to be kicked out of MEA without any say in its affairs, even being deprived of a seat on its board. Their only remaining privilege was to subsidize 40 per cent of the losses, which, judging from experience of Air Liban, would have been inevitable and considerable.

The protocol paid no attention to our warning that, stripped of its rights to control, Intra Bank would withdraw its substantial guarantees. No mention was made of the deal with the French Sud Aviation company for the purchase of two Caravelles, conditional on the sale by Air France to Middle East Airlines of the Air Liban shares. It seemed clear to us, therefore, that the protocol, which nullified the sale of the Air Liban shares, must automatically nullify the purchase of the Caravelles. We were dismayed to find ourselves apparently being coerced into surrendering to Air France and its Air Liban partners everything we had worked for, and thus forced to hand control of Lebanon's civil aviation back to foreign domination. We were not prepared to accept that domination, even if it were French.

But, objectionable as it was, we would not, in the long-term interests of Middle East Airlines, reject the protocol outright. It would have been foolhardy to oppose the President and France, the country still thought of by a large section of the Lebanese community as 'Lebanon's compassionate Mother'. I was a firm believer in the Lebanese saying: 'If you want to cross to the other side of the river, do not swim against the current but with it.' I therefore decided to go along with the protocol. At the same time I was determined to expose *les amis de la France* and call their bluff.

Reliable information had reached me that the Lebanese shareholders of Air Liban would take part in the merged airline only if guaranteed the privileges they had previously enjoyed. It was highly doubtful, on the other hand, that Air France would agree, these costly handouts having been the main reason for Air France's decision to get rid of Air Liban in the first place. Our response was therefore obvious: we would welcome the participation in the newly merged airline of the Lebanese shareholders of Air Liban, on condition that they were granted no special privileges or subsidies. At the same time, we pointed out that Intra Bank had given guarantees of over £L50 million on behalf of MEA, including the one for the purchase of the two Caravelles. These guarantees would be withdrawn and would have to be taken over by Air France and the Lebanese shareholders of Air Liban. Under the last extension of the Caravelle contract, we would be committed to a definite purchase if notice of cancellation were not given by the end of February 1983. To protect ourselves, we therefore gave such notice to Sud Aviation, effective on 28 February 1963.

There was, of course, a danger that Air France and the Lebanese shareholders of Air Liban would accept our conditions. If they did, Middle East Airlines would be lost. It was definitely a risk, but a calculated one, for I knew Lebanon and my Lebanese. My partners and I concluded that the gamble was less dangerous than a confrontation with the President of the Republic and the powerful French influence in Lebanon.

Our unexpected willingness to accept participation of Air Liban shareholders in the merged airline, and the consequent renunciation of control and management, set the cat among the pigeons. Their request to participate had been designed as a trap, opponents of the merger being convinced that the 'Intra Group' would reject such a request, it being impossible for them to imagine that any Lebanese would ever give up advantages of prestige and power. Had we approved the request, we would have been trapped into having turned down an agreement proposed by Air France and approved by the President of Lebanon. Air France would then have been forced to abandon the merger and continue operating Air Liban. Our apparently willing acceptance was a blow to these machinations.

The other thrust of our riposte, the cancellation of the Caravelle contract, was a serious matter for Air France, and for the French authorities opposed to the merger. General de Gaulle had encouraged the production of the Caravelle and personally sponsored its development. This order for two airliners could be expected to open the Middle East market to the sale of the pride of the French aircraft industry. Air Liban had never bought aircraft for itself and had relied on Air France to supply them on lease, because its Lebanese shareholders had always refused to pay for aircraft purchases. Our purchase agreement, guaranteed by Intra Bank, was genuine. Unless the new majority shareholders accepted responsibility for the authentic order, Air France would have to justify cancellation of the purchase contract both to Sud Aviation and to General de Gaulle. At that time, few Frenchmen had the courage to face the General.

The gamble worked. I was summoned to see an agitated and angry President Chehab, who exploded in a tirade of criticism of the Lebanese shareholders of Air Liban. He referred to them as *fromagistes*, an expression he was fond of using to describe a category of Lebanese who sacrificed everything for personal gain. He then told me that they had gone back on their word and refused to take part in the merged airline unless guaranteed by Air France the same privileges they enjoyed in Air Liban. Air France had categorically refused. The President then praised my constructive attitude during the negotiations and gave his approval for the merger to go ahead on my terms.

The French authorities, who had counted on the Lebanese shareholders of Air Liban — the professed 'friends of France' — were equally disillusioned. We, for our part, had won a great victory, with Air France being given the green light to complete the original merger agreement. An addendum to the agreement was signed on 15 March 1963, by which Air France raised its participation from 20 to 30 per cent. MEA confirmed the Caravelle purchase contract. Air France undertook to deliver the shares of Air Liban at the prices already fixed by the 6 August agreement, which was finally confirmed with the approval of the two governments.

The merger became effective on 19 June 1963, when the new airline, named Middle East Airlines–Air Liban, came into being. The first task for management was to integrate staff from Air Liban in the various departments and to set about making them welcome. Before long, they entered into the way of life of MEA and were pleasantly surprised to find it was not the ogre they had been led to believe. At last the foundations had been laid on which to build a sound and viable Lebanese airline. The future looked most promising and we turned our attention to developing the merged company.

Middle East Airline's profits in 1961 exceeded £L4 million. In 1962, those profits were up 28 per cent, and in 1963, despite the extraordinary expenses of the merger, 32 per cent higher than in 1962. Possibly our most remarkable achievement was to have repaid, by the end of 1962, a total of £3,772,835 sterling of debts to BOAC as well as all the aircraft instalment payments guaranteed by BOAC. It was a shock to all those pessimists in BOAC who had believed they would be extremely lucky to receive any repayment at all.

It left us free to devote more attention to re-equipping with a more modern fleet, and a third Caravelle was ordered, to the amazement of the French lobby who had fought the merger. In December 1963, an even bolder step was taken when an order was placed for a supersonic Anglo-French Concorde, intended to inaugurate the fastest ever flight from Beirut to New York with one stop at Toulouse. Such were the ambitions of MEA that we actually took an option on a second Concorde for delivery in 1970 at the then quoted price of $10 million an aircraft. But, with a touch of natural caution born of suspicion of what happens when governments are involved in the manufacture and sale of aircraft, I reserved the right to cancel the contract should the eventual price of Concorde exceed $10 million and delivery be delayed beyond 1970. By 1974, when the asking-price had mounted to $50 million an aircraft and was still rising without a delivery date in sight, the venture was abandoned.

9
The IATA, and Disaster at Ankara

Fierce competition among the airlines serving the Middle East had meanwhile developed and we needed to face the uncomfortable fact that too many aircraft seats were chasing a limited number of passengers. MEA was facing alarming competition from two sides. Government-owned European airlines were busy squandering their taxpayers' money by offering more and more flights in the region, while the airlines of oil-rich Arab states ran their companies with prodigal disregard for cost. What the *nouveaux riches* regional airlines were after was prestige rather than business. In the face of such competition, MEA had done well not only to hang on to its share of traffic but actually to win a greater share.

Even so, we were well aware of the need to rationalize air traffic arrangements by controlling unlawful competition. With this aim, we sought the help of the International Air Transport Association (IATA). An attempt was also made to control the chaos of Arab airlines by setting up the Arab Air Carriers Organization (AACO), modelled upon and closely related to IATA. Thirteen airlines were represented at the inaugural meeting held in Cairo in 1964 to discuss aviation problems.

Middle East Airlines was asked to second Salim Salaam, Senior Vice-President of International Affairs, to help lay the foundation of the new organization and the structure of its administration. Salim was a member of the traffic advisory committee of IATA who knew how the organization worked. He was invited to be the secretary-general of AACO for a period of not more than a year, the time thought necessary to complete its formation. Twenty-two years later, Salim, though now chairman of MEA, was still secretary-general of AACO and managing its affairs. The reason for this somewhat lengthy 'temporary' assignment is that the Arab airlines could not agree on which country should provide a secretary-general. Many wanted that honour. Unable to agree, they settled on leaving it with Lebanon. Finally, in November 1986, Salim was relieved of his 'temporary' appointment and replaced by someone acceptable to all the Arab airlines – a stateless Palestinian.

Back in 1957, I had been elected to the executive committee of IATA: an honour for Middle East Airlines and myself to be admitted to the inner sanctum. The executive committee at that time was made up of a group of pioneers who had greatly contributed to the early development of air transport and the growth of IATA. By then, few of them were playing any part in the day-to-day operation of their airlines but held well-deserved sinecures in their companies. Perhaps because of the standing of its members, and the honorific nature of its composition, the executive committee had adopted the role of a housekeeping committee, leaving the management of IATA to the director-general, then the formidable Sir William Hildred – 'Dick' to his friends – who was charming, capable, efficient and possessed an extensive knowledge of aviation matters. To him must go the credit for the formation and early growth of IATA, and I cherish the memory of the honour Sir William Hildred wished to confer on me when, nearing retirement from IATA, he asked whether I would like to replace him. Overwhelmed by his confidence, I regretfully had to decline because of my work in MEA.

At forty-eight I was the youngest member on the committee, and by far the least experienced. At first I was quite happy and content to attend the meetings and to enjoy the privilege of listening to my experienced colleagues. I had much to learn about IATA and the airline business, and I could not have been in better company. By 1961, the composition of the executive committee was changing. Chairmen, presidents and chief executives of member airlines, realizing the importance of IATA decisions, were gradually replacing the old timers.

During my association with IATA, I was re-elected five times, each for a period of three years, and so served for eighteen consecutive years on the committee. During the last fourteen of those years, I worked hard to draw attention to the defects I saw in the procedures of IATA, the inconsistency of some of its policies, the application of its resolutions and in the behaviour of members, especially the major airlines and their attitude towards IATA. I urged the committee to initiate reforms which were, in my opinion, necessary for the effectiveness of the association and for the welfare of the airline industry. My views and suggestions were politely listened to, but not heeded. All my reports and proposals were courteously recorded in the minutes, but no action was taken.

The purposes, aims and objectives of IATA, as specified in its articles of incorporation, are to promote safe, regular and economical air transport for the benefit of the peoples of the world, to foster air commerce and to study the related problems. There was nothing in the articles to indicate that the main function of IATA could be to fix the fares on international routes. This basic function, because it was deliberately hidden under the general objective 'to foster air commerce', promoted the accusation that the association was a cartel, IATA's valuable contributions to commercial air transport then being brushed aside and completely forgotten.

To refute this accusation and give fare fixing a cloak of respectability, IATA introduced the unanimity rule. No fare was to be adopted unless approved unanimously, in a traffic conference, by all member airlines. Fares were also to be subjected to governmental approval before they became operative.

The unanimity rule had an insidious and disastrous effect. It was democracy at its worst. To start with, it was unrealistic to expect 113 airlines, representing countries from all over the world, with different cultures, different political and social philosophies and at varying degrees of development, ever to reach unanimous agreement on any subject. It was also absurd to give a small airline, with a few local services and limited experience, an equal voting-right with that of a giant airline with vast experience and a network of world-wide international services, especially when the voting was about fares on routes that in no way involved the small airline.

The fare-fixing process was further complicated by the lack of any IATA yardstick, or of any economically scientific rules for calculating fares. Distances, costs and other economic factors were never taken into consideration. It was catch-as-catch-can. The fare finally agreed was the one proposed and not opposed. It was, in other words, what the airlines considered they could get away with.

To avoid anti-trust and anti-cartel retaliation by certain government authorities, procedures were designed to control fares but not to control capacity. In airline vocabulary, 'capacity' means the number of aeroplane seats offered by all airlines on the routes of the air transport market. To control and rationalize fares while capacity is unrestricted is an economic absurdity. There are, of course, strongly held beliefs that control of capacity would eliminate freedom of competition. Certainly, this could happen if the control was flagrantly abused, but so long as it was exercised to cater for the true economic needs of the air transport market, it cannot interfere with freedom of competition. What it can do is eliminate waste, the scourge of the airline business. What could be financially more devastating to airlines than to have aircraft flying all over the world with more than half their seats empty?

Rationalizing capacities would undoubtedly have cut the number of aircraft required by airlines, and this, in turn, would have reduced capital expenditure and lightened the airlines' enormous financial burden. But where it would have been a most welcome relief to the airlines, it would have delivered a painful blow to the aircraft manufacturers, who therefore had a vested interest and favoured government resistance to capacity control.

The unanimity rule and capacity control were among the many IATA rules and procedures which needed modification. The tragedy was that the executive committee of IATA, composed of the elite of airline heads of the utmost integrity, abdicated its responsibility and failed to exert its authority for the general good. Although it had the power and authority to act, its members chose not to do so.

In the end, I gave up all hope of even denting the steel curtain of IATA's fanatical adherence to outdated policies, rules and procedures that had been drawn up some forty years earlier to serve the needs of a young and rapidly growing industry. The harmonious life of this exclusive club was resistent to change, and its committee refused to keep pace with the meteoric growth and evolution of air transport. It would not accommodate or guide the heterogeneous membership which had, back in 1965, almost tripled its original growth to ninety-five airlines. By the 1980s, 133 airlines from all over the world were claiming membership.

Naturally, I fully appreciated the privilege of periodically meeting the most illustrious of airline leaders. Those meetings were time-consuming and entailed frequent travel to distant and exotic places. The last four meetings before I left the committee were held in Japan, New Zealand, western Canada and the United States. By 1975, as chairman and president of an airline engulfed in the problems peculiar to our part of the world and battling each day for its survival, I could no longer afford the time-consuming membership and let it be known I would not be standing for re-election. Nevertheless, my presence on the committee had helped MEA to be elected to serve on most of IATA's important committees, the competence of the MEA delegates thereafter ensuring their re-election for term after term of office. The many hours they spent working for IATA were more than made up by the value of the contacts they made with other airlines and the effect these had on interline sales and MEA's prestige in the airline industry.

At this point, however, I must turn back from the general to the particular, and record how, on 1 February 1963, MEA experienced a tragic incident of the kind that sooner or later inevitably happens to an airline during the course of its operations. It was the first fatal accident in seventeen years of existence. An MEA Viscount, on a regular Beirut–Nicosia–Ankara–Beirut flight had, when cleared for the approach to Ankara Airport, collided with a C–47 aircraft of the Turkish Air Force. The military aircraft was on a blind instrument training-course and heading for the military airport, west of Ankara. There were eleven passengers and a crew of three in the Viscount, and three airmen in the C–47. All were killed.

But fate had not been satisfied with the deaths alone of the passengers and the crews of both aircraft. It had sent the Viscount spinning vertically on to the roof of a bank in a congested residential area, where it burst into flames before falling on to an open market, so inflicting death and injury on many Turkish citizens whose misfortune had brought them there that day. Sixty-eight Turks died in the inferno, of whom thirty-four lost their lives in the blazing bank. Another eighty were injured, about twenty so badly that more died later.

We were appalled, our first experience of a tragic crash leaving us stunned. But we had to pull ourselves together to cope with the repercussions that every airline must face after a disaster. Yet what hit us most unexpectedly was the reaction of certain sections of the public. We were pronounced at fault even before the investigation into the accident began, perhaps because we were a small airline from the Arab Middle East. In similar situations, the technical efficiency of an airline from the so-called developed world, especially that of a major airline, is never questioned, but some of the media in Lebanon, spearheaded by the French-language newspaper L'Orient, were quick to assign the blame to Middle East Airlines.

The Lebanese civil aviation authority issued a press release refuting the accusation, and this was followed in due course by the official conclusion of the committee of investigation, composed of representatives of the Turkish civil aviation authority and of the International Civil Aviation Organization (ICAO). It stated:

Ankara Airport tape recordings confirm absolutely that the MEA Viscount (OD–ADE) was operating strictly in accordance with air traffic control instructions and prescribed procedures. There is no evidence to indicate that Ankara Airport control tower was aware of the presence of the Turkish military aircraft and there was definitely no advice to the Viscount of the presence of this same aircraft in the vicinity.

The Turkish military authorities, however, were not prepared to admit they had been at fault. They rejected the findings of the committee and issued the result of their own investigation. Inevitably, this blamed Middle East Airlines for the accident and absolved the Turkish Air Force of any responsibility. The Turkish Air Force none the less had a bad reputation for hazardous behaviour in Ankara's airspace. While the crash of our Viscount was the first incident in which people had died, Turkish military aircraft had been responsible for a number of dangerous 'near-misses' with commercial airlines. Six weeks after the MEA accident, a meeting held in London of all airlines operating through Ankara decided that a special delegation of the International Air Transport Association should go to Ankara to discuss these incidents with the Turkish authorities. The delegation submitted a number of proposals for improving air-control procedures at Ankara Airport so as to minimize the hazards to civil aircraft. The London meeting, and the visit of the IATA delegation to Ankara, assisted us significantly in establishing Middle East Airlines' innocence in this fatal accident.

The Turkish Air Force's immediate denial of responsibility, combined with the great loss of life, had initially produced a hostile reaction to Middle East Airlines in Turkey. Opinion changed in our favour when, on hearing that hospitals in Ankara were short of plasma to give to the injured, hundreds of MEA employees rallied to my appeal and filed into the American University Hospital in Beirut to donate blood. News of this spontaneous gesture was widely reported in the Turkish press, and added to it was a prompt assurance from Lloyd's that compensation would be made quickly and in full to all Turkish victims. This enhanced our reputation and helped in the amicable settlement of all claims.

Although, as a fatalist, I realized that it was written that all the victims of the Ankara crash should have died when they did, and in the tragic manner prescribed by *kismet*, the loss of so many lives left a deep sorrow in my heart. I was especially grieved by the loss of our crew: Captain Maurice Malcolm Stilwell of Leicester, England; Senior First Officer Farid Abi-Zeid of Alma, Kesrouan, Lebanon; and Air Hostess Aprine Chobanian of Beirut, Lebanon.

Normally, there were two air hostesses on every Viscount flight, and our ill-fated flight had left Beirut for Ankara with two. However, because there were few passengers on the Cyprus to Ankara leg, the captain gave one of them, Miss Liselotte Loedel, permission to remain in Nicosia to attend to some personal business until the plane made its return flight some hours later. It was not written that she should die in Ankara on that day.

We did not forget our lost colleagues, but we had to put our sorrow behind us and continue making our airline, their airline, a success.

10
A Personal Tragedy, and MEA Expands

Between 1962 and 1966, MEA extended its operations to thirty-seven cities in thirty-two foreign countries, and its fifty-five offices abroad were all managed by professionally trained Lebanese nationals. Our total revenue in 1966 was 73 per cent higher than that for 1962, and our operating profits ran at a yearly average of 36 per cent. It was an achievement few airlines could have equalled. Middle East Airlines was flying high. Sadly, it was not the same with my family.

On 11 September 1963, we were struck by a heart-rending tragedy which will live with us for ever. Our elder daughter Rima was murdered in front of our house in Shimlan. The man who killed her was Samir Farah, a graduate drama student, born in Jerusalem, whom she had known while studying at the American University of Beirut. Rima was twenty-two when she died, full of life, a kind girl, talented in writing, poetry, music and everything she did. She had graduated with high distinction from the American University and then enrolled at Cambridge University in England for her post-graduate studies.

Samir Farah followed her to England, determined to win her love. He trailed her everywhere, pursuing her relentlessly, and not taking no for an answer. He acted as if love had made him mad and became suicidal. Rima was frightened and telephoned her mother to come to her help. This is what my wife Ida wrote about the incident in her recently published family history *Maktoob*: 'I left the next day with all my senses wanting and needing Najib beside me, with his wisdom and strength. But he was at yet another Middle East Airlines board meeting.'

In England, Ida comforted Rima, and as the university vacation had started, they packed and left for Geneva. From there, Rima went to Germany and Ida returned to Lebanon. German friends had invited Rima to spend some time with them, and Ida advised her to accept. Rima spent a few weeks with them in the Black Forest and returned to

Lebanon at the end of August. On that tragic 11 September, I was at our farm in the south of Lebanon, enjoying a short break from the office, when Ida phoned to say that Samir Farah had arrived at Shimlan, shot Rima, then blown his brains out. My Rima was dead.

I arrived in Shimlan to find the house full of people from neighbouring villages who had quickly come to us as soon as they heard the news. In particular, the people of Shimlan, women, men and children, were all there to share our sorrow. My grief-stricken wife and children were the first to dash sobbing into my arms. I held them close, very close, praying for strength. Then I hurried to see my Rima. She lay on her deathbed, serene, beautiful and looking very much at peace with an evil world. I kissed her – a final kiss and a final goodbye. I could not believe I would never see her again. I steeled myself to endure our great loss.

My first duty was to support my wife in her agony and to comfort our children. The façade of control we managed to sustain during the day collapsed at night in tears in the privacy of our bedroom. But Ida was a tower of strength and did her best to console us all. She was the perfect example of self-control and of sorrow borne with pious dignity. Before long, my family and many friends arrived from all over Lebanon. They were not allowed by the Shimlanis to help with anything. The Shimlanis took over and looked after everybody. We felt that our loss was also theirs, and that they were grieving for one of their own family.

The funeral took place on the second day, and all Lebanon was represented to share our sorrow. As the coffin was carried to our private family cemetery, the Maronite Christian church tolled its bell all the way. Next day, the Maronite priest held a mass for Rima in his church, and we were there, Christians and Druzes, together in faith and in grief. A Druze boy bore the incense burner during the mass.

A few days later, we left for Europe with all the family, except for my eldest son Makram, who stayed behind to receive condolences from friends who had been unable to attend the funeral. We went to the south of France in an effort to forget, but as Ida and I soon realized, our grief was made more poignant by being in a foreign country among people who were strangers. We therefore returned to Lebanon, to our family and friends, and I plunged once again into my work in Middle East Airlines to try to forget. It was impossible. I shall never forget.

The Druzes, as fatalists, believe that nothing one can do will prolong the ordained span of life, and nothing will ever happen to any Druze before life has run its span. This fatalism should have comforted me and lessened my grief. It did not do so. I had a deep feeling of guilt that, had I given more time to my family and less to my work for Middle East Airlines, I might have helped to save Rima. This feeling lives within me still, and every time I think of my Rima, as I often do, I feel that I failed her, failed my wife and family by not being with them when I was most needed.

Fatalism works only when those who have the faith are living natural and normal lives. To have become a prisoner of my own achievements and to have devoted my life to work at the expense of neglecting the family and failing my wife and children when they needed me, was not natural, not normal. It must have been a form of mental aberration or a peculiar brand of insanity. Fatalism, with its comfort, abandoned me in Rima's death.

As I write the story of my life, I feel more than ever before the weight of my responsibility in Rima's death. I ask myself over and over, in the light of all that happened: was I right in what I did and, if given the chance, would I do it again?

Whatever I felt about my Rima's death, it was my work after the tragedy that saved my sanity. I worked harder than ever before. Working for Middle East Airlines had always resembled the ancient Lebanese sword dance, in which you had to foil strokes and thrusts from all sides, most of which were meant to be fatal. There was no time to relax and repose. Your fight was for survival. For defence, you were allowed the use of a shield, which, in the case of Middle East Airlines, was its commercial success. If this should fail, our chances of survival would quickly vanish.

Because of our modest size as an airline representing a small country in a tough political world, I firmly believed that our commercial policy had to be based on full co-operation with the national airlines of the countries to which we flew. By the end of 1966, MEA had twelve commercial pool agreements with such airlines and were looking for more. These agreements were extremely profitable because, in many instances, they served to control capacity by the pooling partners. We also had agreements to handle the services of twenty-one foreign airlines operating into Beirut, representing over 60 per cent of all the passenger traffic at Beirut International Airport.

Our engineering-department was operating successfully, and by the end of 1966 had obtained the official airworthiness approval of the American, British, French and most Arab and African authorities. Busy workshops attracted business from many foreign customers. By 1967, the engineering-department had fifty customers, including airlines, air forces, oil companies, the United Nations, and various other government agencies. This number had grown to eighty-four by 1974, the year preceding the civil war. Our technical reputation was firmly established, and the workshops were by far the best equipped between Hong Kong and Europe in terms of human skills and modern equipment.

There were also outstanding improvements in all departments, for which the training-centre was largely responsible. A specially designed building was erected, to which the centre moved in 1964. Additional instructors were employed, and international aviation training experts were invited to assist in the programmes. Courses were given in all aspects of the airline business, and in 1966, 2,000 employees received instruction. The company also continued to send a number abroad each year for advanced training. By 1974, seventy foreign airlines and agencies were also making use of the centre's training-facilities. Many sent employees on courses, and others visited the centre to study standards and methods.

Airlines in the Arab world, especially in the oil-producing countries, were mushrooming, and all faced the problem of finding staff. Some recruited foreigners, others followed our example and started their own training-centres. A number raided Middle East Airlines, attracting our employees with much higher salaries. We did not mind these raids, for the training-centre enabled us easily to replace those who took the bait. By aiding the export of Lebanese technical skills, the centre was helping the national economy.

There was another form of poaching that created trouble from the start, but to which we could only gladly give our blessing. On our services to West Africa, our hostesses became the happy victims of marriage raids by Lebanese bachelor emigrants working there. We were losing hostesses at the rate of one a week. Normally young Lebanese, once well-established in their new country, returned home to marry a bride chosen by their parents; a traditional system that worked well in most cases. In some instances, however, the bridegroom found to his chagrin that the bride suited his parents better than himself. Middle East Airlines unwittingly offered the bachelor emigrants an ideal solution. We flew to their doorstep some of the nicest and most beautiful Lebanese girls for them to choose from. Because we flew to West Africa twice a week, the girls stayed three to four days between flights. During that stay, they were entertained lavishly by the Lebanese community, and a golden opportunity was thus provided for the young men to meet them socially, unhampered by the stringent codes of Lebanese mountain courtship, under which the young women's families would have carefully chaperoned them. The benevolent surveillance of the Lebanese community in West Africa meant that, while the courtships engaged in were perfectly proper, they felt much less restrictive.

The marriage raids we accepted with pleasure, and although they meant additional expenditure for training of replacements, we felt it was money well spent. However, we were not so lucky with raids of a different sort: raids by Lebanese pilots, hastily trained in foreign pilot training-schools, who wanted to fly for MEA. In the beginning, almost all our pilots and some co-pilots had been foreigners. The Lebanese, limited in number, had at that stage qualified only as co-pilots. But we never held back on any expenditure for their training in Beirut and abroad, and the first Lebanese pilot in MEA received his command at the end of my first year in Middle East Airlines. In time, others followed.

By 1966, the salary of a pilot in MEA equalled that of a Lebanese government minister, and soon exceeded it. It was therefore natural that a pilot rush should follow. Parents borrowed at excessive rates of interest or sold their land to send their sons to pilot training-schools. There were schools in Cairo, Europe and the United States, but the standards of some of these were far from satisfactory. They would accept applicants who lacked the essential educational background, give them a period of inadequate training and then award flying-diplomas.

I received an official letter from the United States aviation authorities, warning me of the existence of some so-called aviation academies that were virtually selling pilot diplomas to students after a limited period of residence and with little teaching or training. A list of suspect academies was attached, and many of the 'pilots' who were pleading to fly with MEA had been to schools that figured on it.

Unfortunately, these diplomas were accepted by the Lebanese Department of Civil Aviation, and although many of the so-called pilots were not properly qualified, they were officially recognized as licensed Lebanese commercial civil aviation pilots. We found ourselves swamped with applications from such 'fliers'. Politicians, who needed the applicants' family votes, or had other incentives, came to their support in the usual Lebanese style and put pressure on us to employ them. But their pleas got nowhere. I was used to such pressures and could easily ignore them. I was not prepared to take any risks that could jeopardize the operational safety of Middle East Airlines, but nevertheless felt sorry for those misguided and over-ambitious young men, and for their parents who had, in good faith, spent all their money to send their sons to study, as they thought, for a most rewarding career. Unhappily, there was nothing I could do for them.

Our refusal to employ pilots who were inadequately qualified produced angry protests and accusations that we preferred foreign pilots to Lebanese. Public opinion was roused, the media championing the cause of the Lebanese 'pilots'. The parents, who were naturally convinced that their sons were being victimized, solicited the support of politicians and friends in defence of their sons' rightful cause, as they saw it. Cries of: 'Lebanon for the Lebanese!' and 'Out with foreigners!' were beginning to echo in Lebanon – a country that had always boasted of its open-arms policy to foreigners. It is surprising how greed can lurk behind the loudest of patriotic noises.

It did not help matters when a project law was submitted to Parliament aiming to restrict the employment of foreigners in Lebanese airlines. The project was hailed by the Lebanese pilots' union as a much-needed national protection for its members and for the Lebanese in general. The law was not passed by Parliament, but none the less greatly helped to stoke the fire of the Lebanese pilots' rebellion against what they believed to be discrimination. This furore had a damaging effect on our foreign pilots.

One of them was attacked and stabbed while returning home one evening. Luckily, the wound was not serious, and it was later proved that the reasons for the attack had been personal. Nevertheless, when it was reported, the incident was unfortunately related to the employment of foreign pilots in preference to Lebanese pilots who were out of work. The situation became explosive. What exacerbated the problem was our need for more pilots, but only for those who were properly qualified and adequately trained. Since they were not available in Lebanon, we decided to produce them and set up our own cadet pilot scheme.

As soon as the scheme was announced, 120 candidates applied. Applicants had to be of good educational background with baccalauréat or equivalent qualifications; of the right age, sound in health and with an aptitude for flying. A series of examinations and tests produced only ten suitable candidates out of the 120. Pressures to favour politicians' candidates were, as usual, strongly applied but not heeded. Only the best were selected. They were then sent on a two-year course to Air-Work Services at Perth in Scotland. The fact that Middle East Airlines had demonstrated that it was trying to produce more Lebanese pilots of acceptable quality helped to blunt chauvinistic criticism. At the end of the day, MEA had, as a result of its training-policy, rigid adherence to the highest operational standards and cadet pilot scheme, rightly been able to claim that its pilots, Lebanese and foreign, are among the best in the world.

Despite steady growth and increasing prosperity, 1964 produced its share of mishaps and misfortunes. On 18 April, a Middle East Airlines Caravelle crashed into the sea on its final approach to Dhahran Airport. Of its crew of seven and forty-two passengers, there were no survivors. The crew were Lebanese, with the exception of the flight engineer, who was French. A fierce sand storm was raging at the time, and the official investigation revealed that, as often happens in desert sand storms, a whirlwind had been hidden within its depths. It must have struck the aeroplane on its final descent and hurled it into the sea. Nowadays, this phenomenon is termed windshear and is known to have caused several similar accidents.

I was in London when Middle East Airlines telephoned the news in the early hours of the morning. I returned to Beirut immediately and went straight to my office, where the management was gathered awaiting my arrival. There were also representatives of the Lebanese Civil Aviation Department. After I received an account of what had happened, I was taken aside by the most senior of the civil aviation representatives, who whispered to me that, in his opinion, Lebanese pilots were not yet ready to fly in command. We would therefore be well advised to withdraw them and give them more training.

I was furious, and pointed out that the official investigation had not yet even begun. The Lebanese Civil Aviation Department had sent its representatives to join the investigating committee only that evening. How dare he blame the Lebanese pilot without evidence? I reminded him that the Civil Aviation Department had, many years before, issued the pilot concerned with his Lebanese licence, authorizing him to take command of commercial passenger aircraft. If he was honestly convinced of what he said, he only had to send us his opinion officially and we would then call for an ICAO investigation of this most serious charge. At the same time, we would ask for an investigation of his department's licensing procedures. I advised him to shut up until the official investigation had reported.

I feared, from this official's outrageous behaviour, that there would be worse to come from Lebanese and Arab reaction to the first fatal accident to an MEA aircraft piloted by a Lebanese. The Saudi authorities had invited a team of experts from the British Air Registration Board to investigate the accident. Lloyd's Insurance had also sent their investigators. Representatives of the Saudi authorities and of the Lebanese Civil Aviation Department joined the investigating committee. I myself never doubted the ability and qualifications of our Lebanese crew, yet it was a great relief when the investigation found Middle East Airlines and the crew to be completely blameless.

Twenty-three of the forty-two passengers had been Americans, most of them from the Arabian American Oil Company (Aramco). Middle East Airlines had pioneered the air route from Beirut to Dhahran, and Aramco employees were among its most valued customers. I had my fears that this accident, with its high toll of American lives, might alienate our American passengers. My fears proved to be groundless and the reaction of the Aramco American community was most heartening. Instead of criticism, we received messages of sympathy and assurances that Aramco in no way held us responsible. The most touching message came from the American schoolchildren in Dhahran, assuring me personally that they loved Middle East Airlines and would always fly with us. I cherish this genuine gesture of affection and kindness among memories of my work in Middle East Airlines.

Shortly before the accident, I had made a speech to the American Women's Club in Beirut and chosen as my subject the safety of modern air travel. I used statistics to point out the dangers of accidents in the home and on the roads, and to demonstrate that, although flying could never be 100 per cent safe, the comparative risks were relatively small. In a year when IATA members flew 87 million passengers, only 772 had perished. One charming lady present said, in thanking me, that in future she would worry less about her husband's flights in the Middle East. Later, I learned with horror that her husband was one of those who lost their lives aboard our Caravelle. By boasting about air safety, I had broken the golden rule of fatalism – never defy fate. Since then I have kept to it rigidly.

Since several of the crew members who lost their lives were the parents of young children, I decided that MEA must pay for their education up to graduation at a Lebanese university. This established company policy for the future. We took responsibility for the education in Lebanon of all the children of local crew members who died, while the son of the French flight engineer was looked after by us in the same manner in France.

On 4 October 1964, Abdallah Khoury died of a heart attack. By his death, I lost a true friend and an able and constructive board member, one of the trio who had lebanonized Middle East Airlines. Lebanon, for its part, lost one of the pillars of its economy. I invited his widow, Nadia, to take his place, and so she became the first woman to be elected to the board of Middle East Airlines and was soon a most useful

112

member. She always showed genuine care for the airline and took a real interest in its affairs.

When I was elected chairman in 1956, I also continued to be MEA's general manager. But, as the company expanded and the work load grew heavier, I decided to appoint a general manager to carry some of the burden of the day-to-day operations. At the board meeting held on 22 October 1964, I informed the board that I had promoted Asad Nasr from vice-president planning and economics to general manager, a post I had held since 1952. According to Lebanese commercial law, the chairman is also general manager, but may appoint another to assist him, at his own risk and responsibility. I myself continued to be chairman and chief executive of Middle East Airlines, with the title of 'Chairman of the Board and President', until my retirement in December 1977.

Asad Nasr's appointment upset a number of executives who were senior to him in the company's service, and who were convinced that they were more qualified and should have been given the job. I promptly promoted the disgruntled – but efficient – gentlemen to senior positions, reporting directly to me, but unconnected with the day-to-day operations of the company. I found advisory and other important work for them to do, which was also of real value to Middle East Airlines. In this way, I divorced them and their work from the general manager, so avoiding harmful friction.

11
Involvement in Lebanese Governments

While all these developments were taking place at MEA, I was gradually becoming more involved with government. I had no wish to become a politician, but felt it my duty to accept when asked to serve the country. I was appointed to various government advisory councils and ministerial committees: the Superior Economic Council, the National Litani Board, the National Tourist Council, the Town Planning Council, the Board of the Port Authority, the Druze Supreme Council and advisory committees of the Ministries of Public Works, Interior and Foreign Affairs. I was invited to serve, not for any expertise I might possess, but mainly to represent the Druze community, for even advisory councils and committees are subject to confessional distribution in Lebanon. Such bodies are generally set up as public-relations stunts to hoodwink the Lebanese into believing that the government is seeking expert advice to tackle the various national problems. Once the news of the government's initiative has been loudly trumpeted, and after a meeting or two for photographs to be taken and public declarations made, the councils and committees die a natural death. This, however, was not the fate of the National Litani Board nor the National Tourist Council. Both were allowed to live.

The National Litani Board was set up in August 1954 by President Camille Chamoun to harness the waters of the Litani river for irrigation and hydro-electric generation. The project was agreed between the American and Lebanese governments under the Point-Four Aid Programme. The concept was not new. It had been the brainchild of the late Ibrahim Abdul-Al, a Lebanese hydraulic engineer, who sadly died before its adoption by the government. It was modified, refined and improved by the late Salim Lahoud, another brilliant Lebanese hydro-electric engineer, who was chairman of Litani and also a board member of Middle East Airlines and Masco. A loan from the

115

International Bank for Reconstruction and Development of $27 million was concluded in 1955, and the hydro-electric part of the project was completed. The irrigation part was shelved by the Lebanese government for political reasons.

I served on the Litani Board only for the first three-year term, soon realizing that the project was politically explosive. Powerful foreign interests were determined to sabotage it and deprive Lebanon of the waters of the Litani river. The board initially succeeded in foiling these intrigues, but its efforts were not appreciated by the Lebanese government. In fact, they were greatly resented. Although I was re-elected for the second term, I declined to serve in order to save Middle East Airlines from the consequences of further involvement in the international battle for the Litani waters.

The National Tourist Council was formed by President Fouad Chehab early in 1962 to attract more tourists to Lebanon. It was meant to be autonomous and, as such, to stand outside government bureaucracy. This was too much to hope for in Lebanon. As the project finally evolved, the council was denied executive authority and had no official power to come to grips with the many problems it should have dealt with.

Charles Helou, who was elected President of Lebanon two years later, was appointed chairman. He was assisted by a council of members, representing all the religious communities. I was chosen again to represent the Druzes, and my appointment helped to co-ordinate the tourist campaigns of Middle East Airlines with those of the council. We had plenty of experience and MEA had always devoted hard work and funds to this side of the air-travel business. Between 1952 and 1974, before the fighting started, MEA spent £L60 million on tourist publicity. During that period, it invited, at its own expense, thousands of travel writers, travel agents and airline people to experience for themselves the delights of the country. Over 200 international congresses brought in more than 23,000 visitors. Through subsidies and travel facilities, we encouraged and supported the Baalbeck and Tyre Festivals. All forms of Lebanese sporting activities were sponsored. MEA also encouraged handicrafts and artisan works, in particular the Jezzine inlaid cutlery and the Chouf Artisanat. Our offices, all over the world, acted as Lebanese tourist offices and distributed publicity material, including that produced by the Tourist Council.

I left the council in 1965 when I was asked to join the cabinet. My sister Souad replaced me. The council persevered in its efforts to encourage tourism, despite all the difficulties, and especially those of the civil war. Regretfully, it was dissolved in 1982 and its functions transferred to a newly created Council for External Trade. Later this decision was reversed.

My real initiation into the workings of the Lebanese administration began, however, when I was appointed a minister in the Lebanese government for the first time. In the first week of July 1965, I was in London. The telephone woke me at 1.00 a.m. with the hotel operator announcing that the President of Lebanon was on the phone. President Charles Helou wanted me to return and join the cabinet which he and the Prime Minister, Rashid Karami, were forming. I was chosen for the Ministry of Information, National Guidance and Tourism. The President informed me that I was needed since I was the only Druze who would receive universal acceptance by the Druze community. I made no comment about being the only Druze, for I thought the President was pulling my leg. You do not argue with the President of your country over the phone at one o'clock in the morning, and you cannot ignore a call to serve your country.

Returning to Lebanon, it transpired that I was really the only choice acceptable to the two political leaders of the Druze community, who had refused each other's candidate. My acceptance was on condition that I should also continue as chairman and president of MEA. This was accepted, and since the Lebanese government did not work in the afternoons, I devoted those hours to Middle East Airlines.

One sunny Monday morning, I went to the office to take over from the departing minister. The exchange of courtesies and the formality of handing over took less than an hour, most of it being spent in polite conversation, for there was not much to be handed over. Then the director-general came in, followed by the senior executives of the ministry. There was a welcoming speech. My reply was brief.

I then attempted to set about my ministerial duties in a business-like fashion by discovering the objectives and the function of the ministry. Exhaustive inquiries revealed that these had never been officially defined. I called for papers, charts, terms of reference, as well as the decree setting up the ministry, from which I hoped to discover what was expected of the minister. All these attempts met with little success since no files were kept. The outgoing minister had taken his files with him, leaving nothing for me except a report outlining his recommendations on how to deal with a dispute between the two Lebanese TV companies.

Eventually a copy of the budget emerged, but for the rest there were only verbal briefings from the director-general. Apart from that and a

117

rather gaudily furnished office, the only available infra-structure for the minister was the shared services of a secretary and an office boy.

In general, the ministry was a comfortable and peaceful place. The greatest excitement was when the Deuxième Bureau, the government military intelligence branch, requested me to rig the elections of the press reporters' syndicate to make sure that the journalist, Milhem Karam, should not become president. I flatly refused such an outrageous demand. In the election, under official ministry supervision, Milhem won with a big majority. He has been re-elected to that post up to the present day. For my part, I won the enmity of the Deuxième Bureau.

As a gesture of religious courtesy, the director-general, who was a Maronite Christian, had detached a charming and capable young Druze lady from her work in one of the departments and assigned her to my office. She was to act as a public-relations officer to deal with my visitors. I appreciated the gesture, but doubted the thinking behind it: a Druze minister must have a Druze public-relations officer: I had been aware of the divisiveness of confessionalism in the Lebanese government, but had not realized before how deep-rooted this practice had become.

To acquire secretarial assistance for a working minister was quite a problem. I would either have had to deprive a ministry executive of his secretary, or wait until the coming year for the approval of a budget provision for the employment of a new secretary. The same would have applied to procuring the necessary equipment and furniture. Luckily, the ministry was not lacking in office space and, to the astonishment of the established bureaucracy, I brought my secretary over from the airline, together with her typewriter, filing-cabinet and office furniture. I also asked my press adviser to move to the ministry and instal himself near by. To the amazement of the ministry, in which jobs were shared out on a strictly religious basis, both were Christians.

We were then ready to go to work, but one small problem needed to be resolved quickly. The provision of the habitual cups of coffee in the ministry was contracted out to a coffee maker. Since I had decided not to offer coffee to my visitors, the contractor's revenue was substantially reduced and he complained at once.

In MEA, coffee drinking in offices was forbidden. It was a rule that applied to employees and visitors alike. The decision was a social revolution for, in Lebanon, coffee drinking is a deep-rooted expression of courteous hospitality established over hundreds of years. At MEA, in my office, I did not drink coffee and offered none to my visitors. I expected everyone to follow my example. Coffee drinking during office hours is time-wasting and, depending on the individuals' habit — especially the smokers — it can waste up to 25 per cent of an employee's working-time. If an employee shared an office, as many did, he also had to offer coffee to his colleagues as a matter of hospitality. They then stopped work to enjoy a little conversation. In Lebanon, conversation automatically means a political discussion. Since the employees usually belonged to different political factions, discussions would soon become heated. Apart from the loss of working-time, friction and discord was the inevitable result. We were therefore much better off without coffee drinking.

Not offering coffee to visitors was a different matter. It was a long-established social custom in Lebanon and difficult to stop. It was also time-consuming, for it was the custom not to talk business until after coffee. Not every visitor appreciated my flouting of Lebanese hospitality, but since nearly all of them came to ask for favours, they praised the coffee-ban decision if the favours were granted and were critical if they were denied — which they would have done anyway, coffee or no coffee.

I explained to the director-general the MEA rule and why I had decided not to offer coffee in the office at the ministry. I would have liked to stop it in all the offices, but realized this was perhaps too serious a government policy decision. As for the coffee contractor's problem, I suggested he be paid, by me, what he had earned previously, plus 25 per cent as a bonus. But there would be no coffee.

The ministry's task, it seemed, was to issue news items and press guidance considered important by the government, together with the declarations of ministers and politicians in their favour, and to obstruct, whenever possible, those of the opposition. The press was attacking the government daily, and criticizing various ministries and ministers. To enable the Ministry of Information to deal with the criticism and acquaint the public with the true facts, it was arranged for each minister to have on his desk, each early morning, cuttings of all newspapers and magazine articles or news-agency items that concerned him or his ministry. Ministers were then asked to send us their observations on what was published as soon as possible and we would do the rest.

To this procedure, there was no response whatever. I took the matter to the Council of Ministers. The procedure, and its importance to the government and to the Lebanese public, was explained. The ministers promised prompt action. Despite these promises, no comments or replies were received. They all preferred to deal directly with the press.

It was politically more advantageous to trade favours in return for praise or silence. Leaks of confidential or even secret government news, along with other ministerial favours, were valuable barter commodities, and, where the ministers' personal political ambitions were concerned, produced immediate and better results. After a period of patient but fruitless waiting, the scheme was dropped.

Lebanon has an endemic problem with its press, there existing far too many journals and magazines for a country of its size. Before the fighting of 1975, there were, incredibly, 50 daily political newspapers, 43 weekly and 4 monthly political publications, 155 weekly non-political publications, 158 monthly non-political publications and 26 Lebanese news agencies.

The late Afeef El-Teeby, who was, at the time, president of the press syndicate in Lebanon, worked with me on a draft project whereby the government would buy the licences of most of the newspapers and magazines and close them down, except for the number considered adequate to serve the country's needs. Thereafter no licences would be granted. It was what the country needed and we spent a great deal of time preparing our joint recommendations. The project never saw the light of the day because the authorities feared a backlash that might adversely effect their political aspirations.

The ministry had a radio broadcasting department and a newspaper department. In addition, two private companies were given the television concessions. One had French partners, the other British. Naturally, they were highly competitive, and the government had no influence or control over either. With the concessions nearing their end, my predecessor had prepared a project for government approval before their renewal. Since he was a well-known francophile, his project was viewed with suspicion by the Lebanese-British company. The French believed that I was anglophile, and so now my intentions were automatically suspected by the Franco-Lebanese company. There was, however, a difference in the way the two embassies went about the affair. The British Embassy was reluctant to interfere in any trade activities and, in general, kept aloof from British business and British businessmen. Not so the French Embassy. There was heavy pressure to pass my predecessor's project without the slightest modification. I was also made to feel that the Lebanese authorities favoured the French. In the mêlée that followed, ministry officials were automatically split into two factions — those who favoured the French and those who favoured the British.

After meetings with representatives of both television companies, and a careful study of the terms of the concessions, an even-handed project was prepared which favoured neither company more than the other. This embodied most of my predecessor's thinking and recommended a merger of the two companies with government participation. I felt strongly that the government should, in the national interest, have a say in the way this powerful media machine was exploited. Despite being known as a champion of free enterprise in Lebanon, I recommended that, if the merger failed to go through, the government should nationalize television in Lebanon upon the expiration of the concessions. My project was not welcomed and the matter was taken up politically at higher governmental levels. I was gently discouraged from proceeding too speedily with my proposals. The concessions were renewed, without any change, after I left the ministry!

Having failed to rationalize television and the chaotic press situation, I turned my attention to tourism, the second function of the ministry. I thought of creating a government tourist development bank to finance the industry with long-term loans at low rates of interest. This was badly needed because the banks in Lebanon were short-term lenders and charged market rates of interest. I set to work on the project and, in a relatively short time, it was in its final form, vetted by lawyers for its legal wording and by financial experts for its compliance with Lebanon's banking laws. It was placed on the agenda of a ministerial meeting and copies were distributed. The council, on the advice of the Central Bank, remained convinced that, with the number of banks already in existence, there was no need for an additional one. Despite strong pleading that such a bank was urgently needed for Lebanese tourism, the project was dropped. Later it transpired that my proposed bank would have cut across the interests of a joint venture bank set up by certain favoured, interested parties and the government to finance industry. Private interests in Lebanon are given precedence over national interests.

I was not entirely discouraged and still hoped to assist Lebanese tourism. I therefore looked at the National Tourist Council. The most important help I could give, it seemed, was to provide this with executive powers, and so I recommended the formation of a separate Ministry for Tourism which could adopt the council as its child. Again my proposal failed to make headway because, in Lebanon, you cannot create only one ministry. Two have to be created at the same time: one for the Christians and one for the Moslems. The government had no plans for a second ministry just then. The recommendation was shelved until a sectarian distribution of ministries could be accommodated.

With nothing more I could do for tourism, my attention turned to national guidance, the third function of the ministry. To have national guidance, there must be a national policy. The only national policy in Lebanon was the National Covenant of 1943, an unwritten agreement between the Christians and the Mohammedans dating from when Lebanon won independence from the French. It had been hammered out between the political leaders of the two communities and was based essentially on three principles: first, Mohammedan renunciation of an aspiration for Arab union; secondly, Christian acceptance that Lebanon was a part of the Arab Middle East and not an outpost of Europe, especially France; and thirdly, a reconfirmation, but this time with specific ratios, of the constitutional provisions introduced by the French in 1926 for the 'equitable' confessional distribution of seats and posts in the legislative and executive branches of government.

The covenant was a delicately balanced compromise which worked only so long as it served the interests of the political feudal lords from both communities. It was so ingenious that only the Lebanese could have conjured it up: Lebanon's identity was defined as being Arab yet not Arab, Western yet not Western. When Riad Solh, the first Lebanese Moslem Prime Minister after independence, made a speech to Parliament on 7 October 1943, this was how he defined the country under the covenant: 'Lebanon is a homeland with an Arab face seeking beneficial good from the culture of the West.' Politicians defined the 'Arab face' as their interests dictated. When their interests changed, so did their definition. 'Beneficial good from the culture of the West' proved equally volatile in interpretation.

The National Covenant had failed in its purpose and served only to divide the people into separate and discontented religious communities. It actually prevented the Lebanese from being Lebanese. Rather did it divide them more rigidly into factions: Maronite Christians, Sunni Moslems, Shi'ite Moslems, Greek Orthodox Christians, Druzes; and so reinforced the belief in the Lebanese that they are Christians and Mohammedans but not Lebanese.

I disliked and dissociated myself from the feudal political lords' interpretation of the covenant and its distribution of government posts by religion. In fact, I hoped for a chance to change it. An opportunity arose when the director of the broadcasting department was promoted to the Ministry of Foreign Affairs. I decided to promote his number two, who was highly qualified. He had been trained in the Voice of America broadcasting organization, and was also a highly talented

122

journalist. I was told, however, that he could not be promoted because he was a Christian. The director of broadcasting was a post eternally reserved for Shi'ites. The question was raised with the highest authority, but with no success. Confessionalism is the Lebanese government's religion and has to be fanatically observed.

A second opportunity presented itself when it was discovered that the position of the head of the press department had been vacant since the previous promotion elsewhere of its holder. The deputy head was well qualified, with long experience, and was the natural choice. Alas, no, he could not be promoted to the post because he was a Maronite Christian and that particular job was reserved for Druzes. Being the Druze minister, I thought to convince the authorities that the Druzes would be prepared to forego their right to the job in favour of the Christian candidate. The request was denied. The government policy of religious allocation of posts was unchangeable.

I became a target for criticism. Being a Druze, I was expected to fight, as a minister, for the rights of Druzes and not 'give them away'. My reply was that giving the Druzes minor government posts did not give them their rights. They needed more schools, clinics and hospitals, social services, agricultural credits, village industries, better telecommunications, better roads and many other necessities of community life. What good did it do the Druze community if the head of the press department in the Ministry of Information was a Druze?

I refused, during the rest of my stay in the Ministry of Information, to fill these two vacancies by sectarian hopefuls and left the qualified number twos to continue their efficient management of the affairs of their departments. I could only sympathize with their frustration at being deprived of promotion.

The crazy adherence to a sectarian division of government posts and privileges could at times carry over into black farce. Considerable public merriment was caused at one time when a Moslem Prime Minister, who was also Minister of Finance, refused to authorize a subsidy for an urgent surgical operation for a Christian government employee until the ministry produced a Moslem requiring the same operation and the same subsidy. Everyone enjoyed the comic aspect of the situation and no one seemed to care about what happened to the unfortunate Christian while waiting for a Moslem colleague to be produced.

President Charles Helou announced, at one of the council's meetings, that he was determined to purify the government administration of its corrupt elements. There was much excitement. It was a courageous, stupendous undertaking. But, surely, were we not biting off more than

123

we could chew? To draw attention to the enormous difficulties of such a task, I recounted to the council the story of Thompson's cactus fruit. Thompson was an American teacher who came to work at the American University in Beirut. At breakfast, on his first day, the waiter brought him a cactus fruit. He went to work on it with gusto, separating the pips from the rest. But when his task was completed, there was nothing left for Mr Thompson to eat. If he purified the government of all its corrupt elements, I said, the President would find himself left with hardly any government. Nevertheless, despite the implications of the Thompson cactus-fruit warning, everyone was enthusiastic for reform – any reform – to make a start, at long last, on tackling Lebanon's chronic problem.

Such was the enthusiasm that laws were rushed through, the first, intended to reform the civil service, being passed by Parliament on 2 August 1965. A similar law, to affect the judicial system, was passed a month later. Significantly, the military and internal security departments, including any civilians working for them, were excluded from attempts at reform.

The most serious misgivings began to plague me when special committees, set up to purify the administration, recommended the dismissal of a number of senior judges, ambassadors and a few senior civil servants but, strangely, nobody else. It was horrifying that the committees brought no accusations, nor indeed any charges, against those concerned. The shocking consequence of this underhand procedure was that various distinguished and eminent men, who had worked to serve Lebanon all their lives, were to be sacked and destroyed without explanation, and were not permitted by the cunningly concocted Reform Law to defend themselves. At a stroke of the pen, they had been ruthlessly deprived of the right, enjoyed in every civilized democracy, to stand trial or, indeed, be presumed innocent until found guilty.

When four ministers, including myself, objected strongly to these outrageous measures, we were told that they were in accordance with the Reform Law. It seemed that Parliament, under great pressure to pass the law quickly, had failed to detect certain cunningly introduced wording that enabled those who designed the law to dismiss government officials without informing them of the charges against them or allowing them to reply in their own defence.

Not only were the unfortunate victims deprived of the right to know the reasons for their callous dismissal, but the Council of Ministers was also denied this right. The infamous Reform Law stipulated that the council should decide on the recommendations of the various committees. But then we were told that, in accordance with that law, we had no right to know why the victims were to be dismissed and must approve the recommendations with no questions asked. Several of us strongly contested this distorted interpretation of the law, but our objections were swept aside while other ministers approved, robot-like, the recommendations placed before them.

It became clear that the proposed dismissals had nothing to do with the reforms we had so fervently supported. The new laws had been designed and exploited by unscrupulous men in power to take revenge on senior Lebanese personalities who had at some time in some way offended them. It was not reform but personal vendetta. As soon as the enemies of the power brokers were disposed of, nothing more was heard about reform.

Even in this infamous act, sectarian distribution was applied. The high-ranking judges who were ruthlessly recommended for dismissal numbered twelve in all: three Sunni Moslems, three Maronite Christians, two Shi'ites, two Greek Orthodox, one Druze and one Catholic — the exact sectarian formula officially adopted in Lebanon. It may be thought that the distribution happened by chance, but the likelihood of that according to the laws of probability would be 1 in 670 million!

The whole procedure was a violation, not only of human rights, but of the very Lebanese Constitution. I knew quite well how rare it was for Lebanese governments to propose a law to Parliament for the benefit of Lebanon and its people as a whole. Most legislation was prepared with the aim of either benefiting friends or damaging enemies. But the Reform Law was the worst example of all, and one which Lebanese should always remember with shame.

Appalled by events, and seriously concerned at this abuse of power, I resigned, together with Wajdi Mallat, Minister of Labour and Social Affairs, who shared my indignation that more crimes had been perpetrated than any the Law was designed to root out. Strong pressure was at once put upon us to withdraw our resignations. We were given a solemn promise that, if we did so, every step would be taken to see that any mistakes were put right and justice be done in the case of any who had suffered. There was also a subtle hint that our departure from the council might have a harmful delaying effect on such a process. It was argued that setting things to rights could take a long time and that, if we insisted on resigning, nothing might be done at all. Feeling that, by remaining in government, we might help to get justice for those who had suffered, and accepting the promise, we both agreed to withdraw our resignations.

In retrospect, I have become convinced that vendettas and personal revenge were not, in fact, the main objectives of the Reform Law, but only incidental issues. The law was really designed to intimidate senior judges, top government executives and even politicians into submitting to plots that were then being prepared against Lebanon. It was a test case for what was to come. If they could get away with such a law, they could get away with anything. As one well-known politician said: 'The Reform Law was the first nail in Lebanon's coffin.'

Having agreed to remain in government, however, I decided there was no point in staying on at the ineffectual Ministry of Information. I asked, instead, to take over as Minister of Public Works, which post had become vacant. In that capacity, I might at least be able to get on with some useful work for the country. The proposal was accepted and so I moved to one of the busiest ministries – not only the busiest, but also the biggest, embracing over 60 per cent of the public utility services in Lebanon. It employed 70,773 employees, which, for a ministry in tiny Lebanon, was a colossal number. Its budget covered over 50 per cent of total government spending, and it was one of the four ministries traditionally reserved for the two super-privileged communities of Lebanon, the Christians and the Sunni Moslems, the other three being the Ministries of Finance, Foreign Affairs and Interior.

It took nearly a week to receive all the director-generals, directors and heads of the numerous public utility authorities, who came to pay their respects. It was soon clear that no single human being could deal efficiently with such a vast ministry. Road construction and mainte-nance, government building construction and maintenance, transport on air, sea and land, electricity, water, town planning, airports, ports and railways – all came under public works. And the minister had to make and sign all the necessary decisions.

My first discovery was a huge backlog of documents awaiting decision. It was months, even years behind, and each day new recommendations flooded in for rulings from the various departments. After consulting the directors, I delegated each of them with the necessary powers to make all those decisions that were not policy ones and that fell within the approved budget and did not grant contracts above a certain limit. This voluntary delegation of ministerial powers created a sensation. No minister had ever done such a thing. It was also the first time in the history of public works that decisions affecting the urgent needs of citizens were expedited.

I then proceeded to work out a project to divide the ministry into two parts; the first to deal with public works and transport; the second with hydro-electric resources. It would have been even better to have split the ministry into three or even four separate ministries, but I knew I could never get away with such a drastic deviation from the long-established tradition. I was, once again, faced with the sectarian bogey. To create a new ministry for hydro-electric resources, we also had to create another ministry to satisfy sectarian distribution. Fortunately, the authorities were ready to create one, and my previously proposed Ministry of Tourism was this time allowed to be born. The President and the Council of Ministers approved the partition scheme and Parliament passed it in record time after a debate lasting less than half an hour.

Requests for assistance and demands for favours poured in from all quarters: members of the public, deputies, political leaders, the President's entourage, and anyone who hoped to make money out of the ministry in one way or another. Everybody wanted to see the minister to explain why his request was so essential. A system was instituted whereby deputies and politicians came to see me by appointment, and I assigned each Thursday as an open day for the public when I heard their requests and had them recorded. They were told that, if they returned the following Thursday, they would have a definite answer, yes or no. The arrangement worked well and was popular with the people.

It soon became clear, however, that I was becoming unpopular with deputies and politicians, who were accustomed to ambling into the minister's office without appointment and did not take kindly to the new system. But what hurt them most was that I was rejecting their requests because nearly all of them were illegal. Never to be forgotten was the occasion when I told a deputy that what he was requesting was against the law. 'I know that,' he replied, 'for if it was in accordance with the law, why should I come to you?'

Soon, the backlog was cleared and it became possible to decide on and sign all ministerial documents each day by noon. It was an experience both new and unsettling to the ministry. One day a director came in and asked permission to speak frankly. 'Your Excellency, Mr Minister,' he said. 'May I say, out of friendship and loyalty, that this is not how ministerial work ought to be done?'

'How should it be done?' I asked. 'Please feel free to tell me.'

'Mr Minister,' he said, 'you are signing all decisions very quickly. Usually, when a document reaches the minister for signature, it must find its way unsigned to one of the minister's desk drawers.'

'Why should that be?' I enquired.

'To force interested deputies and politicians to come begging to you,' he said. 'They will then be obliged to you, and their votes are important for the government to stay in office.'

'My friend,' I replied, 'my duty is first and foremost to serve the Lebanese public by expediting the ministry's decisions, and secondly, I don't care two hoots for the votes of the deputies for or against the government. I joined it reluctantly, and after what I have seen, I should be very happy if the deputies voted the government out of office and I was able to return to the pleasure of my work in Middle East Airlines.'

I was treading heavily on the toes of the powers that mattered in Lebanon. There were villages deprived of water and electricity, of roads or road maintenance, because their inhabitants were loyal to and had voted for political feudal lords who were in the opposition. Disregarding the political game, I supplied villages with their rightful services. Displeasure was also caused in high places, despite forewarning, by foiling a plot designed to annoy the Maronite Patriarch, who had not given certain people his blessing or support. A road scheme had been concocted in the ministry to use a large proportion of a valuable piece of land owned by the Patriarchate. I was told of the scheme, and when I examined it found that the road was neither necessary nor desirable, and that its only purpose was to ruin the value of the land. The scheme was stopped at once and steps taken to ensure it would not be reintroduced.

My unpopularity with the politicians was rapidly increasing, and my attempts at introducing progressive improvements were mysteriously being delayed, if not actually sabotaged. I had managed to organize the partition of the ministry, but all other projects ran into trouble, including a new system of land appropriation, under which the government would appropriate all the land needed for a road at one time and not in yearly portions. This would have saved hundreds of millions of Lebanese pounds. Another plan was to modify the regulations and procedures for granting contracts, which would have plugged the many loopholes, provided better control and would have also saved hundreds of millions a year. Studies for a sewage network for Beirut's suburbs and the mountains around it were to be seriously developed and priority given to the construction of this badly needed public utility. Town planning was to include the mountain resorts so as to preserve the phenomenal scenic beauty of Lebanon and its picturesque architecture. Strict measures were to be introduced for the prevention of sand removal for construction purposes from the beautiful shores and beaches of

Lebanon. And there were numerous other much-needed public utility projects.

It was getting tiresome, constantly to be asked to break the law by those whose sworn duty was to uphold it. Most of my improvement projects were being obstructed, and I also became convinced that the authorities had no intention of carrying out their promise to correct the injustices of the Reform Law.

One evening, after the council's weekly meeting, I asked President Helou for a chat. We went to his home, next to his offices, and, over a glass of whisky, I told him that I would like to depart so as to look after the interests of Middle East Airlines. I explained that I thought I could assist Lebanon more through MEA than through the ministry. The President tried to convince me otherwise. This went on for a while, and after the second whisky the President leant back in his armchair and burst out laughing. He said, 'You know, had anyone been listening to us, he could have never believed his ears: a President of Lebanon trying to persuade a Lebanese to be a minister, and what is more incredible, a Lebanese who does not want to be a minister. Absolutely unbelievable.' We enjoyed the joke, but did not achieve my release on that occasion.

During this period of my preoccupation with ministerial duties, MEA got along well enough. For the first time in its turbulent history, it basked in the sunshine of financial security and the Lebanese shareholders were happy to finance expansion. Negotiations to buy new long-range jets had begun as early as 1964. Studies were made of the Boeing 707, Douglas DC–8 and BAC Super VC–10. All three aircraft looked excellent, but the Super VC–10 was chosen. Our pilots preferred its excellent flying capabilities, and its passenger appeal was spectacular. The problem was that the British Aircraft Corporation (BAC) did not enjoy the financial resources of their American rivals and could not offer the same attractive terms.

In an effort to overcome these difficulties, I flew as minister to London in November 1965 on an official mission to suggest a barter deal to the British government: apples for aircraft. In Lebanon that year we had a glut of apples, and the export to the United Kingdom of some of that surplus could have more than compensated for the unfavourable VC–10 terms.

We wanted to pay 30 per cent of the purchase price of the aircraft in apples, but were prepared to accept the 10 per cent suggested by the British Ministry of Aviation. The proposal created a sensation, and the media gave it wide publicity. British humour took a hand and a slogan appeared in the press: 'An apple a day keeps Boeing away'. A caricature appeared of BAC employees queueing to receive their weekly wages in apples. 'Plane deal flop upsets the apple cart,' was among other similar witticisms.

Despite public enthusiasm, both in Britain and Lebanon, for a deal that could have helped the continued manufacture of the best passenger aircraft ever produced by Britain, the British government refused to give BAC the financial backing it requested.

There was a public outcry. The collapse of the deal was tantamount to killing off the VC–10. The *Sunday Express* of 23 January 1966, under the headline 'Lunacy in the Air', attacked the government's decision and its consequences, and ended its onslaught with the indignant outburst: 'It is a lunatic situation. How has it arisen? Has Mr Wilson done a deal with President Johnson? Has he, as the price of dollar dole to rescue the British economy from the wreckage to which socialist policies have led it, agreed to destroy the British aircraft industry?'

Despite all that had happened, we were still interested in the VC–10. Our hopes were shattered when BOAC announced that they were cancelling what had been a firm order for ten Super VC–10s, preferring to pay the heavy cancellation penalty rather than go through with the deal. We could hardly be expected to be more royalist than the king and consequently, on 18 February 1966, signed an agreement to buy three DC–8s. To meet the financial requirements of our purchase, a general assembly of shareholders decided on 3 September to increase the capital of Middle East Airlines from £L25 million to £L50 million. Air France, to our amazement, refused to participate in the increase of capital, but Bedas, for Intra Bank, readily agreed to take up Air France's share.

Our affirmed intention of being an up-to-date company had made it even more important that our employees should enjoy progressive and modern working conditions and a full right to social justice. Salaries were improved; annual holidays were given for periods exceeding the provisions of the Lebanese Labour Law; generous scholarships were awarded to the children of company employees; and efforts were maintained to bring about a social revolution within the company. With discreet encouragement from myself, a trade union in MEA came into being. It seemed a healthy development, giving employees machinery for communicating with management. It fostered a spirit of 'togetherness' in the airline, and generally played a constructive role. And, as a result, our pioneering work in the field of labour relations received a great deal of complimentary publicity all over Lebanon. What made this publicity especially pleasing was that it was spontaneous.

Our peaceful revolution was to play a part in Lebanese politics. In the late summer of 1965, a row broke out between some politicians of the right and left. They hurled accusations and insults at one another, and the storm developed into a war of words, attracting politicians from both sides on to the public platform. On 9 October 1965, with the quarrel still raging, I made a speech at the distribution of scholarships to the children of MEA employees in which I outlined the social benefits enjoyed by those employees. Emphasizing that the relationship between employer and employee is that of a partnership in which both parties respected each other's right to the equitable sharing of benefits and profits, I declared that social justice was not a favour or a charitable donation. It was the sacred right of every Lebanese citizen. I was as critical of the ugly face of capitalism as I was of destructive extremist socialism.

The press hailed my speech with banner headlines: 'A Revolutionary Step', 'Between the Ignorant Right and the Foolish Left', 'To Create Stability and Social Justice', 'To Save Private Enterprise', 'Social Justice is the Lawful Right of Every Citizen', 'The Socialism of Najib Alamuddin', 'A Partnership between Employee and the Employer', 'Stability and Social Justice', 'Alamuddin Rings the Warning Bell', 'Unions Support Najib Alamuddin'. This unanimous press reaction fanned the flames of the enmity of the Lebanese business establishment towards me and my 'socialist principles', and towards MEA, which had, in their opinion, become a dangerous socialist organization.

They were, of course, totally opposed to our social revolution within the company. My friendship with the late Kamal Jumblatt, the Druze socialist leader, further convinced them that the course I had embarked on was a danger to them and to their fortunes, and they feared that others might follow my example. They waged a clandestine war against me and Middle East Airlines, using their powerful influence to aim blow after blow below the belt. Some of them went so far as to accuse us of pro-communist Russian sentiments, because of the warm reception the employees gave to Valentina Tereshkova, the Soviet astronaut, when she visited MEA and its engineering installations during her brief stay in Lebanon. As she entered MEA grounds, she was showered with rose petals which happened to be red in colour!

Later we learned that the campaign was carried beyond the Lebanese frontiers into the 'moderate' Arab countries, where socialism is often confused with communism. The social policies embraced by MEA were pictured as Marxist ideology. The same false accusations were whispered into the ears of several United States agencies. I can only hope those agencies were better informed than to believe such self-interested lies about a company that never, during my twenty-five years there, had a strike or even an acrimonious quarrel between management and employees. Such a company is hardly a leftist danger. It is rather an example to be followed, not only in Lebanon but everywhere in the Arab countries where true socialism must replace autocratic feudalism. Only genuine social justice applied with compassion can halt the rapid advance of fanatic communism.

This belief remains unshaken. In common with the late Kamal Jumblatt, I was convinced of the urgent need to improve the living-standards of the 'have-nots' of Lebanon. I stood for moderate socialism and opposed extremism and the use of violence as a tool for change.

My friendship with Kamal Jumblatt had been intensified following the troubles of 1958. A group of young men who joined his forces and held leading military positions during the fighting, went to him after it was all over and asked for jobs to compensate them for their material losses and for their loyalty in the fighting. But Kamal Jumblatt possessed no personal fortune to satisfy their demands. The Jumblatts had, over the years, squandered their feudal wealth and only a small fraction remained, tied down in agricultural land, part of which Kamal Jumblatt had distributed to the peasants who lived on it. The revenue from his real estate was barely adequate for his domestic needs. He was constantly in debt, yet money meant nothing to him. He saw it as a means to an end, not an end in itself.

Knowing of our friendship, the supplicants asked me to intercede on their behalf. They needed work and money and were considering following the Druze tradition: warriors, unable to earn their living with dignity, will never beg but prefer to become Robin Hoods of the highway. I was certain that some of them were not only capable of following the Druze tradition but were enthusiastic about doing so. What really worried me was the knowledge that, unless these young men were given honest employment, some of them would reluctantly become recruits to serve as mercenaries or subversive agents for those who planned trouble for Lebanon. I promised the young men that I would talk to Kamal Jumblatt.

Coincidentally, it happened that MEA needed a force of security guards after the move to its new installations at the airport. This need provided the solution for the problem of the Druze fighters. A security department was formed and employment offered to more than fifty of Kamal Jumblatt's tough young men. It proved a great success. They

132

gave MEA excellent security and saved lives and property on a number of occasions. Sadly, Kamal Jumblatt was to be assassinated on Wednesday, 16 March 1977, by unknown forces. He was and is still greatly missed in Lebanon. The most appropriate *cri de coeur* for his murder was given by the *Herald Tribune* on 19 March 1977, under the heading: 'Murder of a Gentleman'.

'The Role of Private Enterprise in the Economic Development of the Middle East' was the title I chose for an address in 1966 to the Middle East Institute in Washington. Representatives of the United States government agency who extended the invitation to me also offered to write my speech to save me time and effort. Naturally, I refused their kind gesture, preferring to write it myself and be personally responsible for what I had to say!

In my speech, I emphasized that private enterprise had contributed much towards the economic development of the area and still had immense potential for the future. But, I also argued, private enterprise needed to face the challenge of the newly created socialist movements in the region. It was not enough for private enterprise to increase the total national product; it also had to ensure that the masses received their fair share of the increase. The failure of private enterprise to bring about this fair distribution was mainly responsible for its downfall. Private enterprise ignored the pressing and urgent demands for social justice and did little to improve the condition of the masses, either on its own or in co-operation with the public sector. In Lebanon, there was also a frightening gap throughout the country between the prosperous minority and the majority of its people. A survey had shown that over 61 per cent of the national income was monopolized by 18 per cent of the population.

The short-sighted policies, love of quick profits, control and corruption of governments, unreasonable hatred of any social reform, blind opposition to any form of labour movement or labour legislation, association with foreign interests in order to protect their own, schemes for exporting capital, and their extravagant living while their countrymen were starving, must lead inevitably to the explosion of the masses. This must lead, in turn, to the overthrow of what the masses considered to be régimes of injustice, corruption and inhuman exploitation, and to the establishment of state-controlled economies.

I then made the point that the leaders of such *coups d'état* were, in most cases, military officers educated in the West or in Western-managed schools, not in Moscow. And that these were mostly honest patriotic men who felt deeply the suffering of the masses and the

133

humiliation of having to tolerate governing régimes that did little or nothing to improve the inhuman conditions of poverty, ignorance and need in which their people lived. It was the misery of the people and the hatred of injustice inflicted upon them which led to the overthrow of régimes. It needed to be realized that, although communism takes advantage of revolutionary situations, it is not always responsible for their origins.

The speech was well received by the audience and, sponsored by Congressman the Hon. Charles E. Goodall, was inserted in the *Congressional Record*. I was well pleased with it, and with the additional honour of having it inserted in the record. But you may imagine my embarrassment in August 1969 when Miles Copeland published his book *The Game of Nations* in which he disclosed that it was the US Central Intelligence Agency (CIA) which had inspired and set up the various *coups d'état* in the Arab Middle East, not my honest, patriotic Arab military officers, 'who deeply felt the suffering of the masses'. I still blush when I think of that speech, and seriously wonder, in these days of the CIA, the KGB and other agencies, how many leaders who are hailed as national heroes, especially in developing countries, are in fact mere puppets. Are the patriotic utterances we hear being so loudly voiced and so fervently praised genuine, or are they a part of the political tragi-comedy of the 'Game of Nations'?

Shortly after the Washington speech, and to my great relief, the government resigned for 'normal' Lebanese political reasons and so I was left free to resume full-time work at MEA.

12

Intra: The Murder of a Bank

President Charles Helou telephoned one evening in October 1966, saying he wanted to see me urgently the next day. Despite the fact that I had arranged to fly to Paris, he insisted I should call on him at his official residence before catching the plane.

The President asked me to tell him what I knew about Intra Bank's financial difficulties. I was astounded by such unlikely news and told the President I was certainly unaware that Intra had any financial troubles. On the contrary, to my knowledge it was embarking upon an expansion programme and had plans to open new branches in Athens and Cyprus as well as in certain African countries and in South America. There had also been the matter of a substantial increase in the capital of MEA, decided upon two weeks earlier. Intra, in addition to its share, was going to take up Air France's portion of the increased capitalization since the French did not wish to subscribe to that increase. Furthermore, with Intra's financial guarantee, Middle East Airlines intended to buy three big modern jet aircraft for over £L100 million. I had recommended cheaper, used aircraft, but Bedas had insisted that new aircraft, though much more expensive, would be better for the image and prestige of MEA. I was, in fact, on my way to Paris to meet him and work out the final details of this purchase. Taking into account all these facts, there could be no truth in the story of Intra being in difficulties. It must be one of those rumours that were constantly being spread by those jealous of the bank's spectacular success.

'No,' the President replied. 'I have been requested by Bedas to ask the Central Bank to help Intra because it is in real trouble.'

The Central Bank of Lebanon, founded in 1963, was successor to the privately owned French Banque de Syrie et du Liban, which had, until then, fulfilled the official function. The Central Bank was staffed at executive level by the unqualified protégés of political parties, who were

135

totally incompetent and inexperienced, most of the rest of the staff having previously worked for the French bank.

I promised the President to find out the true facts and report back. His revelation about the request for assistance was very disturbing, though I found it hard to believe that, as a member of Intra's board and as a close friend of Yousif Bedas, I could have known neither of any sign of the need for such assistance nor of such a request being made.

Because of arriving late in Paris, I was not able to contact Bedas that night. Early next morning, I phoned his apartment. His Sudanese manservant told me he was still in New York. His Paris office told me he had been attending meetings of the World Bank but was expected in Paris soon. I felt uneasy. It seemed unlike Bedas to miss an important meeting without letting me know. I therefore phoned his hotel as soon as it was morning in New York and heard from Yousif a most incredible story.

He said that President Charles Helou had sent for him before he left for the World Bank meetings and asked him to increase the bank's investment in Lebanon. The country, said Helou, needed more investments, especially in tourist projects. Bedas replied that Intra had, in fact, over-invested in Lebanon. It now had plans for expansion in other countries and therefore could not possibly tie up more capital internally. President Helou brushed aside the objections. 'The government will help you,' said the President. 'You must have important assets in your Lebanese investments. Why not use these as collateral to get a loan from the Central Bank? It is there to help you. You should make use of it.' The President then mentioned a possible figure of £L150 million — 'Go and see Joseph Oghourlian, the deputy governor of the Central Bank.' Bedas found nothing unusual in this, since one of the functions of the Central Bank was to help banks in their plans for investment in Lebanon. Furthermore, Joseph Oghourlian was the President's brother-in-law, with whom it would have been only natural to discuss such investment plans. Bedas did as he was told. In Washington, he discussed the President's directive with Oghourlian, who was also attending the World Bank meetings.

In his memoirs, which have never been published, Bedas tells the story of this meeting when he proudly explained to Oghourlian Intra's splendid work in Lebanese investments and the consequent contribution to the Lebanese economy. 'Why did you do it? Who asked you to? You are not Lebanese and Lebanon does not want your control of its economy,' was Oghourlian's unexpected outburst. Bedas remonstrated strongly and was very firm with the deputy governor of Lebanon's Central Bank who was, anyway, an Armenian!

My first reaction was to challenge Bedas's account of the affair. Until then, I had always regarded Charles Helou as a personal friend. Moreover, he had, as President of the Republic, insisted that Intra Bank was in trouble and Bedas had asked him for help. But Bedas now swore to me on the lives of his children, which I knew to be his most sacred oath, and I was convinced he had told me the truth.

I asked why he had not told his fellow directors about his audience with the President. He said the question was not pressing and had come up only the day before he travelled to the United States. A request to invest more in Lebanon was hardly urgent and there would have been plenty of time for him to discuss it with the board after his return. He then remarked angrily: 'You know me and my love for Intra. Would I have left Beirut to attend a routine World Bank meeting had I felt the least suspicion that my bank was in trouble? And had I wanted assistance from Charles Helou, would I not have asked your help to get it?'

Bedas well knew of my personal friendship with Charles Helou at the time. Helou and I had worked closely together in the National Tourist Council and I had been a minister in his government the year before. Bedas also knew that, before his election as President of Lebanon, Helou had asked me to help him by persuading Kamal Jumblatt to support him, which I did.

It was truly bewildering. It seemed impossible, at the time, to reconcile the two versions of events. I did not want to doubt the President, but, knowing Bedas and his fanatic devotion to Intra, I could not imagine he would ever leave his bank in trouble and travel to Washington for a World Bank social gathering.

Bedas, greatly distressed, convinced that the President's story would spark off a run on the bank, pleaded with me to return immediately to Beirut to ask for the necessary government intervention. I telexed Beirut, asking for an urgent appointment with the President, and left on the first available flight. When I arrived at Beirut Airport, I was told the President was waiting for me at his office. Paul Parker, personal adviser to Bedas and a former regional director of the Bank of America for the Middle East, and Joe Salameh, Bedas's brother-in-law and manager of the Intra branch in New York, were waiting at the airport to brief me on the rapid deterioration in the situation. News was spreading like wildfire that Intra was in trouble and depositors were withdrawing their money. The banks which used Intra as a 'bankers' bank' and had substantial deposits were also withdrawing funds. Unless the government came to Intra's assistance, it was certain that the run on the bank would become a deluge. But, they assured me, the bank had important assets in shares, bonds and other semi-liquid funds to give a full and adequate collateral to the Central Bank for any liquidity help it needed.

After driving to the Palace where the President awaited me, I argued for immediate help from the Central Bank to avoid the biggest financial catastrophe in the history of Lebanon and the destructive blow to the economy that must inevitably follow. The President listened to my arguments and asked me to return at 10 p.m. for a meeting with him and Prime Minister Abdallah Yafi, who was also Minister of Finance and the ultimate government authority on the Central Bank.

That evening I faced a stormy meeting with the Prime Minister, who stated that Bedas was a crook, that the bank was in very bad shape and had been involved in questionable and unsavoury transactions. Agitatedly, the Prime Minister rejected every request for help to avoid the financial havoc which would follow the collapse of Intra. He asserted that no financial assistance given to the 'failing' bank could possibly save it and would only be money down the drain.

'I have received a report giving me all the details of Bedas's thieving, and of the hopeless situation of the bank,' he said. 'I am assured the bank is in very bad shape and nothing can save it.' I asked to see this report and to know the name of its author. 'The report,' he said, 'has been sent to me confidentially. I can neither let you see it nor disclose the name of its author.'

The meeting lasted into the early hours, both the President and Prime Minister insisting that Bedas must return to Lebanon before any assistance could be considered. I argued that the government had a responsibility to help the bank, its shareholders and its depositors and to save Lebanon's banking-system. I told them I was not only arguing to save Bedas but also pleading to save Intra. If there was a valid case against Bedas, he should stand trial and answer for it. If he was not guilty, he should be honoured for all he had done for Lebanon. The saving of the bank should not be conditional on his return.

Despite all my arguments, the Prime Minister would not shift an inch. There was no purpose in trying any more. As a Lebanese saying about the futility of argument when the other party is determined not to listen puts it: 'No matter how long you pound water, it will remain water.' This was the point at which we had arrived.

I said I would convey their demand for Bedas's return, but wanted a guarantee that he would not be arrested on arrival in Lebanon, or molested in any way. He should be given an opportunity to explain. The President gave his word but the Prime Minister remained silent.

I left the President's office smelling a rat. Indeed, the meeting had been charged with the stench of rats. How could a bank, even the biggest, ward off a run if the President of the Republic and the Prime Minister spread the news that it was in financial difficulties and that it had applied for government assistance which they were convinced should not be given? I was also afraid that, despite the President's assurance, Bedas would be arrested on arrival by the evidently determined Prime Minister, who was also Minister of Finance and Minister of Justice. Nevertheless, I felt Bedas must take the risk and return to defend his bank.

At the Phoenicia Hotel, Paul Parker and Joe Salameh were waiting for my report on what had taken place in the meeting. When I said that Bedas must come back, they both felt doubtful whether Bedas would do so. He feared he would be arrested as he stepped off the plane and never given a fair chance to explain. But, I said, the President had given his word that no such thing would happen and, I insisted, the bank's survival depended on Bedas's return to Lebanon. They took the point and suggested that, as Salameh was leaving for New York the following day, he should convey the message. If anyone could get Bedas to return, it would be Joe, his brother-in-law and intimate confidant.

As it came about, the government did not wait for his return. The crisis escalated and the conspiracy against Bedas and Intra went into full swing. The conspirators did not want Bedas in Lebanon and, as it emerged later, he was threatened with assassination should he set foot in the country. The story he set down in his memoirs made a chilling one, a precursor to much that has happened since in Lebanon. Bedas wrote: 'A leading Lebanese politician has vowed publicly, "Yousif Bedas will never again set foot in Lebanon." He sent an emissary to tell me his agents would kill me if I ever returned to Lebanon.' The politician was named in the memoirs, but they were never published since Bedas was also threatened with the assassination of his children if he dared to do so — or, indeed, if they should be published after his death. The threats were serious enough, because of the scandals they would have unveiled and the number of 'famous' Lebanese politicians who would have been exposed — especially the 'leading one' who made the threat.

Bedas was also advised — badly, I believe — by some of those closest to him, not to take the risk of returning. They assured him that the Lebanese government could not afford to let Intra collapse. The bank would be helped to overcome its liquidity problems and all would be well; the national interest of Lebanon and common sense were bound to prevail. Bedas, they said, could then come back safely after the dust had settled. Alas! It did not turn out like that. Intra Bank was ruthlessly destroyed and Bedas never again saw the Lebanon he so loved, but died in exile on 28 November 1968 at Lucerne in Switzerland, just over two years after Intra Bank closed its doors on Black Friday, 14 October 1966.

The news of Intra's closure triggered off financial shock-waves throughout the world. Bedas's version of what really happened when he was summoned to see President Helou gathered momentum and credibility as the plot against Intra unfolded. *Time-Life* magazine told the story on 12 December 1966. This account was later reiterated by Bedas in a message to the Lebanese people in August 1968, which was prominently published in the Lebanese press. It was told again at a press conference held on 28 October 1970 by Moustafa Moured, the lawyer representing the heirs of Yousif Bedas. Subsequently, Bedas's version of the story was never challenged or denied, and although a great deal has been written about the conspiracy and its after-effects, I feel it my duty to place on record everything I know. My most compelling reason is that I am convinced the affair was the beginning of the disintegration of Lebanon and its old type of Lebanese government – a system corrupt in style and morals that had plagued Lebanon since independence and finally plunged the nation into a civil war that threatened its very survival as an independent state.

While I remained at the head of MEA, I had to remain silent about the Intra affair in the course of protecting the airline and its employees. Certain of the conspirators remained firmly entrenched in positions of power in the government, and also in MEA's majority shareholder, Intra Investment Company, which finally replaced Intra Bank.

Yousif Bedas, the creator of Intra Bank, was born in Jerusalem in December 1912, and educated at St George's School up to the age of sixteen, when he went to work to help his family. He held two minor government jobs for a short time, and then joined the staff of Barclay's Bank in Jerusalem, where he learned about finance and banking. After eleven years, he went to work for the Arab Bank in Jerusalem. He married Wadad Salameh, a bride of Lebanese origin, in December 1946. Two years later, when Arabs and Jews were fighting for Jerusalem, he fled with his pregnant wife to Beirut where his first son was born.

Together with a few friends, Bedas then founded a Lebanese import-export company called International Traders. His wife's uncle,

140

Mounir Abu Fadel, a prominent member of the Lebanese Parliament for many years, and its Deputy Speaker, joined International Traders in May 1949. They were later joined by Badr Fahoum, today the President of Arabia Insurance Company, who also contributed effectively to the success of Intra Bank.

International Traders was a successful venture, but Bedas remained a banker at heart. So he persuaded his partners to form a bank which was given a licence in 1951 to operate with a capital of £L6,400,000. The bank was given the widest scope for activities, as well as a licence to participate in commercial, real estate and other forms of investments. The partners chose Intra, the cable address of International Traders, as the bank's name.

From a small bank operating from a two-roomed office, Bedas and his colleagues built, within fifteen years, the Intra Bank empire. By 1966, the bank had subsidiaries and branches throughout the Arab world, in New York, Paris, London, Frankfurt, Rome, Geneva, Brazil, the Bahamas, Nigeria, Liberia, Sierre Leone and others in the final stages of establishment. Intra had investments in twenty-six important companies in Lebanon, seven in France, three in England, three in Switzerland, one in Canada and one in Brazil. In most of these companies, Intra had the controlling interest.

While executives of foreign and Lebanese banks were basking lazily in the enjoyable social life of Beirut, Bedas and his colleagues were busy scouring the Arab Middle East for business. They succeeded in attracting substantial deposits from the Arab oil-producing countries. Rulers, sheikhs, merchants, contractors and entrepreneurs were among the important depositors. Naturally enough, depositors soon became prospective shareholders. Intra widened its shareholding base in Lebanon and was ready to welcome new shareholders, both Lebanese and Arab. It became by far the biggest of the ninety banks in Lebanon.

By 1966, Intra Bank had 750 shareholders, 79.68 per cent of whom were Lebanese. The remaining 20.32 per cent were Arab, the most important of them being the Al-Sabah Kuwait ruling family, with 5.9 per cent, the then Ruler of Qatar and family with 4.2 per cent, important Saudi businessmen with 3.4 per cent and Jordanian businessmen with 1.8 per cent. The remaining 5.02 per cent were small shareholders from all the Arab countries.

This Arab shareholding, small as it actually was, enabled Bedas's enemies to exaggerate Arab participation and to accuse Intra of being Lebanese in name only while spreading the fear that, as a result of their shareholdings in the bank, Arabs would ultimately control Lebanon's economy. Lebanon is, because of its mixed population, viewed according to taste as a Christian outpost in the Moslem world or as an Arab forward base on the Mediterranean. But the Lebanese, worshippers of ambiguity and compromise, had agreed in the National Covenant of 1943 for Lebanon to have an Arab face — a flexible interpretation! Participation by Arabs in the shareholding of Intra was, in the opinion of some Lebanese, not an acceptable aspect of its Arab face.

The Intra Bank Arab shareholders, whose participation was so much resented, were without doubt the best you could ever have hoped to win from the oil-rich dreamland. In time, they became billionaires many times over. Had the bank survived, they would have invested an important part of their fortunes, through Intra, in building up the Lebanese economy, thereby raising the standard of living of the deprived people of Lebanon — the people on whose sufferings the civil war has always fed.

It is both ironic and a compliment to the far-sightedness of Bedas and his friends that President Amin Gemayel of Lebanon was reported in the Lebanese newspaper *An-Nahar*, after a visit to Saudi Arabia on 15 November 1982, as having declared that Lebanon's reconstruction motto would be 'economic participation' not 'financial aid'. It had taken sixteen years and a long, bloody civil war to convince the Lebanese that Arab participation in the economy of Lebanon was no act of monetary colonization to be feared and rejected, but an act of co-operation to be solicited and gratefully acknowledged.

Bedas, who had a Lebanese mother and a Lebanese wife, and who acquired Lebanese nationality, was never accepted as Lebanese. To most Lebanese, he was a foreigner and a resented Palestinian. He paid not the least attention to this and attributed it all to jealousy of success. He loved Lebanon with all his heart and his dearest ambition was to help secure Lebanese ownership for the many enterprises which were under foreign control. In a long and emotional statement to his adopted compatriots in 1968, he declared that, even though political independence had been won, Lebanon was still a prominent target for the business interests of the colonial powers: France, Britain and America, anxious to exploit the new flow of oil wealth from the Gulf.

'It was equally clear that no substantial economic progress, indeed, no actual political independence, could be achieved without the prior achievement of economic independence,' Bedas stated. 'This, I knew, could only be done through the true Lebanonization of the hordes of nominally Lebanese enterprises which were in the grip of foreign interests. My associates and I initiated the Lebanonization plan in the

142

full knowledge that in so doing we were challenging, not only powerful foreign interests, but also a small but highly influential group of Lebanese. This group, a cluster of no more than fifty families, had since the days of the [French] mandate depended for their livelihood on serving foreign-controlled enterprises in Lebanon in nominal capacities. My associates and I then suspected from the outset that any Lebanonization plan would be met by their vicious opposition and our suspicions were soon to be justified.'

Many of the foreign-controlled companies mentioned by him were, in fact, French-dominated. The most notable were Air Liban, the Port Company, Radio Orient – the wireless company – Société Fonçière du Liban and the St George's Hotel When Yousif Bedas and Intra offered generous prices for shares, the foreign investors, already alarmed by political instability in the region, were only too happy to sell out and leave. But official France, and the Foreign Ministry in particular, were most unhappy about this development which struck a blow at the *présence Française* in the Near East.

Instead of blaming their citizens for selling out, they turned on Bedas and Intra, in which they were joined by the Lebanese 'men of straw' who had derived substantial benefits from their nominal participation in the Lebanonized enterprises. They started and sponsored, with the help of their principals, a campaign against Bedas and his bank and spread all kinds of stories to discredit what he was trying to achieve. The most damaging rumour alleged that Bedas said he could remove or appoint the President of Lebanon with a snap of his fingers. This infuriated the then President, Fouad Chehab, and turned him against Bedas and his 'Intra Group'. To set the French and their friends in Lebanon against Bedas and Intra, a rumour was circulated that he was the channel for Arab money subsidizing the Algerian FLN, then fighting France. When he refused a loan without security to an Arab League staff member in Geneva, the man denounced him to the league on a false charge of selling to Israelis Arab land in Palestine.

Curiously enough, the only Arab country to pay any serious attention to this obviously malicious lie was Lebanon. The Lebanese authorities suddenly became patriotically Arab and felt tremendous zeal to protect the Palestinians and their land against Bedas and the wicked Israelis. They dispatched a special investigator to Switzerland, hoping to trap Bedas. But the investigator was assured by all the Arab embassies in Switzerland, as well as by others he approached, that the story was a fabrication. One ambassador was reported to have told him sarcastically, 'Israel does not need to buy Palestinian land. It takes it.' The

143

Lebanese authorities, disappointed with the failure of the investigation, and to humiliate Bedas, asked the military prosecutor in Beirut to summon him and question him publicly on his sale of Palestinian land to Israel. Bedas had to appear before the prosecutor, who asked a few questions and then dismissed the story.

Bedas paid not the slightest attention to the campaign against him and his bank. He was too busy, expanding, growing and Lebanonizing more and more enterprises which were in the 'grip of foreign interests'. Using Intra as a solid base, he embarked on ever more ambitious schemes which brought him into conflict with the international money men. One involved the creation of what he called the 'new Hollywood' in Beirut. He told President Charles Helou, 'The climate is perfect for pictures 320 days a year. That is why I bought Baalbeck studios and a big piece of land for a whole new complex of studios and luxury apartment hotels for stars making the pictures . . . the world's biggest movie companies were enthusiastic about my plans.'

Bedas moved into even more dangerous territory when he bought a controlling interest in the grandiose Casino du Liban, where both the Lebanese and the new rich of the Arab world combined to pour money out at the gambling-tables. Not content with that successful venture, he planned a linked network of casinos all over the world. He firmly believed that Arabs were more entitled than anyone to profit from Arab money, but, by threatening to break into the world of international gambling, he made yet more enemies, many of them extremely dangerous.

Bedas's most ambitious plan was the one that was to prove his undoing. Inspired both by patriotism to Palestine, the land of his birth, and loyalty to Lebanon, his adopted country, he sought to create a financial empire, based on Beirut, which would be powerful enough to take on the might of Zionist financiers and the international groups that supported them. Already he had established a strong base in New York, where the Intra Bank branch was located in an Intra-owned twenty-seven-storey skyscraper on 5th Avenue. His motives were clearly explained in his memoirs:

> I had come out of Palestine with the firm conviction that the major factor behind the loss of Palestine was our inability to utilize our potential in both the financial sector and the political one. Our adversaries have a financial power and a well-organized machinery which we could not match. I dreamed of a Lebanon wielding similar power.

He had begun to believe that Intra Bank was ready to take on such a Herculean task, using Arab investments of oil money from the boom in Arabia during the 1960s. This was his fatal mistake, for the bank was not yet ready, nor was Lebanon in a state to accommodate the necessary growth and expansion of Intra. In addition, there was a strong Lebanese faction in power totally opposed to the ambitions of Bedas, the aggrieved Palestinian, to engage in a campaign to fight the 'financial might and well-organized power machinery of his adversaries — the Zionists'. This helped the conspiracy against him and brought about the destruction of Intra Bank.

Too late, Bedas realized how he had got it wrong. 'I was going too far too fast,' he wrote. The timing of the attack on Intra was masterly. It came just at the moment when, because of a general tightening on world credit, interest rates were rising in the United States, Europe and Lebanon. Intra's deposit account rate of only 5 per cent was being outbid, even in Beirut, by branches of foreign banks, such as Chase Manhattan, which was offering 8 per cent. In London, during October 1966, ICI (Imperial Chemical Industries), called for a £60 million loan at 8 per cent on only 98 per cent payment of nominal value, and this contributed indirectly to Intra's difficulties.

The truth was that Arab depositors of huge sums of money failed to carry out what Bedas considered their loyal duty to invest in his Arab bank in Lebanon and were tempted elsewhere by higher rates. He had calculated that they would not consider a few points extra in the rate a sufficient incentive to shift. In this, he was sadly mistaken. The Arab mandarins, in search of even more money, and alarmed by political crisis in the region, were the first to withdraw their huge deposits. They spearheaded the panic. Within a year of the collapse of Intra, the interest rate had fallen back to 5½ per cent, and there were even those who believed that the rise and fall was itself part of the plot to sink Intra.

I myself came firmly to believe that Intra Bank was deliberately destroyed in a devious campaign mounted by an unholy alliance of Lebanese, Zionist and international interests, determined to prevent Yousif Bedas carrying out his ambitious plans. The destruction of Intra may also have been part of the forward planning by the international banking 'fraternity' to pre-empt the consequences of the impending Arab–Israeli wars. As a result of these wars, they perhaps calculated, the Arabs would react patriotically and deposit more of their oil fortunes in Intra Bank and its branches than in foreign banks which they controlled. Therefore Intra had to be eliminated.

145

The attack on Intra was certainly carried out with an astonishing skill. A major run on the bank was sparked off by the two highest authorities in Lebanon, the President of the Republic and the Prime Minister, and then reinforced by a well-planned campaign of letter writing, round-the-clock telephoning, personal visits by carefully selected agents and even door-bell ringing to urge thousands of Intra Bank depositors to withdraw their money before it was too late. Along with this went the strange behaviour of the Central Bank when Intra asked for a loan to see it through the crisis.

On a collateral of over £L120 million of assets, including shares in the most important and profitable Lebanese companies, the Central Bank agreed, after days of protracted and gossip-generating negotiations, to give Intra a loan of a mere £L15 million, just 12½ per cent of the value of the assets. The collateral was a van load of shares and bonds, which Intra was ordered to take to the Central Bank, where, in an extraordinary public scene, they were displayed for all to see in the entrance hall. There, for hours, the shares and bonds were slowly counted, recounted, checked and verified.

Normally, so large a collateral in shares and bonds would have been left in the borrowing bank's vaults, to be verified in the utmost secrecy by officials from the Central Bank and then kept sealed in the vaults. Najib Salha, who was elected chairman of Intra when Bedas did not return to Lebanon, requested and even begged that this procedure be followed, but Joseph Oghourlian insisted on having the bonds and shares at the Central Bank. He promised discretion by suggesting they should be delivered very early in the morning, before the bank opened its doors to the public. This was done. But when they arrived, discretion was deliberately thrown to the wind and the heaps of shares and bonds were placed on exhibition. It was also reported that some Central Bank employees, influenced by the spectacle of the heaps of shares in the entrance hall, telephoned colleagues in other banks and business friends to alert them to the difficulties of Intra and advising them to withdraw their deposits before it was too late.

The run on the bank was started on Wednesday, 12 October 1966, and the refusal of the Central Bank to give the required assistance forced Intra to close its doors on Friday, after paying out more than £L100 million in an effort to halt the run. On Saturday there was a general run on Lebanon's banks. Many bankers, who had spread rumours about Intra and helped to trigger its ruin, themselves fell victims to their intrigues and were faced with disaster. The government, hoist by its own petard and fearing the collapse of the whole Lebanese banking-

146

system, promptly panicked. In an emergency meeting on Sunday, 16 October, the Council of Ministers declared a three-day bank holiday starting on the Monday. The Central Bank was instructed to give immediate and practically unlimited financial assistance to all Lebanese banks to enable them to resume their normal activities. All banks, that is, except Intra.

Intra was excluded, despite the strong pleas of some ministers, headed by the late Kamal Jumblatt. The government used the pretext that Intra had closed its doors and had applied to the courts for a 'Concordat Préventif' (Stay of Execution). This was untrue. Intra did not apply for a 'Concordat Préventif' until ordered to do so by the Prime Minister/Minister of Finance on the following day – Monday, 17 October.

To cover it up, the Prime Minister summoned Intra's lawyers that Monday morning and demanded the application for a 'Concordat Préventif' be submitted by 1 p.m. or else he would declare Intra bankrupt, notwithstanding that Lebanese commercial law stipulates a period of ten days during which an application for a concordat could be submitted. It is significant that Yafi was the first and the last Prime Minister simultaneously to hold, in addition to the premiership, the two Ministries of Finance and Justice – an unusual and intriguing concentration of power. He was also well versed in banking affairs, for he was, during all his working life, legal adviser to the French-owned Banque de Syrie et du Liban. As such, and as an experienced lawyer, he must have known what he was doing to Intra Bank.

For its part, Intra, badly advised by its lawyers and fearing the Prime Minister's threats and the consequences of bankruptcy, although knowing full well it was solvent, was forced to apply for the 'Concordat Préventif', undertaking 100 per cent payments of all liabilities over a period of three years. Although the courts in Lebanon do not open in the afternoons, the Prime Minister, in his desire for an immediate cover-up, ordered the court to remain open until evening so as to receive Intra's application. As the court records show, the application for a concordat was made at 5.30 p.m., and not only was the court open after office hours, but ready and prepared. It appointed, the same evening, a team of Lebanese experts to audit the accounts of Intra and to value its assets – a remarkable combined feat of pre-planning and crystal-ball gazing.

The Prime Minister, when questioned in Parliament about his role in this sorry episode, admitted he had summoned Intra's lawyers to his office on the Monday and 'advised' them to apply for a concordat.

147

'Advise', however, was not the word he had actually used in his office, but apart from this, His Excellency's admission in Parliament that he had summoned Intra's lawyers on Monday the 17th and advised them to apply for a 'Concordat Préventif' provided irrefutable evidence that the Council of Ministers was not told the truth on Sunday the 16th, that Intra had already applied for the 'Concordat' and was consequently disqualified from receiving government aid like all other Lebanese banks. The distortion of the truth in the Council of Ministers, and the threat by the Prime Minister to bankrupt Intra, were confirmed in the annual report of the Lebanese Bankers Association (31 March 1967, pp. 11–12).

The court appointed two teams to study different aspects of Intra. The first was composed of six accountants and a retired judge, Shawkat Al-Munla, who had no knowledge whatsoever of banks and banking and whose only qualification was that he was a trusted friend of the Prime Minister. Its task was to audit Intra's accounts and investigate its banking policy and practices. The second was composed of four experts appointed to evaluate Intra's assets. The court ordered both teams to submit their written reports within a week. This time limit to investigate and audit the accounts of Intra, with twenty affiliated banks and branches world-wide, and evaluate its assets and investments in forty-one companies, twenty-six in Lebanon and fifteen overseas, was proof of the government's ruthless haste to destroy Intra. No court, not even in Lebanon, could have been so incompetent as to believe that such a colossal task could be truly and accurately done in so short a period.

The clumsy fiasco, as well as the choice of the 'experts' and their lack of experience for such a task, provoked a storm of angry protests. Most critical were the important Arab depositors, who feared the loss of their deposits if Intra was allowed to collapse. In response to their protests, and upon their insistence, the government commissioned Price, Waterhouse, auditors to the World Bank, to audit Intra's accounts and evaluate its assets.

After a brief audit, Mr Eric McMillan, senior partner of Price, Waterhouse, told the British journalist, Patrick Seale, that the bank was basically solvent. Its problem was liquidity. He felt it was vital for the future of the Lebanese economy to keep Intra operating as a going concern. But, before it could reopen its doors, it would no doubt require some financial backing. He felt this was a very attractive opportunity for any international banking group wishing to extend its Middle East business. If the Lebanese government agreed, he said, 'I would discuss the affairs of the bank with any intending purchaser.'

148

When this was reported in the *Observer* on 5 November 1966, the Lebanese government was enraged, promptly dismissed Price, Waterhouse and cancelled its commission to continue with the audit. Nobody should be allowed to reveal that Intra was solvent when the Lebanese government had decided it must be found insolvent. Eric McMillan was asked to leave Lebanon and was, indeed, lucky not to have been prosecuted for telling the truth!

After the abrupt dismissal of Price, Waterhouse, the task was left to the two teams of Lebanese experts originally appointed. The ludicrous deadline of one week was generously extended, week by week, for three weeks, until 14 November 1966, when their reports were finally submitted. They showed a deficit of nearly £L25 million, or 3.7 per cent, on assets of £L627 million. But the experts, harassed for time, had omitted to include the value of the bank's skyscraper in New York, and branches in Rome and Frankfurt had also been forgotten. Had the true value of these assets been included, the report would have shown a surplus, not a deficit, and Intra would have been saved. This was quickly pointed out to the government in the hope of saving the bank, but the truth continued to be smothered as the plot proceeded along its skilfully planned course.

One prime example of the inexperience of Lebanese experts in international finance was their evaluation of the Londonderry Hotel in London. They valued the hotel at zero pounds sterling! Shortly afterwards, it was sold for £2,600,000 sterling, but the damage achieved by this absurd evaluation was never undone.

The powerful Arab depositors, already incensed at the dismissal of Price, Waterhouse, brought further pressure to bear on the government, expressing displeasure at the hasty and inaccurate reports of the investigating teams. And so, on 23 December 1966, the government called on Cooper Brothers, another internationally known firm of British auditors. This firm was also put under pressure to produce a report quickly and given no time to verify all the information made available. In their report, Cooper Brothers confirmed this, and further stated that they were unable to obtain information from Bedas's top executive aides responsible for running the bank or from the auditors of the bank. The government had deliberately prosecuted these people and would not allow them to set foot in the bank. Thus was Intra left defenceless and Cooper Brothers obliged to rely mostly on information provided by Shawkat Al-Munla and his carefully chosen aides. The information was presented in such a way as to leave Cooper Brothers with no alternative except to allow extra large provisions for what they

لجنة تقييم بنك الاهلي الموضوع اليد عليه

المادة ٣٠ من قانون ٦٧/٢٨

العنوان : مصرف لبنان ص.ب ٥٥٤٤ - بيروت

بيروت في ٢٦ /٥/ ١٩٦٩

حضرة رئيس هيئة ادارة قسم ادارة . مصارف المحترم

مصرف التسليف الزراعي والصناعي والعقاري

بـبـيـروت

افادة مؤقـتـة
==========

بناءً لطلبكم تفيد لجنة تقييم البنك الاهلي الموضوعة اليد عليه
ان شركة جستبلان التي تملك حق استثمار اوتيل لندن دريفي لندن هي
مدينة لبنك الاهلي بتاريخ وضع اليد اي في ١٨ /٦/ ٦٨ بمبلـــغ
٤/ ١/ ٢٦١٣٣٦ ليرة استرلينية وقد خمنت اللجنة حق استثمار الاوتيل
بقيمة هذا الدين لعلمه ان قيمة الاوتيل المذكور هي صفر بعد دفـع
كامل ديونه . كما ان شركة سيجست التي تملك شركة جستبلان هـي
مدينة للبنك الاهلي بتاريخ وضع اليد اي في ١٨ /٦/ ٦٨ بمبلـــغ
/ ٥٤٦٥٢٦٤٠٩٣/ ليرة لبنانية و ٢٥٠٦١٥٠١٧ فرنك بلجيكي وان
هذا الدين اعتبرته اللجنة هالكا بكامله لان هذه الشركة لا تملك شيئا
سوى حق استثمار الاوتيل المذكور وليس ملكيته .

وتفضلوا بقبول فائق الاحترام

لجنة تقييم البنك الاهلي الموضوع اليد عم

Figure 1. The text of the document of evaluation for the Londonderry Hotel, London. (Note: Ahli Bank was heavily indebted to Intra, and the Londonderry Hotel was part of the collateral.)

With reference your request, the committee for evaluation of the Ahli Bank, now under seizure, declares that the company Gestplan, which owns the right to exploit the Londonderry Hotel in London, is indebted to the Ahli Bank at the date of seizure, i.e. 18 June 1968, for the sum of £461,336 sterling, and the committee evaluated the right of exploitation as equal to the sum of that debt. The value of the hotel is therefore zero, after payment of its debts. Furthermore, the company Sejest, which owns the company Gestplan, is indebted at the date of seizure of the Ahli Bank, i.e. 18 June 1968, by the sums of £L5,465,264.93 and 250,615.17 Belgian francs, and the committee considers these debts to be completely uncollectable since the company only owns the right to exploit the said hotel and not the hotel itself.

The committee for the evaluation of Ahli Bank
[Signatures]

were told were doubtful and bad debts. The most ludicrous examples from among many similar cases were 30 per cent provisions for the debtor accounts of known billionaires (in any currency), Kamal Adham, brother-in-law of the late King Faisal and a member of the board of Intra, and Jasim and Abdallah Darwish, a famous trading family of Qatar. It must have been one of Shawkat Al-Munla's 'innocent' aides who informed Cooper Brothers that these debts were doubtful. There were many similar cases, but these were the uncontested prize-winners.

The most malicious and illegal act forced on Cooper Brothers by the Lebanese authorities was the appropriation, without court sanction, of the credit balances of Bedas's personal account, and those of the savings accounts of his wife and children. Over £L7 million were illegally taken over by the bank. Had Bedas been aware that Intra Bank was in financial difficulties, as President Helou claimed, he would at least have withdrawn his and his family's balances. Had he been a dishonest personality, he could also have withdrawn many additional millions. In fact, after the troubles started, he refused his American lawyers' advice to withdraw at least $5 million from the New York branch, which was still open for business, to put aside for legal and defence expenses. 'I will not rob my bank,' said Bedas.

The effect of excessive provisions for bad debts was compounded by an odd and illegal government decision which ruled that no reconciliation of accounts should be allowed after Intra closed its doors. A client who therefore had, say, a credit of £L1 million in one account and a debit of £L600,000 in another, was not allowed to take both into consideration. The credit balance of a million was frozen while he was asked for immediate payment of the debit account of £L600,000.

Naturally, clients who found themselves in this situation, and there were many, were outraged by such unfair treatment. However much they argued, they could not get the government to change its decision. The settlement of many debit accounts was therefore delayed, which led the auditors to increase heavily provisions for doubtful debts.

Because of the lack of time, Cooper Brothers were also unduly conservative in estimating the value of assets. For example, they estimated that Intra would make a profit of only $1.5 million on the sale of its New York skyscraper, yet, when the building was sold by public auction a few months later, Intra's profit came to $6.5 million. They valued the Rome branch at well under $600,000 dollars, yet, when it was sold, it fetched $1.5 million. And returns from the disposal of these two assets would have been very much higher had the sale been a normal one and not one of liquidation. Even Intra's 82 per cent

152

shareholding in La Ciotat, the biggest French shipyard, was valued at only 39,922,000 French francs, or 90 frances a share, when, by contrast, the French government had valued these at 200 francs each in March 1967, shortly after Cooper Brothers' evaluation.

Cooper Brothers submitted their first report to the Minister of Finance on 3 February 1967. Assets were estimated at £L737,827,000, and liabilities at £L788,813,000, showing a deficit of £L50,986,000 or 6.9 per cent – 'which could be less or could be more', Cooper Brothers said, had time and opportunity been provided to verify the figures supplied. Yet had the assets been correctly estimated, not to mention the 'bad' debts which were nothing of the sort, the Cooper report could only have confirmed Price, Waterhouse's findings that Intra Bank was solvent.

Badr Fahoum, one of the senior aides to Yousif Bedas, presented to the Prime Minister/Minister of Finance a detailed analysis of the Cooper report, calling attention to the undervaluation of many assets and to the exaggerated bad debts, most of which, as Badr Fahoum pointed out with documentation and proof, were not bad at all. The Prime Minister/Minister of Finance paid not the slightest attention. He seemed set on massacring Intra Bank, come what may.

While the experts' reports were left dormant, the Council of Ministers decided to push through legislation authorizing the government to borrow up to £L50 million from the Treasury or the Central Bank to pay small depositors and savings-account holders in Intra whose deposits and balances did not exceed £L15,000, and to acquire all their rights in the bank. Those for whom this law was designed were mostly Lebanese and they numbered many thousands. The pretext was to help the poor, but it was not compassion that prompted the government, but fear of an expected outcry and fury for its failure to help Intra. All Lebanese have equal rights, says the Constitution. Why should a depositor or a savings-account holder of £L15,000 or less be paid in full by the government, and others, whose balances were slightly more, not be paid?

A second law was passed on the same day to legitimize the help the Central Bank had given to other Lebanese banks. The two laws were debated in stormy sessions in Parliament, where the general consensus of opinion felt that the Central Bank had been much at fault and the government responsible for what had happened to Intra and the consequences of its failure. Unfortunately, this was no more than an ineffective parliamentary noise that could not prevent unjust government legislation.

A certain body of politicians had, however, mounted a vicious attack in Parliament as early as 31 October 1966, two weeks before the very first committee of accounting experts had submitted its official findings. They accused Bedas and the bank of all the crimes and dishonest dealings they could think of, offering no evidence, proof, documentation or corroboration. You would have thought it was the behaviour of aggrieved politicians whose demands for loans from Intra had been denied, but, as Bedas reveals in his memoirs, these were people to whose assistance he had come whenever they were in a financial fix, which was quite often. Their debts to Bedas were substantial. It was after this incredible display that I asked my administrative assistant to seek out the best calligrapher in Beirut and commission him to write, on a sign of reasonable size, the Arabic saying: 'Beware those to whom you have been charitable.' That sign hung prominently in my office for nearly six months until, one day, I called my assistant and asked him to remove it. 'It seems to apply to nearly all my visitors,' I said. 'I'd rather not have such an ugly reminder facing me!' Although the sign was physically removed, the saying has continued to live on in my mind.

The Central Bank was in fact advancing to the other Lebanese banks huge sums that would, by the end of 1967, amount to £L221 million. Despite this generous financial assistance, many were unable to survive the crisis and faced bankruptcy. Bankrupting Intra had been the object of the conspiracy that the government favoured and abetted. Bankrupting other Lebanese banks was a different kettle of fish. The majority of their owners and top executives were closely related to the establishment — relatives, friends and friends of friends. In the government's view, they must be protected at all costs to preserve the traditional structure of feudal and factional Lebanese society.

The government again panicked and, like a conjuror producing a rabbit out of a hat, rushed into producing yet another law. This one barred the bankruptcy of any bank in Lebanon, with retroactive effect to include Intra. This time Intra was not excluded; they had other plans for it. The law gave the governor of the Central Bank authority to ask the appropriate court to appoint a temporary manager and a management committee, which would then assume the powers and responsibilities of the board of directors, those of the ordinary general assembly of shareholders and, at the same time, represent creditors. The move was also unconstitutional and violated the Lebanese Commercial Code by usurping shareholders' rights.

Then came the big surprise. Just seven days *before* Parliament

154

approved the special law to prevent the bankruptcy of Lebanese banks, the court made a special ruling of its own and, on 4 January 1967, declared Intra bankrupt. The court was clearly determined to sabotage any rescue action, ruling that the experts' reports had found that Intra's assets did not cover its liabilities and refusing to take into consideration the failure to include the correct value of assets in New York, Rome and elsewhere. The action demonstrated the power of the enemies of Bedas and his bank. As the Beirut newspaper *An-Nahar* commented: 'The intention was to bankrupt the bank despite the fact that it was solvent.'

The bankruptcy was given extensive national and international publicity and, once it had achieved its objective of smearing Intra so as to pre-empt any possible rescue operation, the sentence was, quickly and with less noise, reversed by the Court of Appeal. Lo and behold, Intra was no longer bankrupt! Immediately after the reversal, the commercial court appointed a well-qualified Lebanese executive of a foreign bank in Beirut as manager for Intra, and also appointed a management committee of ten. The manager was to administer day-to-day affairs, and the committee was given six months to report on the accounts of Intra and the true value of its assets.

To the astonishment of many, the court appointed, as chairman, Shawkat Al-Munla, the same retired judge previously included among the so-called financial 'experts' of the investigating teams. Four members of the committee refused to serve, so the committee was authorized to function with its chairman and the remaining six members. The committee was later reinforced by the appointment of three other members. But there was another problem, for the newly appointed manager was conveniently taken ill and not replaced.

The committee formed a sub-committee of two competent accountants together with a representative of Cooper Brothers to verify the valuation of assets. Cooper Brothers, however, submitted a separate report dated 11 May 1967, increasing further the provisions for doubtful debts and decreasing again the valuation of assets. In defence of their action, they stated emphatically that they were obeying instructions from Shawkat Al-Munla. To a large extent, their report was based on figures given to them, and accepted, without any verification, as was confirmed by Cooper Brothers in a letter to me dated 3 August 1967.

Chairman Shawkat Al-Munla had given Cooper Brothers both the instructions and the figures, without informing the committee. When this action was strongly challenged by the committee, the chairman admitted to having done so inadvertently and proposed that the said

Cooper Brothers' report be completely laid aside. He instructed the secretariat not to distribute it to anybody, but the committee none the less insisted on placing in the official record the chairman's extra-ordinary directive to Cooper Brothers as well as his instructions to the secretariat to have that report disregarded. Yet, despite the recorded solemn promise of the chairman and his instructions to the secretariat, the report somehow found its way to the authorities and was leaked to the press to drive yet another nail into Intra's coffin.

One of the basic elements in Cooper Brothers' report of 11 May was the abnormally high provision for bad debts. They took good care to point out that the figures, which they had had no time to verify, had been given to them. The Association of Intra Depositors, in a memorandum to the government, offered the following account of these provisions:

> Total debts payable to Intra were £L190,478,626. Provisions taken by Cooper Brothers for bad debts were £L115,611,378, i.e. 61 per cent. Interests payable on the so-called bad debts amounting to £L25 million were removed from the assets of the bank because the debts on which these interests would have been due were considered not collectable. However, the truth was that over 80 per cent of the doubtful debts had been collected by 1974.

This was confirmed at the general assembly of shareholders, held on 25 April 1974. In actual fact, only £L18,322,276 remained as bad debts, and these were more than adequately covered by the £L24 million already provided for doubtful debts in Intra's 1965 accounts. There could hardly have been a more blatant example of rigging the facts.

Notwithstanding Cooper's separate report, the sub-committee arrived at a result showing that Intra had a surplus of over £L50 million. Every item revalued or modified was discussed and approved separately and unanimously in regular committee meetings until their report was ready for final approval as a whole before submission to the court. During the meeting called for this purpose, the chairman, Shawkat Al-Munla, provoked a raucous quarrel with one of the members, walked out and claimed he had been insulted. He refused to call any further meeting of the committee, justifying his action by claiming he had not received a proper apology from the offender. Despite frantic appeals from the rest of the committee, he refused to call a meeting until the six months' deadline set by the court for submission of the report had expired.

Five of the most prominent members of the committee, however, undaunted by the chairman's refusal to call a meeting, submitted to the court the report that should have been presented by the committee as a whole and which showed a surplus in Intra of over £L50 million. The court refused to accept the report since it was not the formal one of the management committee. It then warned the chairman that the committee must submit its report within a week. This did not happen because the chairman was still 'sulking'. The court therefore charged the chairman with dereliction of duty, but no further action was taken against the obviously guilty Shawkat Al-Munla, nor was any attention paid to Intra's proven solvent position. The management committee was dissolved on 17 August 1967.

Once again, the government had meanwhile resorted to legislation. Remembering the earlier parliamentary row, it had bypassed Parliament and issued Decree Law No. 44, dated 5 August 1967, ten days before the management committee's deadline. Here was another brilliant feat of crystal gazing, for how could the government know the committee would fail to submit a report — unless it had instructed Shawkat Al-Munla to prevent the report being submitted if it proved favourable to Intra?

The decree authorized the government to appoint yet another committee, to which it delegated vast powers in addition to those given to the previous committee. The new committee was also charged with finding buyers for Intra Bank, its affiliates, branches, assets and investments, subject to the approval of the commercial court. The law gave the court only one month to approve any agreement submitted. It went on further to violate the Lebanese Constitution and all democratic laws by banning appeal or any other form of recourse.

The new committee was composed of Elias Sarkis, the newly appointed governor of the Central Bank, as chairman, and, as members, the President of the Supreme Court, the Director-General of Finance, a well-known Lebanese economist, and the ubiquitous Shawkat Al-Munla. Even as the committee went about its business, inspired attacks on Intra Bank continued with ferocious intensity. False information was leaked to the press, accusing Intra of having lent substantial amounts of money to its board directors as well as to affiliated and associated companies. No mention was made of the fact that practically all these loans were secured by solid collaterals, and were all later collected in full. What is wrong in lending money to directors, if the loans are secured? What would have happened to the reputation of Intra had it become known that its directors preferred to take their business to other banks? As for giving credit to affiliated and associated companies,

157

surely that was the wisest course of action, considering that these companies were, and still are, among the most successful in Lebanon, the loans therefore being adequately secured. Furthermore, Intra exercised direct or indirect control over all these companies and knew everything about their financial status.

The government, to justify its crime, played a major role in the attacks by giving these reports the widest possible circulation. It leaked false information to the press, and in many instances led the attack itself. It let it be known, for example, that one of the reasons for refusing Intra the requested Central Bank loan was its fear that Bedas would personally pocket the money instead of using it to pay depositors and creditors. But Bedas, having been warned not to return to Beirut, had at that stage been replaced by Najib Salha. It was Najib Salha, not Bedas, who was chairman of Intra when the request for the loan was made.

Salha was a Lebanese businessman of well-known integrity, an important shareholder in Intra, a Member of Parliament who had served as a minister on a number of occasions. To insinuate that he might have passed on the bank's much-needed loan to Bedas for personal use was preposterous. To accuse Bedas, who built the Intra empire and spread the reputation and prestige of Lebanon internationally, of being liable to take a loan for his personal use instead of using it to help his bank was equally grotesque. To imply that the members of the board of Intra, all eminent personalities, could have been guilty of collusion in dispatching such a loan when the survival of Intra depended on it was monstrous.

The government also claimed that it would have been reckless to save Intra by providing financial assistance. Such action would, they said in an argument of topsy-turvy logic, have undermined the value of the Lebanese pound and have caused international speculation at the expense of the currency. Then, in a final impressive display of contradictions, the government excused the role of the Central Bank in not giving Intra assistance by saying that this action was irrelevant and unimportant since Intra Bank had, in the government's opinion, been bankrupt long before the run on it. This conveniently ignored how the respected auditors, Price, Waterhouse, appointed by the government to audit Intra's accounts, had found Intra solvent and were, as a result, dismissed for telling the truth.

The facts as they emerged showed how false and unfair was the government's claim that Intra had been bankrupt before the run. Of all the Intra affiliated companies in Lebanon, not one failed, despite the looting, obstruction and lack of support, especially over the three years following the collapse of Intra. Twenty years later, despite the thieving, wasteful expenditure and mismanagement, Intra would remain the strongest financial enterprise in Lebanon, busily buying available banks for sale in Lebanon and elsewhere. Ironically Intra, forbidden to function as a bank, speedily became an international consortium of banks with no lack of its own funds.

At the time, many schemes to save or buy Intra were submitted to the new committee, among the most credible being one from a Swiss finance company closely related to Crédit-Suisse, a major Swiss bank; and another from Jules Piquet, the eminent French financier who, in 1946, nationalized the Banque de France for General de Gaulle and later helped to launch the New Franc. Piquet was making his offer on behalf of the Union Européenne des Banques. The Swiss plan was rejected and Piquet's offer never materialized because of a letter sent to those concerned in Paris from the French Embassy in Beirut, asserting that, contrary to all other reports, the deficit of Intra amounted to £L350 million. No one knew where this figure originated, but the surprising incident was confirmed by the committee in its final report.

Another offer came from Kidder Peabody, the American finance brokers, who submitted a plan for Intra to be transformed into an investment corporation. Shares in this corporation would be owned by the bank's depositors in proportion to the amount of their deposits. The offer was conditional on Kidder Peabody being given a contract for three years to assist in the conversion of the deposits into shares.

The new Sarkis committee, which I shall call the 'terminal committee' since it ended the life of Intra as a bank, accepted this proposal and signed an agreement with the major creditors: the governments of Lebanon, Kuwait, Qatar, and the United States Commodity Credit Corporation (CCC), assigning to them all assets. The government of Lebanon was included because of the £L50 million it had paid to Intra's small depositors. CCC came into it because Intra Bank had issued a guarantee for $21 million in its favour for the account of a joint American-Lebanese company for the purchase of American wheat. Although not all the wheat had been delivered at the time when the protocol was concluded, and despite the fact that the partners of the American-Lebanese company were financially capable of meeting their commitments, CCC was nevertheless included among the four major creditors. The committee also approved and sponsored the signing of a protocol between Intra's four major creditors and Kidder Peabody.

In its final report, the committee admitted that all the audit reports, asset valuations and other related documents concerning Intra were contradictory, inconsistent and inaccurate, including the Cooper report on 11 May which had been discarded by the previous committee and ordered not to be distributed. In the committee's opinion, the reports could not be depended on. Its doubts were genuine, but, strangely enough, the fact of the matter was that all offers to save the bank, and the committee's own decision to terminate the life of Intra as a bank, were based on these very reports.

Despite its admission of these inaccuracies, the 'terminal committee' concluded that a large deficit existed and claimed that the lack of firm offers to buy the bank was irrefutable proof for such a deficit. It was this, they claimed, that had scared away prospective bidders, while they also concluded that the deficit exceeded the capital of the bank. Then, usurping the role of a general assembly of shareholders, the committee reduced the capital of the bank to zero and ruled the shares valueless before finally conjuring up a masterpiece of legal hocus-pocus. The valueless shares, the property of the old shareholders of Intra, were appropriated by the committee and used to transfer the assets of Intra Bank to the four major creditors: the governments of Lebanon, Kuwait, Qatar and the Credit Commodity Corporation of the United States of America. This was in blatant violation of Article 15 of the Lebanese Constitution, which states that ownership rights are protected by law and no one may be divested of these rights except for reasons of public interest, as defined by law, and only after being justly compensated. No shareholder of Intra ever received compensation.

The court approved the committee's action, which could not be challenged, Decree Law No. 44 deliberately banning appeal or any form of recourse. The committee then authorized the four major creditors to transfer £L3 million from Intra's assets to a mini-Intra Bank which would act as trustee for the assets pending the formation of an investment corporation to be owned by the depositors. The Kuwait government appointed two representatives to the board, and Qatar and the Credit Commodity Corporation appointed one each. It took the Lebanese government six weeks to choose its representatives. Pierre Dagher, a former Lebanese judge, lawyer and close friend of President Charles Helou, was named chairman.

Had the Lebanese government wished to save Intra Bank, nothing would have been easier than to suggest that the four wealthy major creditors lend the funds necessary. The Kuwaiti and Qatari governments would have been more than willing to do so. In fact, the government-owned Kuwaiti Investment Company made a determined attempt to refloat Intra and a draft agreement was drawn up, ready for signature. The Lebanese government rejected this generous offer with no reasons given. It was rumoured that the Lebanese authorities opposed any plan to refloat Intra with Kuwaiti or any other Arab money for fear that the Lebanese economy might then fall under Arab control. The truth of the matter was that Intra had, as a bank, been sentenced to death, the intention being to transform it into an investment company in which the depositors became shareholders.

It now, however, took an incredible three years for the four major creditors to value Intra's assets for the fifth time, call a general assembly of shareholders and officially form the investment company. During those three years, Intra's activities were frozen and the affiliated companies left on their own without Intra's financial backing. Expenses soared through the appointments of relatives and protégés of political leaders, and salaries were substantially increased. Every branch of the bank was either sold cheaply or dismantled at a loss. Cooper Brothers were asked to value the assets yet again, and Lebanese accountants were asked to perform the same task. The costs and fees of all this were colossal. Marwan Iskandar, a well-known Lebanese economist, published in *An-Nahar*'s economic and financial issue of 12 August 1972 a carefully documented analysis which concluded that £L142 million had been squandered to form the Intra Investment Company with its capital of £L280 million.

The 'terminal committee', by arbitrary make-believe, wiped out all the shares of Intra Bank, 79.6 per cent of which had been owned by Lebanese. They then converted the deposits, most of which were foreign, into shares in the new company. Thus did Bedas's vast Lebanese empire become a foreign institution located in Lebanon and easy prey to the 'chosen few'. All affiliated companies of Intra, including Middle East Airlines, became non-Lebanese in the eyes of the law. Could this ingenious swap have come about by accident, or was it by cunning design that all the companies Bedas Lebanonized were automatically de-Lebanonized? Curiously, although these companies were not legally considered Lebanese, they continued to be controlled and exploited by the Lebanese government.

No one is perfect. Yousif Bedas was not always right in his decisions, as he readily admitted in his memoirs: 'Could I or anyone else create this huge international enterprise in such a short time without making mistakes? You can avoid mistakes only by doing nothing.' He made legal mistakes, but these were in form only, not in substance. The new banking law had given all the banks in Lebanon a period of five years to put their houses in order, and Bedas had still two years before the final date. He was, therefore, within his legal rights and did nothing criminal. The Lebanese government – keen as it was to do so – never proved any malpractices, such as fraud or embezzlement, or established that any personal benefits had illegally accrued to him. The government was not even able to present an acceptable case to the Swiss authorities to support a request for extradition. The Swiss Federal Public Prosecutor in Lucerne, in charge of examining the file, became both convinced of Bedas's innocence and revolted by the unjust behaviour of the Lebanese authorities. He became, as a result, a faithful friend and, apart from the family, was one of the few who remained close to Bedas until his death.

Bedas proved himself a genius by building the Intra empire in so short a time. He was, however, equally a genius at making powerful and vindictive enemies. He was hounded, libelled, falsely accused of fraud, his character smeared, his achievements maligned and the bank he built shamelessly taken over and looted. The colleagues who helped him to build the bank were similarly treated. Middle East Airlines owed its independence, its growth, its establishment as the sole Lebanese passenger airline to Yousif Bedas and Intra. No one connected with MEA should ever forget Bedas and his valuable contribution to its prosperity. Bedas loved Lebanon more than most Lebanese and tried his best to serve the country's interests. The Lebanese, especially the authorities, did not reciprocate his love. Nevertheless the crimes they committed against him and his bank did not stop him from making a deathbed wish for two cedar trees to be planted by his grave in Lucerne, Switzerland.

Yousif Bedas, 'the genius from Jerusalem', built a financial empire for a country that did not deserve it and allowed it to be ruthlessly destroyed for the personal benefit of certain politicians. The lesson to be learnt by the Lebanese from the story of the life, success, destruction and death of Yousif Bedas is that, if crimes against Lebanon continue to go unpunished, that beautiful country and its proud heritage must continue to crumble and eventually be lost for ever, destroyed by greedy men lusting for riches and power. In August 1968, Bedas addressed a message of warning to the Lebanese, 'Be on your guard, let not those who have caused irreparable harm to Lebanon take further advantage of your docile attitude of life in general and of your willingness to be trusting. Make them accountable for their deeds. The destiny of your country is at stake and with it the future of your youth.'

The warning went unheeded and Lebanon is as it is today!

13
Intra: The Aftermath

My joining Intra Bank as a shareholder and board member took place two years before it was forced to close its doors. I became involved, early in 1964, simply to protect the interests of MEA after distressing rumours arose that Yousif Bedas was planning to sell Intra's substantial holdings in the airline. He was said to have been engaged in talks, both in New York and Paris, with Carlos Arida of Lebanese International Airways, and with the American tycoon, Daniel Ludwig. It was not that I blamed Bedas for wanting to sell MEA's shares at a substantial profit – indeed, I was grateful for all the help he had given in the past. My objection was to the idea that foreigners might regain control of the company, and so I wrote a letter of protest.

In typical fashion, Bedas replied, 'I told them I was ready to sell anything except my wife and my children. Anything at a price.' But, he went on, 'I made it so clear to them that in the case of Middle East Airlines, the final say rested with Sheikh Najib, and secondly with Air France, to whom I have moral obligations.' He then added, 'There is no need to assure you, dear Najib, that I shall never attempt to think of disposing of Intra's shares in MEA until you advise me to do so.'

I accepted his assurance, though I knew his philosophy was to make profits for the bank and that any chance to make big money would tempt him. At least my letter had made it clear that I would do all in my power to prevent an unsuitable sale. To set my doubts at rest, he suggested I sell to Intra my 12 per cent holding in the airline and in return take a substantial quantity of Intra shares. He argued, as only he knew how, that if I accepted the offer I would be in a much better position to defend the interests of MEA. He urged the advantages of a seat on the board of the mother company, and duly succeeded in convincing me. As a result, I committed the greatest error of my life. I sold MEA shares to Intra and bought 5,000 shares in the bank. Duly elected to the board of Intra in May 1964, I then lost everything in the crash of October 1966. Of course, Middle East Airlines did survive the Intra Bank disaster. But, to my mind, the saddest outcome was to see the company which Bedas, Abdallah Khoury and I had been so proud to have Lebanonized, after its founders sold it all to BOAC, emerge from the crisis as non-Lebanese.

The subsequent creation of Intra Investment Company brought about a self-destructive change in the shareholding of Middle East Airlines. Intra and Yousif Bedas were replaced by representatives of the four governments concerned, three of which own national airlines in direct competition with MEA. The representatives thereafter needed to refer every important boardroom decision for approval by their respective governments. From 1966 to 1977, eleven of the most difficult years in the history of Middle East Airlines, I had to live and deal with this shareholding circus. It was a miracle that the airline survived. One government in an airline is a paralysing disadvantage. Four governments make it like sitting in a minefield.

I tried on more than one occasion to find a solution to this complex and paralysing problem and was, at one stage, close to success. Nearly eight weeks before the Intra Investment Company was formed, I approached Maître Pierre Dagher, chairman of the committee in charge of the mini-Intra Bank, and explained to him the dangers to MEA, to Lebanese civil aviation and to the economy of the country of continuing to live with a faulty shareholding structure. Middle East Airlines, I told him, needed a widely based shareholding if it was to be assured of a sound financial foundation and regular financial support. It should not again be exposed to the perils of single ownership. Maître Dagher listened with interest, and I proceeded to tell him that a solution to the problem had opportunely presented itself and could be adopted with minimum difficulty.

The court experts had just submitted their report evaluating the assets of Intra at £L339,148,527, and it was intended to form the Intra Investment Company with a capital of only £L280,000,000. There was thus an excess valuation of £L59,148,527. The same experts had valued Intra's shareholding in MEA at £L48,948,600. The constituent general assembly of Intra Investment Company was to be held on 25 June 1970, and I proposed that it should be asked to approve the formation of Intra Investment Company with a capital of £L280,000,000, to cover all the assets of Intra, except the shares of MEA. The assembly would then be asked to approve the distribution of the MEA shares owned by Intra among the depositor shareholders of the new Intra Investment Company in proportion to the shares they owned in that company. There were 8,366 shareholders in the new Intra Investment Company, and so, if they were to replace Intra in the shareholding of MEA, the desired wide-based shareholding structure would be achieved.

Of the shareholders, 46.7 per cent were Lebanese, and this, in addition to Nadia Khouri's shares (2.5 per cent), would provide a substantial Lebanese shareholding. The Lebanese government owned 10.6 per cent of the shares in the new Intra Investment Company, and consequently would become a shareholder in MEA without any fresh outlay. This would provide MEA with direct government interest, and a seat on the board would enable the government to be well informed about MEA. The obligation for any increase in the capital of MEA would thus be lifted from Intra Investment Company and spread over the 8,366 new shareholders and the other shareholders of MEA. Intra Investment Company could then use its capital resources to assist other Intra-owned companies.

I further recommended that the employees should hold shares in the company. Their participation would increase the shareholding to a Lebanese majority and would be healthy and generally beneficial. Moreover, I stressed, the proposed solution would liberate Middle East Airlines from the meddlesome control of four governments and give it a wide Lebanese shareholding base.

To my surprise, Maître Dagher was greatly interested and even enthusiastic. He asked me to submit a report, even going so far as to ask for the proposal to be produced in the form of a brochure in Arabic, English and French for eventual submission to his general assembly. It seemed too good to be true, and I had some genuine doubts, but could not afford to allow these to dampen my hopes. For the first time since the collapse of Intra, I felt optimistic. At last there seemed a chance of being rid of the four-government nightmare.

The brochures were printed in Arabic, English and French and held ready for distribution. The report was sent to Maître Dagher, together with copies of the brochures. But now, it seemed, Maître Dagher had gone into reverse. After careful consideration, he said, he could not agree to my proposal, nor would he submit it to his board. I tried to talk him round, but talked in vain. Finally he admitted that the authorities did not approve the proposal. It became clear that they hoped to control Middle East Airlines through Intra Investment, a hope they had cherished ever since the takeover of Air Liban. It was a hope against which I fought successfully until my retirement from MEA.

Few believed that MEA could possibly survive all the disasters and complications of the Intra Bank crash. Many were convinced that the destruction of Intra was partly motivated by a scramble to gain control of the airline. As the conspiracy against Intra unfolded, so did I also become convinced. The London *Sunday Telegraph* in October 1966 commented:

> The collapse of Intra which has sent reverberations round the world, is not simply the story of imprudent banking or of anti-Nasser intrigue, though without these factors the débâcle could not have occurred. An important factor in the exploitation of these weaknesses, which together led to Lebanon's biggest bank closing its doors, has been a struggle for control of the prosperous Middle East Airlines of which Intra holds 60 per cent of the equity. It may well have been the crucial link in the chain.

The unseemly rush to buy Intra's shareholding in MEA was led by Daniel Ludwig, the American billionaire and proprietor of National Bulk Carriers, which had a large holding in LIA (Lebanese International Airways).

Dr Hanna Asfour, in his book *Intra Bank* (1969), tells the following story:

> While the council of ministers was discussing the Intra crisis on 14 October 1966, two days prior to its closing its doors, Alphonse Arida [of LIA] entered the council's waiting-room accompanied by a foreigner who was introduced as Ludwig's lawyer. He had arrived in Beirut that evening to attempt to buy the shares of Intra in Middle East Airlines. These two individuals were seen to meet aside with Minister Fouad Boutros, who left the council's meeting more than once to talk to them.

This anecdote demonstrates that LIA was attempting to gain control of MEA even as talks were going on about Intra. As the late Kamal Jumblatt declared, ministers at that meeting were more interested in selling the shares of MEA than in saving Intra Bank. It seems certain that the Arida family were actively stirring the pot by spreading stories of Intra's financial troubles. But they were not the only people interested. Ludwig's bid was followed by many others, most of which were straightforward business propositions without political or ulterior motives. Direct approaches came from the Niarchos Group, National Airlines of the United States, Lufthansa and Air Canada. Mr Robert

Anderson, a former Secretary of Finance in the US government, made a personal offer, and so did the Aga Khan by way of his representative in Beirut, Mr Kamal Khan.

The Niarchos proposal was to purchase Intra shares in MEA, and then resell a proportion to Lebanese investors so that the Greek group would end up with a 40 per cent interest. They offered to provide £L25 million to increase MEA's capital and give a guarantee for the purchase of new equipment. To make the package more attractive, Niarchos also offered to promote Lebanese tourism and help in the development of holiday facilities. He additionally threw in a further offer of financial help to refloat Intra Bank, thus misjudging Lebanese determination to finish the bank off. His excellent offer was no doubt turned down for that very reason.

Troubles were piling up for MEA. Douglas Aircraft Corporation unilaterally cancelled the contract for three DC–8 airliners because of the bank crash. For the same reason, Eximbank cancelled its loan. The plan to double the company's capital, previously approved by the shareholders, was annulled. The working capital deposited in Intra was blocked, and deposits abroad were frozen on instructions from the Intra committee, even though other depositors in foreign branches were paid in full.

In short, it became obvious that MEA was the next target for the very interests that had ruined the bank. The Lebanese government showed malicious intent by issuing Decree Law No. 28, dated 5 August 1967, so taking powers to form a mixed Lebanese government and private enterprise airline, either by merging existing ones or by forming a new company to take over all or part of Intra Bank's stake in MEA. The right was reserved to cede appropriated shares to third parties of the government's choice and to retain not less than a 10 per cent holding in the new company. This minority holding would none the less give it the right by the Decree Law to control the company, its management and choice of shareholders.

The objective was to ensure the success of a proposal made by Robert Vergnaud, who had reappeared on the scene. He recommended the merger of MEA with LIA, with joint participation by Air France and the Lebanese government in over 50 per cent of the shareholding in the new airline. The transparent aim of all this was to place Lebanese civil aviation under the more compliant control of Air France and selected shareholders.

I went straight to President Helou and fiercely attacked the new law and its thinly concealed objectives, pointing out how it violated democracy in Lebanon and the rights of private enterprise. I told him, further, that it was in blatant breach of the constitution and of the commercial code. Finally, I informed him that MEA employees and the trade unions opposed the law, since any merger might cause unemployment. My arguments, combined with the fact that we had mounted a press campaign against the decree, calling in legal opinions from both French and Lebanese constitutional lawyers, finally convinced the President that a mistake had been made. He assured me that the validity of the decree was only for six months and that it would never be implemented. The Decree Law and Vergnaud's ingenious proposal died a natural and simultaneous death.

One curious aspect of this business came to light later. Unknown to us, Air France had sent a team of experts to Beirut to study MEA's financial position. Its members neither consulted anyone in the company nor set foot in the airline offices. They compiled their report during a short stay at the French Embassy, and submitted it to the President and to Elias Sarkis, chairman of the 'terminal committee' enquiring into Intra Bank, who himself became President of Lebanon in 1976. Even though the report was about MEA, and dealt with our financial situation, we were never shown a copy. Despite insistent requests, I had to make a serious issue of it before we were given one.

The Air France experts had reduced the value of the shares to the lowest possible level, and a well-informed friend in Air France admitted that this was deliberately done since they were potential buyers. The oddest fact of all, however, was that the Air France experts' report was dated 4 August 1967 and Decree Law No. 28, which authorized the government to merge or appropriate the shares of Lebanese airlines, was dated 5 August 1967, a date shared with Decree Law No. 44, which authorized the appointment of the 'terminal committee' to find buyers for Intra, its assets and investments. The report and the circumstances in which it was produced will always leave an unpleasant taste in the mouth.

The true connection between Decree Law No. 28 and the report of Air France's experts came to light in an item of news published in the January/February 1969 issue of the prestigious French legal magazine *Révue Trimestrielle de Droit Commercial*:

Dans la lutte d'influence qui s'est livrée autour de la Middle East Airlines–Air Liban (MEAL) après le Krach de la Banque INTRA, en octobre 1966, Air France, qui détient 30% du capital, n'a pu s'assurer 'le contrôle' de la société, qui est passé à la nouvelle Banque INTRA, appartenant au groupe de la 'Credit Commodity Corporation of America' (see Appendix for translation).

14
Airport Raid

The evening of Saturday, 28 December 1968, was one of those winter evenings in Lebanon when, after a few days of rain, the clouds shed their last drops and fade away to reveal a sky washed clean of man's pollution, full of millions of twinkling stars. We could see afar off from our house up in Shimlan, and the lights of Beirut glittered like diamonds. The Christmas festivities had just ended and their message of peace on earth lingered as the people of Lebanon prepared to take their vows on New Year's Eve.

We had just finished supper when we heard an explosion from the direction of the airport. As we ran on to the veranda and looked towards the airport, there were more explosions and fires began to blossom on the tarmac and runways. The size of the fires, and the speed with which they spread over the airport, made it look for all the world as if the devil was stoking his furnace. Our hangars and workshops appeared to be ablaze. We could hardly believe our eyes and watched, stunned for a while, until the telephone rang. It was MEA to announce that Israeli helicopters were raiding the airport. MEA executives living in Beirut had managed to reach the airport, braving machine-gun fire on the access road from an Israeli helicopter which was trying to prevent reinforcements reaching the airport, but the full story did not emerge until morning.

Four Israeli helicopters, flying low across the sea from the south-west, had approached Beirut International Airport. Attempts from the control tower to make radio contact with them met with silence, and they reached the airport at about 9.15 p.m. One landed in front of MEA's hangars and workshops on the western side, another near the TMA hangar on the eastern side and one by the terminal building near the fire station, while the fourth strafed the airport road. Commandos, jumping out of the helicopters, proceeded to blow up all

Lebanese aircraft parked on the apron. Thirteen were destroyed. Of these, eight belonged to MEA – a brand-new Boeing 707–320C, a VC–10 on lease from Ghana Airways, three Comet 4Cs, two Caravelles and one Viscount. LIA lost two Coronados and one DC–7, and TMA lost one DC–6 and one DC–4. Partly because no resistance was offered, and partly by good luck, there were no casualties. Only planes belonging to Lebanese companies were destroyed. A Pan-Am Boeing and a BEA Comet were left unharmed.

Despite our earlier fears, MEA hangars and workshops proved to have escaped damage. The blaze I had seen from Shimlan, which made me think they were burning, was the funeral pyre of two MEA aircraft parked in front of the hangars. Unexploded shells and bombs, found near the hangars and the office buildings, were dealt with next morning by bomb-disposal experts of the Lebanese Army. It was reported that the raid had been conducted under the direction of the then Israeli Defence Minister, General Moshe Dayan. Each helicopter had carried twelve Israeli commandos, these helicopters most probably having been bought from or given by the United States on condition that they were used by Israel for defence purposes only. Since then it has become internationally accepted that 'attack' can be explained as 'defence' if the aggressor so wishes, even where the act is conducted against civilians.

The next morning, despite the fact that Sunday is a non-working day in Lebanon, all employees of MEA reported for duty without being called. They had heard the news and rushed to the airport to help. It was not the first time they so loyally came to the rescue, nor was it to be the last. Our fleet was badly crippled but not completely destroyed, five aircraft having escaped the devastating and unprovoked Israeli attack. Four of these were out of Lebanon at the time, and one was under maintenance in a closed hangar. They consisted of a Boeing 707, a VC–10 on lease from Laker Airways, a Comet 4C, a Caravelle and a Viscount.

My office became like a dynamo humming with activity. Journalists, radio and television reporters, foreign and national, all wanted to hear our side of the story. Lebanese visitors flocked in to express sympathy. Meetings were held with MEA executives to make emergency plans. There was a suggestion from management that we should halt operations for one month to give us time to replace the aircraft lost. It was a suggestion I rejected out of hand. I was convinced that, if we stopped flying, even for the shortest time, it would have taken us a very long time to restart – if ever.

We made the best use of what was left of our fleet by linking destinations. Paris was combined with London, and as soon as one runway was cleared of wreckage, our Paris–London flight took off at 11 a.m. with seventy-seven passengers. Rome was combined with Athens, Baghdad with Teheran, Dhahran with Abu Dhabi and so on. In this way we lost not a single flight out of our scheduled services, despite the destruction of more than 60 per cent of the fleet.

Kuwait Airways were signalled to lease three Comet 4Cs, which we knew were surplus to their requirements and which were identical to those of MEA. The response was immediate, and the first KAC Comet 4C landed that afternoon, the second on Tuesday, the third on Wednesday. Ethiopian Airlines, from whom we had leased aircraft in the past, were requested to lease one of their Boeing 720Bs. On Monday, it arrived in Beirut and was put into service. With these planes, and the five which had escaped destruction, we continued our services without interruption. The temporary arrangements were soon replaced by more permanent ones, and we quickly consolidated our fleet. The lost Boeing 707 and the VC–10 were replaced by two Boeing 707s; the three Comet 4Cs and the two Caravelles were replaced. The destroyed Viscount had been up for sale anyway, and was not on active duty.

News of the raid reverberated around the world and reactions to the outrage varied in intensity from country to country. It is fair to say that there was an international condemnation of the Israeli aggression against Lebanese civil aviation. All through Sunday and Monday, messages of sympathy and offers of assistance poured in. The first came from King Hussein of Jordan, whose offer of support and call for an Arab summit to deal with the outrage greatly boosted our morale. King Hassan of Morocco offered us a Caravelle free of charge for a whole year. The Ruler of Kuwait ordered Kuwait Airways to lend us a Comet 4C free of charge for six months. All Arab airlines offered unlimited support.

Equally touching were the warm offers from nearly all international airlines; not only from the airlines of the West, but also from those of the Eastern Bloc, headed by Aeroflot. There is a comradeship among airlines in times of crisis, but the spontaneous messages of sympathy and offers of help received the day after the raid could only be proof of the political reaction to an unprecedented act of aggression.

Although I was used to the dedication of the employees of MEA in any crisis, I was overwhelmed with affection and pride by their reaction to the raid. No one in Lebanon or MEA offices abroad failed to rally to face the challenge, and to tell all that was done would make a long tale.

I shall mention only two incidents. Early on Sunday, the head of the Sales and Traffic Department walked in with two employees, carrying heaps of envelopes that were placed on my desk. The envelopes, he said, contained individual contributions of the employees who were on duty on Saturday night. Without exception, they had emptied their pockets of cash and put it in envelopes as a contribution. Thanking him, and through him the employees concerned, I explained that I would always be grateful for their gesture but was happy to be able to return the money since we did not need it.

Soon after the envelopes were carried away, the council of our union told me they had called an urgent meeting and taken a unanimous decision on behalf of all members to work without pay as long as was needed for the company to get back on its feet. I thanked them and gave them the same encouraging news that we were insured and could weather the storm without recourse to their generous offer. I did, however, ask for their members to work overtime without pay as long as necessary, and to this they readily agreed. Everybody worked overtime without pay until July 1969, when I stopped the 'no pay for overtime'. With such employees, MEA could not fail.

Although fully covered, our insurance troubles started immediately after the raid. The insurance brokers and Lloyd's underwriters had assured us that our claims would be paid in full without delay. Nevertheless, for one reason or another, we were not paid until May 1969. Our insurance premiums rocketed and I personally had to go to London to speed up payments of claims and to battle for reasonable premiums. MEA's public image was tarnished as we were proclaimed to have caused Lloyd's a massive loss. The British press was badly misinformed and came out on 30 December 1968 with such headlines as 'Airport Raid Means 14 Million Pound Sterling Bill for Lloyd's' in the *Daily Express*; 'Raid Cost Britain 14 Million Pounds' in the *Daily Mail*; 'Twenty Million Pounds Israeli Raid Bill for Lloyd's' in the *Sun*. Many other newspapers came out with similar misleading information when the total claim was, in fact, for £7.5 million sterling (then $15,875,000). Only 18 per cent of this was Lloyd's, the rest being reinsured outside Lloyd's. It was reported, at the time, that one of the reinsurers was an Israeli underwriter. But why be so dismayed about a claim of less than $16 million for MEA, which had lost two-thirds of its fleet through no fault of its own? The insurance market in 1968 had paid $33 million to Pan-Am and $17 million to Air France for accidents that year and no one raised an eyebrow.

The UN Security Council unanimously condemned Israel for its

174

attack on Beirut Airport and declared Lebanon entitled to appropriate redress for the destruction of thirteen civil aircraft. It was a memorable decision in which both the USA and the USSR agreed, almost for the first time. Israel rejected the resolution and denounced the Security Council as 'morally, politically and juridically bankrupt'.

Curiously, the Lebanese government, for reasons of its own, and without consulting the Lebanese airlines, rejected the award of compensation. Considering that the Lebanese airlines were privately owned, the government's rejection was highly prejudicial to the airlines, and more so to the insurance companies, who would have had, in case of compensation, a rightful recourse to claim the insurance money paid as a result of the raid. Whether the Lebanese airlines or the insurance companies would have actually received any compensation is another question, for there was never the slightest hope of the Security Council resolution being obeyed or even recognized by Israel.

We were the only Arab airline to be covered by a full war-risk policy, but the raid none the less cost a great deal of money. Some destroyed aircraft had to be replaced by leasing planes at high rates. As ground equipment was not insurable against war risk, all the equipment destroyed was a total loss. With few exceptions, the media all over the world reacted sympathetically, and the Lebanese press was violent in its condemnation of the raid and of the mishandling of the situation by the government.

Sections of the international press friendly towards Israel praised the operation on the grounds that it had been ably planned, and they made much of the fact that it was carried out without loss of life. But there is nothing surprising in this. In the nature of things, civil airports are unprotected and not designed to receive surprise peacetime attacks by commando forces from neighbouring countries. For this reason, there was no resistance, and consequently no casualties. As for the happy chance that no one was killed when the thirteen aircraft, with full fuel tanks, were blown up close to the crowded airport terminal, the fact of nobody dying was the result not of careful planning but of an act of God.

The Lebanese Minister of Public Works blamed the ministers concerned for the absence of airport security measures, especially since he claimed that he had warned of the possibility of such an attack. This ministerial row, and the attacks of the Lebanese press, hastened the fall of the cabinet by the end of January 1969.

The departure of the cabinet was greeted with sighs of relief and hopes for a change of attitude. Alas, attitudes did not change. It may

175

sound incredible that a government should wish to harm an airline which had done so much for the country's economy. In Lebanon, however, passions and private interests take precedence over the country's welfare, even its survival. The destruction of MEA would not necessarily, in certain people's opinion, have deprived the country of its major airline, but would merely have provided the opportunity for the establishment of another airline, differently composed and differently controlled.

Four of the most eminent French jurists, commissioned to advise on whether MEA could get governmental compensation for its losses, produced a forty-six-page study which concluded that 'the government could legally be held responsible and the Lebanese airlines were entitled to compensation'. I was certain that the government would never agree to compensation, having learnt the futility of such hopes from past experience. Nevertheless, we tried, but of course had no success.

There was also the case of King Hassan's Caravelle. The Ministry of Foreign Affairs telephoned to say His Majesty King Hassan of Morocco had kindly placed a Caravelle at the disposal of the Lebanese government for a whole year for use by MEA, who were asked to insure the aircraft and undertake all other formalities. To our stupefaction, the new Prime Minister decided that, as the Caravelle had been loaned to the Lebanese government, it could not be used by MEA, a privately owned company, without payment. A committee was formed to determine the charges MEA was to pay. Furious at this highly dubious attitude, I refused the aircraft. When the Ministry of Foreign Affairs argued that my refusal threatened serious diplomatic repercussions, I referred them to the Prime Minister. They said they had already pleaded with him without success, and asked me to see him.

I put it to the Prime Minister that this aircraft had been given solely to help MEA because of the loss of most of its fleet and should be used free of charge, as was intended. The Prime Minister insisted that the aircraft had been sent to the government, and the government must charge for its use. MEA would have to pay rent to the government, as determined by the specially appointed committee, on the basis of the international rate for the lease of Caravelle aircraft. I was restrained from telling the Prime Minister what he could do with his proposition only by the thought of the adverse effect my refusal would have on a noble and generous Arab ruler. After all, King Hassan had come to the aid of Middle East Airlines and never meant his gift to go to a greedy government. I would have felt most ashamed, as a Lebanese, if news of this incredible behaviour had ever reached him — as it would have done

176

had we refused to use the Caravelle. Therefore I told the Prime Minister that, while I would not pay rental charges, I was prepared to use the aircraft and to share profits from its use with the government on a 50:50 basis.

Believe it or not, the Prime Minister proceeded to bargain and ask for a 60:40 share-out – 60 per cent for the government and 40 per cent for MEA. I accepted with distaste, wishing to avoid any more ministerial bargaining, though the temptation to operate the Caravelle only on loss-making routes and later present the Prime Minister with a request for the government's 60 per cent share of losses did cross my mind. But this was not how Middle East Airlines behaved. At the end of the contract, we settled by paying the Lebanese Treasury the sum of £L6,823 (less than $2,000), the government's 60 per cent share of the profits made by the donated Caravelle.

As life began to return to normal, and the pressures of the consequences of the raid subsided, I attempted to analyse Israel's unprecedented act of carefully planned aggression against Lebanon's civilian airport. Israel must have had extremely important reasons to have mounted such a military attack, fully aware that it would produce world-wide condemnation from friend and foe alike. The Israelis themselves declared that they had carried out a punitive raid in retaliation for the Palestinian attack two days earlier on an El-Al aircraft in Athens. But this left unanswered the key question: against whom was the retaliation directed? The camps of the Palestinian resistance organizations, held responsible by the Israelis for the Athens affair, were within a stone's throw of Beirut Airport. But the Israeli raiders took great care not to approach the Palestinians or damage their camps. In fact, it might be argued that the Palestinians benefited from the world-wide interest which the raid focused on their cause.

Airport installations that belonged to the government of Lebanon remained unscathed among the wreckage of our aircraft. The state of Lebanon was not therefore the target, despite being constantly accused of 'harbouring Palestinian terrorists and allowing them freedom to mount attacks on Israel'. Undoubtedly the Lebanese government suffered a considerable loss of public confidence, and had its prestige badly shattered, but that alone could have hardly made the raid a worthwhile operation for Israel. Certainly there was no question of Lebanon being provoked by the raid into making war upon her powerful neighbour. Lebanon was the most peaceful of Israel's surrounding states. Our small army, trained for internal security, was incapable of attacking, however willing its officers and men might have been to do so. The only real victims of the raid were the Lebanese airlines, and MEA in particular, which took the heaviest loss. Arguing backwards from this indisputable fact, I have come to believe that the main objective of the raid was the destruction of MEA. It may seem incredible that this should have been the purpose, but the facts are there and I can think of no other credible explanation. Yet it still goes against the grain to believe what one very well-informed source told me, that the raid was carried out on a specific request to Israel from someone in Lebanon.

If the objective was the destruction of MEA, then the opposite was achieved. After a loss in 1969, for the first time in a decade we emerged stronger than ever. LIA collapsed as a result of the raid, and we were thus able to take it over and finally unify the Lebanese passenger airlines. The destruction of our heterogeneous fleet and the insurance payments enabled us to standardize our fleet using second-hand aircraft of the same make — the answer to an undercapitalized airline's prayer. The substantial profits we made as a result saved us during the troubles of 1975–6. In addition, we received invaluable publicity. For weeks, MEA was the talk of the media world-wide, and, last but not least, the raid brought the employees together, for nothing gives unity and strength of purpose more than an attack by an outside force.

15
LIA and TMA

One of the great difficulties of óperating an airline in Lebanon has been that no government can ever be persuaded to formulate a proper aviation policy and no rational laws have ever been passed to control civil aviation. Nor have there been any restrictions on permits for new airlines.

During my time at MEA, I tried very hard to remedy the situation, and was once able to persuade a government to invite a famous Italian jurist, who was a specialist on civil aviation legislation, to come to our assistance. He came and, taking the official invitation seriously, produced a comprehensive draft for a modern civil aviation law. It never saw the light of day and slept comfortably in the desk of the Director-General of Civil Aviation. The same exercise was later repeated, this time with a famous French jurist. That project was killed, along with thousands of Lebanese, during the fighting of recent years.

On the question of a civil aviation policy, all airlines in Lebanon had, at one time, spent numerous days and evenings with the Director-General of Civil Aviation and his experts to hammer out an agreed policy. Like the civil aviation law, it never saw the light of day. When General Fouad Chehab assumed power as President of Lebanon after the 1958 civil troubles, he had been anxious to reform the administration and the existing system of government. He appointed, for the purpose, a central reform committee of Lebanese experts and men of experience, on which I was included. My task was to help in recommending reforms in the Ministry of Public Works and the Ministry of Posts, Telephones and Telegraphs. Civil aviation was a department in the Public Works Ministry, and I took the opportunity of recommending, as a useful measure of reform, the creation of a Superior Civil Aviation Board with powers to make policy decisions. It was to be composed of the directors of civil aviation, town planning, foreign affairs, national economy and tourism. It was to be chaired by the Minister of Public Works, and directors-general of Lebanese airlines were to be non-voting members of the board. The board was formed, but with crippling modifications. It was deprived of the powers of decision and could only recommend to the minister, who, in turn, referred the matter to the Council of Ministers which had the power of final decision. It turned in the end into yet another bureaucratic body delaying urgently needed decisions.

In the free-for-all world of Lebanese civil aviation, which successive Lebanese governments proudly misnamed 'free and liberal trade', two new operating-licences had been granted in 1955. One went to Trans Mediterranean Airways, a freighter airline, the other to Société des Transports Terrestres Maritimes et Aériens SAL, later called Lebanese International Airways (LIA), for passengers and freight.

MEA was never unduly worried by competition. I have always believed that fair and just competition is healthy and is one of the pillars of private enterprise. The real irritants in the uncontrolled licensing of airlines in Lebanon were the consequent demands on the government for traffic rights. Having granted them a licence to operate, the government was under an obligation to provide traffic rights. But while free to grant unlimited operating-licences, the government was not equally free to grant unlimited traffic rights, which were governed by bilateral agreements with foreign countries and based on the internationally accepted principle of reciprocity. Traffic to and from Lebanon, from any destination, justified not more than a maximum of one daily flight. Consequently, we found ourselves in a most difficult situation when seven flights had to be divided among four Lebanese airlines. On routes where weekly flights were fewer than seven, the position became even more intolerable.

There was no economic justification for four airlines in Lebanon, and since there were foreign interests in the airlines, there was no possibility of unification. The result was a suicidal trading position for each of the four and a cut-throat war for survival.

In October 1966, LIA concluded a purchase contract with American Airlines and took delivery of two Convair Coronado aircraft. It then defaulted on payments and remained in default until June 1968 when the company suspended operations. Its biggest creditor was Banque Sabbagh, a subsidiary of the French Banque d'Indochine. Pressure was immediately applied by the Lebanese government on MEA to bail LIA out under the pretext of avoiding a social crisis resulting from the loss of jobs for hundreds of LIA employees. The Franco-Lebanese bank was to be helped to recover its funds.

Elias Sarkis, who was then governor of the Central Bank, was also closely involved in 'Operation Sauvetage', during the course of which a ministerial committee was formed to study the crisis and recommend a solution. They wanted MEA to make an offer for LIA, substantial enough to pay off the Banque Sabbagh debts and leave something over for the Aridas. The applied pressure, mixed with menacing hints, left us no option except to make the desired offer. The Aridas, reluctant to sell their LIA holding to MEA, had meanwhile talked American Airlines into leading negotiations with other major creditors for a recapitalization and reorganization of LIA that would enable it to resume operations. American Airlines and the other creditors agreed to convert their debts into shares, an arrangement that gave American Airlines 31 per cent, National Bulk Carriers 30 per cent, Banque Sabbagh 30 per cent, and left a balance of 9 per cent for the Aridas and other minority shareholders. But as American Airlines quickly realized, LIA's routes were inadequate for a viable operation. They were promptly assured by the Lebanese authorities that more routes would be granted and a project for a redistribution of all Lebanese routes was prepared, under which some of MEA's routes were to be given to LIA. We put up a ferocious fight and the Lebanese authorities withdrew the project, claiming it was only an academic study.

Having failed to plunder routes from MEA, tactics were changed and the Lebanese authorities asked MEA to come to an agreement through American Airlines with the newly restructured LIA. An agreement was reached in principle whereby MEA would take over LIA, its traffic rights and all employees, and in return would give the new American LIA group 12 per cent of the shares of MEA. This would have added a new dimension to the MEA shareholding circus — the unlikely co-operation of Air France and American Airlines. As it happened, before this agreement could be finalized American Airlines became disillusioned with LIA. The Americans were especially put out when, after the Israeli raid on the two American Airlines Coronados, it was discovered that LIA had failed to renew its war-risk insurance when this expired three months before. So American Airlines left the scene and the Lebanese government re-entered.

MEA was asked, in the government's usual request-command style, to conclude a satisfactory agreement with LIA which would involve its liquidation and the transfer of its traffic rights to MEA, provided we undertook to give jobs to all LIA employees and paid the salaries due.

181

Failure to do what was asked could lead the government to find another airline interested in the proposed arrangement. Furthermore, since LIA's traffic rights did not form the basis of any viable operation, it was hinted that the government might resuscitate the project to redistribute traffic rights.

MEA was thus forced to conclude an agreement, which was signed in April 1969. The traffic rights were transferred to MEA, while all the employees were taken on and their long-overdue salaries paid retroactively. In return, the Lebanese government, admitting the exorbitant charge on MEA, promised compensation in an official letter from the Minister of Finance, confirmed in the Council of Ministers' Decision No. 83, 1969. In addition, the Council of Ministers undertook not to issue any new permits for passenger airlines for a period of twenty years.

But when MEA tried to get the government to pay the agreed compensation, fruitless meetings followed with ministers and responsible authorities. Middle East Airlines was told it had no right to compensation. MEA therefore asked for arbitration, a procedure specified in the Minister of Finance's letter, but a new Minister of Finance refused to honour his predecessor's assurance. We then came under a governmental pressure that sadly lacked finesse. MEA's requests for additional frequencies and additional routes, although approved by the Superior Civil Aviation Board, were held in abeyance by the Council of Ministers. It became clear that, unless we gave in and forfeited our right to compensation, our requests would be frozen and our growth stunted. So we could only surrender unconditionally, and in this manner the turbulent LIA chapter was finally closed.

At least we had LIA and, at last, one Lebanese passenger airline, but there still remained TMA (Trans Mediterranean Airways), the all-freighter airline to worry about. This had begun with a licence for an Air Taxi Company granted to Charles and Victor Sa'd some time before 1950. The air taxi had never operated, but this did not stop the Sa'ds and Mounir Abou Haidar from submitting a request to the Directorate of Civil Aviation in 1955 to transfer the Air Taxi licence to Mr Abou Haidar. Nor did it stop Civil Aviation approving the request and turning the Air Taxi into a freight charter company. Thus was TMA born. The charter company was later converted into a regular freight airline on the recommendation of the then Director-General of Civil Aviation. We, Air Liban and LIA protested strongly at the time, but the Council of Ministers confirmed the recommendation with the usual politicians' proviso, given but never to be respected, that granting

TMA a licence for a regular freight airline should never prejudice the rights and interests of other Lebanese airlines. This proviso was constantly violated and there was nothing to be done about it.

TMA owed a great deal of its progress and success to the strong personality of its founder, Mounir Abou Haidar, and the assistance it continually received from the Americans. When it started operation, Aramco (the Arabian American Oil Company) helped with important freighting contracts. All Aramco freighting had previously been done by MEA with the help of Mounir Abou Haidar, who was employed by Aramco in its Beirut office. Ambitious to start on his own, he was, at first, encouraged by Air Liban and began his operation by chartering freighters from Skyways operated in the name of Air Liban. Later he bought the aircraft from Skyways and employed their crews once he had obtained the necessary operating-licences. TMA went from strength to strength and, with the support of the government, obtained traffic rights for a vast network of services eventually crowned by an extremely special privilege granted by the American authorities for TMA to operate round-the-world services. American banks had been prominent in providing financial assistance and American technical assistance was provided under contract. TMA rivalled MEA in a constant competition for traffic rights, and periodic discussions took place in an effort to find a formula for co-operation. They were a waste of time and effort and, for various reasons, never meant to succeed.

Mounir Abou Haidar is a true Lebanese entrepreneur. He built a freighting airline whose competition was feared by practically all major airlines. He is a reincarnated Phoenician trading buccaneer, and our personal relations, outside the everlasting fights for traffic rights, were always good and friendly. Sadly, however, TMA had to cease operation because of losses incurred during the civil war. In the end, no amount of pleading by its founder and owner was able to convince the Lebanese government into giving it the financial assistance necessary to keep it in the air. When its shares were acquired by a new Lebanese group, on the other hand, the government gave the airline nearly five times the financial assistance denied to its founder and former owner.

16
Hijacks and Wars

I have always been superstitious about Friday the thirteenth and, in August 1971, the day lived up to its reputation. Middle East Airlines received its first serious threat from a Palestine guerrilla organization. It came in the form of a message delivered to the airline and to the news agencies in Beirut early in the afternoon. Addressed to MEA and all passengers to Amman, the stencilled message in Arabic was clear and to the point:

After the closure of Syrian skies to Jordanian aviation only Middle East Airlines now carries passengers between Beirut and Amman. As this will help the Jordanian government, the imperialists' agent, to act through Lebanon, we are issuing a warning to Middle East Airlines not to use its aircraft on the Amman route. We will not be responsible for any aircraft going to Amman. We also appeal to the public not to travel on these aircraft because we will not be responsible for their lives.

It was signed: 'The Palestine Revolution'.

I was away for the weekend at our family farm in south Lebanon, which lies in a beautiful area north of the Litani River across a couple of small valleys from Beaufort Castle and commands a grandstand view across the Litani of what was then known as Fath land. It was called Fath land because it was acquired from the Lebanese authorities by the Palestine Liberation Organization (Fath) under the controversial Cairo Agreement. The Israelis were to change that in their invasion of Lebanon in 1982.

The farm consists of forests and fertile valleys, with many springs and a small stream that flows into the Litani. It was the place I dreamed of for my retirement and that I used frequently at weekends to refresh my

185

mind and body. It is amazing how quickly the problems of sheep, bees and fruit trees can replace those of running an airline. Alas, our farm, like much that was beautiful in Lebanon, was destined to be laid waste in the successive waves of fighting. The house we had built for retirement was shelled three times. Twice we rebuilt it, but when it was shelled a third time, my son Karim, who looks after the farm, and I decided to build a shelter instead. This was greatly appreciated by Karim and the farmworkers, who made good use of it, but all of that lay unforeseen in the future on the day when MEA's vice-president traffic telephoned to tell me of the threat from the so-called 'Palestine Revolution'.

I asked that he delay the departure of the Amman flight, which was to operate early Saturday morning, and give passengers the classic aviation excuse of a technical snag. Then I returned to Beirut immediately. In the meantime, however, the Lebanese Minister of Public Works and Transport had tried to take matters into his own hands. On learning of the threat, he had given orders that the flight to Amman must not be delayed or cancelled but that MEA simply take extra security precautions.

Having heard the views of those directly concerned in Middle East Airlines, I nevertheless decided to delay the flight from the morning to the afternoon of Saturday, until after I had talked personally with the minister. When I saw him early on Saturday morning, he remained adamant that we should not delay or cancel. It would be most embarrassing for him, he said, since he had received a personal appeal from his colleague, the Jordanian Minister of Transport, and had promised he would not allow us to interrupt our service to Jordan. How the Jordanian minister could have known so quickly of the threat remains an unanswered mystery.

I tried to explain the seriousness of the threat and the devastating consequences that could follow if we ignored it, risking not only the aircraft but the lives of crew and passengers. I told him we had been lucky so far to have had no trouble with the Palestinian organizations, and that I was not prepared to risk it now. He was unconvinced, but I most certainly was convinced, and our flights to Amman were discontinued until further notice.

The minister grew angry and contacted the Prime Minister, and so an urgent meeting was called for the morning of Sunday, 15 August 1971, at the summer residence of the President of the Republic, situated more than 100 kilometres away in the mountains of north Lebanon. I was asked to attend, along with the Prime Minister, the Minister of Foreign

186

Affairs and the Minister of Public Works and Transport, the latter opening the meeting with an account of his exchange of views with his opposite number in Jordan. He emphasized the urgent appeal from the Jordanian government for us to maintain air communications between Lebanon and Jordan, and said he had given his own promise to that effect. The Minister of Foreign Affairs then stressed the adverse effect any disruption of services would have on the friendly relations between the two Arab countries. The Prime Minister assured the meeting that he had asked the Palestinians about the threat and they had denied any knowledge of it.

President Suleiman Franjieh then asked for my views. To begin with, I asked the Prime Minister, Saeb Salaam, which of the Palestinian organizations had he approached.

'Fath [the PLO], of course,' replied His Excellency.

'What of the twenty-two remaining splinter Palestinian resistance organizations? Have they been asked? Does Your Excellency really believe that if the PLO is behind this threat it would have admitted the fact?'

He could give no convincing answers and so I told the meeting that, if the government gave MEA a written order to fly to Amman and guaranteed all losses the airline could incur from defying the Palestinian organizations, whose camps overlooked our runways within rocket and machine-gun range, then naturally MEA would abide by those instructions.

President Franjieh thereupon gave his verdict. MEA being a private company, he said, it was up to its chairman to take whatever decision he considered to be in the best interests of the company. I thanked the President, the Prime Minister and the ministers, and left the meeting, leaving an exceedingly angry Minister of Transport behind.

A week later I went to see President Franjieh to thank him and to show him proof that, had we not cancelled our Amman flight on the 14th, the threat from the 'Palestine Revolution' could well have been carried out. I had with me the passenger manifest of our flight to Baghdad for the evening of the 14th, as well as our passenger reservation records. These showed that Leila Khaled, the well-known Palestinian woman hijacker, had been booked to Baghdad on Middle East Airlines on the 14th but had cancelled her trip just before the flight took off. It could have been a simple coincidence, but we did not think so.

I also told the President that I had learnt, by way of our Palestinian grapevine, that had we flown to Amman on the morning of 14 August, we would have been taught a lesson that evening. President Franjieh commented that he needed no proof of the validity of my judgement in stopping Amman flights. He was the only Lebanese Head of State, during my service with MEA, who ever appreciated what the airline was doing for Lebanon. By contrast, his indignant Minister of Transport showed his displeasure by bringing pressure to bear on the Superior Aviation Board to approve more licences for the creation of private airlines in Lebanon — airlines which, even if they failed, would take passengers and traffic rights away from MEA. We fought back, and he failed to persuade the board, but he maintained a hostile attitude towards MEA until the end of his mandate as minister, which luckily was not long.

Services to Amman were eventually resumed after nearly two years and a considerable loss of revenue, but while the decision to give in to Palestinian threats may be viewed by some as submission to blackmail, I chose to look upon it as sympathetic compliance in the interests of Middle East Airlines. This attitude, and the fact that various services were rendered to the resistance organizations, did give the company a certain immunity from the plague of hijacking. But, although we were fortunate enough to have no hijacking trouble from the Palestinians, MEA was less fortunate with the Israelis.

On Friday, 10 August 1973 a Middle East Airlines Caravelle chartered to Iraqi Airways on the Beirut–Baghdad run, carrying seventy-four passengers and eight crew, was intercepted soon after take-off, while still in Lebanese airspace, by two Israeli Air Force fighters. It was ordered to fly to Israel and land at Ramat David military airport.

While this was going on, several Israeli patrols flew at varying altitudes over south Lebanon, Sidon and Tyre, as well as over Damour — a village only a few kilometres from Beirut International Airport. Consequently the airport had to be closed and traffic diverted to Cyprus. The Israelis allowed the Caravelle to resume its flight to Baghdad only after they had carried out a precise two-hour check of the passengers. Moshe Dayan, then Israel's Minister of Defence, announced that the Caravelle had been diverted in an attempt to capture Dr George Habash, head of the Popular Front for the Liberation of Palestine (PFLP). Israeli agents evidently reported that Dr Habash would be flying to Baghdad on that flight.

There was a world-wide condemnation of this skyjacking of a civil aircraft and its passengers by the air force of a member state of the United Nations. The Guild of Air Pilots called it 'an act of piracy' and called for Israel's expulsion from the International Civil Aviation Organization. IATA, the International Air Transport Association, termed the Israeli act 'reprehensible' and said it posed a threat to the reliability and safety of public air transport. The Canadian Air Line Pilots Association (CALPA) called the action 'violation of international law and civilized behaviour'. In London, the *Daily Mail* commented, 'Jet fighters acting under orders of a supposedly civilized nation kidnapped a law-abiding civil airliner . . . It was an act of piracy.'

The Lebanese government referred the case to the UN Security Council, and after a few days of the usual debates, the council voted unanimously on the 15th to condemn Israel for sending warplanes to skyjack the MEA Caravelle. The United States, which chaired the meeting, joined the vote, while Israel, not unexpectedly, rejected it. In this case, as in so many others when it has been the aggressor, Israel told the United Nations that its action was justifiable, being made in self-defence.

Israel's Prime Minister, Golda Meir, declared that 'her country would continue to capture and force down foreign passenger planes if she considered it necessary to her national survival'. Joseph Tekoah, the Israeli representative in the United Nations, attacked Arab terrorists and all those who sympathized with them, romanticizing that 'Arab terrorists had begun their actions in the 1920s and later collaborated with the Nazis in the extermination of the Jews'. He then declared that Israel would 'continue to fulfil its obligation of self-preservation, self-defence and the protection of its people', adding 'surely the sanctity of human life comes before the sanctity of air'.

How quickly Mr Tekoah seemed to have forgotten the sanctity of the lives of 108 passengers and crew who perished six months earlier in the shooting down by the Israeli Air Force of a Libyan aircraft which wandered by error into Israeli airspace. In contrast to Mr Tekoah's smokescreen of justification, Yitzhak Shaked, the president of the Israeli Pilots Association, condemned the action of his government and said that pilots were continuously 'fighting against air piracy and interference with civil aviation'.

Only the Soviet Union and Egypt asked for sanctions to be applied to Israel. Lebanon, the injured party, could only muster sufficient courage to hope 'that the Security Council would adopt a resolution that would condemn the "abominable act" of Israel'. There can be no surprise that the United Nations failed to do anything more than issue a routine condemnation when Lebanon itself proved so faint-hearted.

Hardly had the reverberations of this affair begun to settle than another MEA aircraft was hijacked to Israel on 16 August 1973, just six days after the first incident. This time a Boeing 707, carrying 109 passengers and 10 crew on a regular flight from Benghazi in Libya to Beirut, was hijacked over Cyprus and ordered to change course and head for Israel. The hijacker was a man carrying two pistols and a bag which he claimed was full of explosives. The plane was escorted by two Phantom fighter bombers after it entered Israeli airspace, and landed at Lydda Airport, amid extreme security measures, to be met by Defence Minister, Moshe Dayan, and his chief of staff, David Elazar. Israeli commandos forced open an emergency exit door and easily overpowered the hijacker. The passengers, among them the Libyan Ambassador to Iraq, were checked, and, after nearly five hours, plane, crew and all passengers were allowed to leave for Beirut.

The hijacker was described by the Israeli authorities as a Libyan, aged thirty-seven, who had said, according to news from Israel, that he 'hijacked the plane to prove to the Israelis that not all Arabs are bad'. Captain Adel Kawas, who was in command of the flight, stated in his official report to Middle East Airlines: 'At 13.39Z an armed man entered the cockpit and ordered me in broken English to head for Israel. As he appeared to be an Arab I tried to talk to him in Arabic but he persisted in using his broken English.' The Libyan Ambassador to Iraq maintained that the hijacker was not Libyan. 'His accent was not Libyan,' he insisted. The last heard of the hijacker was that he had been committed to a mental hospital in Israel.

Although it is now regarded almost as history, the most spectacular set of political hijackings took place on 6 September 1970. Even today, the full significance of that fateful event is not generally recognized, involving, as it did, four international flights being hijacked by Palestinian commandos on the same day, and a fifth being taken three days later.

Around noon on the 6th, a Transworld Airline Boeing 707 with 145 passengers and 10 crew on its way from Frankfurt to New York, was hijacked over Belgium. It was forced to fly to Dawson's Field, an abandoned desert airstrip north of Amman in Jordan, built by the British and named after Air Chief Marshal Sir Walter Dawson. Few, even in Jordan, knew of its existence. About an hour and a half later, a Swissair DC–8 flying from Zürich to New York with 143 passengers and 12 crew, was hijacked over France and also forced to fly to Dawson's Field.

Early in the afternoon, an attempt was made to hijack an El-Al (Israeli Airlines) Boeing 707, flying from Amsterdam to New York with 145 passengers and 10 crew, as the aircraft was over Essex, England. The hijackers were a woman and a man. An El-Al security guard shot the male hijacker dead, and an American passenger courageously tackled the woman, rugby style, and brought her crashing to the cabin floor where she was set upon and bound hand and foot. Even so, a grenade was released, which rolled across the floor with the firing-pin out, but failed to explode.

The plane made an emergency landing at Heathrow, where the woman hijacker, Maria Martínez, was arrested and later identified by British police as Leila Khaled, aged twenty-four, who had gained international fame and world-wide publicity by leading the hijack of a TWA aircraft flying to Syria in August 1969. This time, however, she was completely isolated and no one was allowed to see her face. The male hijacker, shot dead in the same incident, was identified from fingerprints by the US Federal Bureau of Investigation as Patrick Joseph Arguello, aged twenty-seven, a US citizen living in Nicaragua.

Some hours after Arguello's death and Leila Khaled's capture, a Pan American jumbo Boeing 747 was hijacked soon after take-off from Amsterdam, with 158 passengers and a crew of 18 en route to New York. Its captors forced the crew to set course for the Middle East. After landing at Beirut to refuel, it was flown that same evening to Cairo. The next day, after all passengers and crew had been released, the hijackers blew it up in a multi-million-dollar explosion in the middle of Cairo Airport. Why it was not taken to Dawson's Field to join the other aircraft was never satisfactorily explained. No political hijacker could have deliberately overlooked the value of adding such a further valuable prize to the other aircraft under siege there. Three days later, on the 9th, a British VC–10 with 105 passengers and 10 crew on its way from Bombay to London, was hijacked over the Arab Gulf and also flown to Dawson's Field.

All the hijackers belonged to the Popular Front for the Liberation of Palestine (PFLP), a movement originally set up at the American University of Beirut by Dr George Habash while he was studying there. It pursued a highly radical policy in its efforts to reclaim Palestine from the Zionists. One of its provocative operations was an attack, in December 1968, on an El-Al aeroplane in Athens, to which the Israelis retaliated with the raid on Beirut International Airport.

The Dawson's Field mass-hijacking produced an international furore which bordered on the hysterical. Not only governments of the airlines and passengers affected, but other governments not directly involved, the International Red Cross, the International Air Transport

Association, the Holy See, the United Nations and the Council for the Advancement of Arab–British understanding, all became caught up in the affair. A five-nation committee was set up in Bern, Switzerland, to co-ordinate negotiations for the release of hostages. This was composed of representatives of the governments of the United States, Britain, West Germany, Switzerland and Israel.

So fierce and universal was the reaction that it almost gave the impression of being part of a well-orchestrated plan. Naturally, no one condoned these outrageous acts of air piracy, and the Arabs had more cause for anger than anybody, their reputation having been compromised and irreparably damaged. Some years later, it seemed astonishing when the West displayed nothing like the same degree of universal and co-ordinated anger in reaction to the massacres at the Sabra and Chatilla camps in Beirut in 1982, when thousands of Palestinian and Lebanese civilians, mostly women, children and old people, were butchered in cold blood. The only exception was in Israel itself, where the public anger shown at the massacres softened the hearts of the Arabs towards the Israeli people — but certainly not towards their government.

The hijackings also created uproar in the Middle East. The Jordanian Cabinet went into continuous session. President Jamal Abdel Nasser intervened personally. The Iraqi government, a strong supporter of the PFLP, appealed to that organization and to the Central Committee of the PLO to release the hostages. The committee, representing all the Palestine resistance organizations, decided, after a relatively short meeting, that all the hostages should be taken to Amman for humanitarian reasons. It then announced that the PFLP had been suspended from PLO membership, declaring that the PFLP's actions had provided the enemies of the Palestine resistance movement with a 'propaganda bonus which has caused practical losses to the Palestine revolution throughout the world'.

The 402 hostages from Dawson's Field were transferred to Amman on 11 September, after an unpleasant ordeal, lasting several days, of sweltering in the summer heat of the desert with restricted sleeping accommodation and inadequate sanitary services. Soon after the departure of the hostages, the three aircraft at Dawson's Field were blown up and reduced to heaps of scrap metal. Unfortunately, the ordeal for the hostages was far from over. On arrival in Amman, they found themselves in the middle of a full-scale battle. Fighting had broken out all over the city between the Jordanian Army and the Palestine resistance movement. The Intercontinental Hotel, where the hostages were lodged, was caught in the crossfire and they had to sleep in bathrooms and corridors for safety. It was a miracle that none of the hostages came to harm during the battle, even as complicated negotiations were going on to secure their release.

Finally all were released and the Dawson's Field drama passed without loss of life. Not one hostage was harmed during the ordeal, and all declared they had been treated with humanity by the hijackers, who shared with them their meagre supplies of food, water and medicine. The most vociferous of the hostages were the six last to be released, on 29 September. They were all Americans, consisting of two officials of the US Defence Department, a US diplomat, two rabbis from Brooklyn – both possessing dual US and Israeli nationality – and a professor of chemistry, also a Jew. In a statement in Athens on their way to the States, Rabbi Abraham Harari-Raful of Brooklyn said 'the guerrillas treated us like friends' and 'hugged and kissed us goodbye'.

I wonder whether those who planned this drama realized the grave consequences which would follow their action. It was mounted at a time of increasing friction between Jordan and the Palestine resistance movement, with the Palestinians demanding freedom of action and the Jordanians fearing the Palestinians were about to take over their country. It is impossible for guerrilla organizations to co-exist with a disciplined government which believes in law and order, and it is foolish to think otherwise. The Jordanians and Palestinians were no exception. Their quarrels were growing each day and the Dawson's Field drama brought them to boiling point. King Hussein's and his army's patience with the Palestinians finally ran out. It only required the setting down of the hijacked planes on Jordanian territory for Hussein to take the action his army had been demanding. He set up a military government on the 15th and unleashed his soldiers – the Arab Legion, predominantly consisting of men of the desert tribes – against the Palestinian guerrillas on the 17th.

Although the guerrillas fought well, they were not militarily equal to the Jordanian Army, whose tanks slowly but surely ground down their resistance. But now the fighting assumed international importance. Syria ordered its army to move on Jordan to rescue the Palestinians. The Israeli Army was put on alert and dispatched an armoured division to the northern border with Jordan. The United States and the Soviet Union were dragged into the squabble. The Iraqis hovered on the fringes of the fighting.

President Jamal Abdel Nasser telephoned the Syrians and asked them not to become involved militarily in Jordan, then called an urgent meeting of the Arab Heads of State in Cairo. There was an immediate response, but King Hussein did not attend. The meeting, held on the evening of 21 September, lasted into the early hours. A delegation sent to Amman succeeded in arranging a ceasefire, but it was only short-lived. In a telephone conversation with President Nasser, King Hussein offered to fly to Cairo to explain Jordan's position to the Arab Heads of State.

After lengthy discussions, an agreement was reached and the Arab Heads of State departed. It was a most fatiguing and strenuous week during which President Nasser hardly slept, even for three hours a night. He was satisfied that he and his colleagues, especially King Faisal of Saudi Arabia, had managed to pull the Arab nation back from the brink of a tragedy and had possibly helped prevent a confrontation between the two super-powers which could have led to a Third World War.

After wearily bidding farewell to his last guest at Cairo Airport, Jamal Abdel Nasser died at his home on 28 September of a heart attack. The Dawson's Field hijacking, the subsequent fratricidal battles between the Jordanian Army and the Palestine resistance movement and his efforts to bring about a reconciliation, had put too great a strain on his heart. There is no doubt that the hijackings started a train of events which eventually killed Jamal Abdel Nasser.

The ruthless crushing of the Palestine resistance movement in Jordan drove tens of thousands of armed and trained Palestinian commandos into Lebanon, where they joined their comrades in an intensified guerrilla campaign against Israel. In 1973, they clashed with the Lebanese Army, and in 1975 were a major party to the civil war in Lebanon. Their very presence in Lebanon, and everything that has stemmed from that presence, can be traced back directly to the drama at Dawson's Field. Who could have looked into the future and seen that Jamal Abdel Nasser's death would produce Anwar Sadat, who in turn would produce the Camp David Agreement? If they could have done so, would they – or would they not – have gone through with their plans?

A further consequence of the Dawson's Field affair, and the subsequent crushing of the Palestinian commandos by the Jordanian government, was the birth of the Black September Organization – a movement shrouded in mystery which launched itself into acts of extreme violence. Its most notorious operation was the taking hostage of Israeli athletes on 5 September 1972, during the Olympic Games at Munich. Eight Black September commandos climbed the wire fence of the Olympic enclosure and went straight to the sleeping-quarters of the Israeli athletes. They were resisted by two athletes, whom they killed, and then succeeded in taking nine hostages while others escaped. Panic followed and the games were disrupted. The German authorities committed a ghastly blunder when, thinking they could outsmart the commandos, they gave promises they did not intend to keep and, in an incredible misjudgement, mounted an attempt to rescue the hostages. In the resulting shoot-out, all the hostages, five hijackers and one German police sniper were killed. The three survivors of the Black September group were captured, but then, a few weeks later, Black September commandos hijacked a Lufthansa plane on a flight between Beirut and Ankara and threatened to blow it up if their comrades were not released. The German government capitulated and the three were released to be given a hero's welcome in Libya.

The death of the Israeli athletes and the disruption of the Olympic Games was the straw that broke the camel's back. The world was shocked, especially the Western world. The Munich terror was denounced and the Palestinians and Arabs universally condemned. In Germany, the fury reached unprecedented levels and the Arabs were branded as *Unmenschen* – inhumans. Hundreds of Arab residents were indiscriminately expelled from Germany, and Arab visitors were not welcome. In cafés and restaurants, the old Nazi signs reappeared, but this time said not *Juden sind hier unerwünscht* – 'Jews not wanted here' – but *Araber sind hier unerwünscht*. It was not only in the eyes of the Germans that the Black September organization and the Palestinians appeared as 'barbarians'. It was the same throughout the Western world, and especially in the United States. Nevertheless, the Western world seemed to show no shock when, three days after Munich, the Israeli Air Force retaliated with massive raids over Palestinian refugee camps in Lebanon and Syria, killing between 300 and 500 civilians, many of them women and children. This act of twenty eyes for one, which is the new Israeli interpretation of biblical law, did not mitigate the traumatic effect on the world which the untimely deaths of eleven Israeli athletes had produced.

The 'Munich Operation' was designed to produce an unforgettable shock, and did exactly that. But it was the wrong shock for the Palestinian cause. It was the turning-point at which Western public opinion, and especially that in the United States, swung not only against the Palestinians and their cause, but also against the Arabs, who were summarily accused of sympathizing with barbaric terrorism. The Munich drama damaged the image of the Arabs and branded them as the world's arch-terrorists. Any terrorist act was immediately pronounced as Arab or by terrorists trained or financed by Arabs.

A typical example of the world's Arab terrorist phobia was the storming of the offices of the Consulate-General of Israel in Johannesburg on 28 April 1975, when two people were killed, thirty-two wounded and nine, including two children, held hostage. The newspapers printed glaring headlines: 'Children Held in Raid in Israel Consulate'; 'Children as Bomb Hostages – Grenades Tied to Embassy Prisoners'; 'Human Bomb Siege – Terrorists Wired Hostages to Hand-grenades in the Besieged Israeli Consulate in Johannesburg'. The terrorists were said to number six, three Lebanese and three Japanese. There were lengthy tales of the terrorists' siege of the consulate, their demands, their inhuman behaviour, the concern of the Prime Minister of Israel and his Defence Minister and a firm declaration by the South African Prime Minister that South Africa would under no condition yield to guerrilla demands. The world was shocked at this barbaric behaviour. What could be worse than tying bombs to innocent children?

Two days later, on 30 April, the true story emerged. This is how the *Financial Times* told it: 'A heavy pall of shock hung over South Africa's Jewish community today, for the gunman who seized the Israeli Consulate turned out to be not an Arab terrorist but one of their own – 24-year-old David Protter, a security guard in the Consulate and Orthodox Jew brought up in Lower Houghton, one of the city's wealthiest suburbs.' Other newspapers gave a brief account of David Protter and his background, but little was said to offset the horror of the world at 'the Lebanese terrorists who were supposed to have savagely wired children to hand-grenades'. But who, at the start, gave the media the news that the terrorists included Lebanese? Surely the South African Security Forces, who claim to be among the best in the world, must immediately have known the identity of the Johannesburg terrorist.

Whenever I think of the Dawson's Field drama, I can only feel bewildered and mystified at certain very odd and peculiar elements that it contained. Surely those who planned it, and very intelligent they were, must have realized the international furore it was bound to create. The argument that terrorism is the only weapon available to the weak must have been weighed against the international tempest of horror and dismay such a massive act of terrorism against innocent people was bound to create. It should have been obvious that such an act was against, not for, the Palestinian cause.

Then there was the timing of the drama. Relations between the Palestinian resistance movement and Jordan could not have been worse. To choose Jordan for the scene of such a traumatic event could only produce a bloody confrontation, as it did, and the Palestinian resistance movement was, with all its factions, chased out of Jordan, their natural habitat. Jamal Abdel Nasser and King Faisal, the Arabs' hope for unity and effective action against Israel, were having, each in his own way, acute problems with the West, and the Dawson's Field challenge to Western nations could not have come at a worse time for them.

I also wonder if the Dawson's Field drama would have followed its dramatic course had Dr George Habash, the all-powerful PFLP leader, been in the Middle East when it took place. *Keesing's Contemporary Archives* record that Dr Habash was visiting North Korea at the time.

The hijackings themselves were performed with super expertise and perfect co-ordination. They had all the trademarks of the sophisticated Western planning that must have been available to those who carried them out. But, effective as the planning was, it strangely failed miserably in the choice of Leila Khaled to hijack the El-Al plane — Leila whose photo had, the year before, been on every television screen, every front page of every magazine and every journal when, as the first woman hijacker, she hijacked a TWA flight to Syria. Surely, it must have been evident that she could not escape the strict scrutiny of the El-Al security guards, nor those of the Dutch airport authorities. Why choose Leila Khaled, when there was an abundance of other equally capable volunteers? In fact, the others did better than Leila, for she was the only one who failed. And why choose an American as her partner, even if he was living in Nicaragua? Since when was the Palestinian resistance movement enlisting Americans in its ranks, and how often had it shown any especial confidence in Americans or vice versa?

Last but not least, there was the Pan-Am jumbo, hijacked with its passengers on the same day as the others but flown to Cairo and not to Dawson's Field. Its crew and passengers, most presumably Americans, were set free the next day in Cairo and spared the seven-day ordeal of the crews and passengers of the other hijacked aircraft. If the mass-hijacking was meant to call the attention of the world to the plight of the Palestinians, surely a US jumbo jet and its American passengers would have admirably served their purpose. Why therefore let it go?

The Palestinian resistance movement in Lebanon theoretically came under the authority of the Lebanese government. It rapidly became obvious, however, that the government had no effective control over the guerrillas. Continued friction and clashes between the Palestinians and the authorities started in 1969 and escalated until they exploded into a major confrontation in May 1973. The spark that set it off came when the authorities arrested three men, two Lebanese and one Palestinian, with suitcases full of explosives at Beirut Airport. Their destination was Paris. On the following day, five commandos were arrested near the American Embassy in Beirut. They, too, were carrying explosives.

The Palestinians retaliated by abducting three Lebanese Army soldiers and demanding the release of their comrades. The government issued an ultimatum for the immediate release of the soldiers and the army took up positions around the Palestinian camps in the suburbs of Beirut. But the soldiers were not released on time, the army came under fire on 2 May 1973, and fighting broke out. Commandos shelled Beirut International Airport and forced it to close, but MEA continued to fly by moving its operational centre to Nicosia in Cyprus.

At the time, I was a member of the government as Minister of Public Works and Transport. The government, formed on 25 April 1973, was almost immediately plunged into the first major armed confrontation with the Palestinian commandos in Lebanon. The fighting lasted two weeks, from 2–16 May, spreading to Tripoli, Sidon and other parts of the country. Commandos from Syria crossed the border and attacked Lebanese positions along the frontier. Syria, working with the Palestinians, closed its frontier with Lebanon and moved up troops and tanks.

The Secretary-General of the Arab League, the Syrian Minister of Foreign Affairs, and all the Arab ambassadors in Lebanon descended on the President's Palace and started a frenzied waltz of mediation and bargaining. They all vied with one another in demonstrating their patriotic Arab love for the Palestinian commandos and their just cause. But they turned a diplomatic deaf ear to the national demands of Lebanon and its need to maintain sovereignty and control over its own security. None of them would accept that Lebanon should apply the rigid rules of behaviour imposed on the Palestinian forces in their own countries. Nevertheless, the President of Lebanon and the government maintained a firm stand against the Palestine resistance movement because of its disregard for law and order in Lebanon.

The most remarkable fact to emerge from the conflict was the national unity of the Lebanese Army, which acquitted itself splendidly. Although the officers in command during the confrontations in Beirut, Tripoli and Sidon were Moslems, they did not hesitate to use force against the Palestinians. As they imposed control, it was reported that the commandos were running out of ammunition. It seemed success was within reach and Lebanese national integrity would be preserved. And this could have been achieved had it not been for Syria, the other Arab countries and certain Lebanese political feudal lords who insisted we should reach a settlement with the commandos rather than impose control over them.

A settlement was finally reached on 18 May 1973, between the Lebanese government and the Palestinians, though 'settlement' is hardly the right word. The Lebanese government was rather forced to accept a hastily arranged compromise that was ostrich-like, vague and not meant to last. This unrealistic arrangement was used to gain time for preparing the later rounds of fighting which escalated into the civil war. The Palestinians and their Lebanese allies then began an arms race with the 'Lebanese militia forces', who resented the Palestinians' assumption of the right to operate a 'state within the state' in Lebanon.

The way in which the Lebanese government was coerced into accepting such an unrealistic compromise convinced me more than ever that the Arab governments' determination to protect the Palestinian commandos and their freedom of action in Lebanon was motivated solely by their even stronger desire to confine the Palestine resistance movement to Lebanon and keep it as far away as possible from their own countries.

The closing of the Syrian frontiers produced an immediate crisis for the Lebanese exporters to Saudi Arabia and the Gulf of perishable goods – vegetables, fruit and day-old chicks. Daily losses of millions of Lebanese pounds were not easy to ignore, and Middle East Airlines made aircraft available to fly the produce. I then established an airbridge to carry the perishables to their markets. The operation was a success and the satisfied exporters promptly joined the majority of Lebanese who wanted the government to maintain its firm stand against those Palestinians who refused to respect Lebanese sovereignty.

The Prime Minister and the Minister of Foreign Affairs, however, became extremely worried. They feared that, because of my 'airbridge', the Syrians would close their airspace to Lebanese aircraft. I assured them that I knew what I was doing, and that Syria would not take such a step. The closing of airspace was the last thing any country would want, except in time of war, and we were not at war with Syria.

As it happened, the government survived only about two months. Its formation had been an attempt by President Suleiman Franjieh to break away from the deep-rooted practice, dating from Independence in 1943, of reserving the post of prime minister for one of the Sunni Moslem political feudal lords. President Franjieh decided it was time to change this restrictive practice and called on Dr Amin Hafez, a respected Sunni Moslem, Member of Parliament for Tripoli, doctor of economics and political science and chairman of the Parliamentary

199

Foreign Relations Committee to form a cabinet. The choice seemed a good one. The country needed, and was ready for, a change. But then the selection of the cabinet ministers was done in the usual Lebanese manner. Every religious community was satisfied with its representatives in the new cabinet, except the Sunni Moslems. The Sunni political lords joined forces and declared that the Moslems were not suitably represented and that the designated Prime Minister and the two Sunni Moslem ministers chosen were not really qualified to represent their community.

Like the Prime Minister, both ministers were, in fact, highly qualified. They came from respectable and well-known Beirut families. One was a lawyer with a doctorate in law, the second had a master's degree from the American University of Beirut. President Franjieh paid no attention to the protests and went ahead with his experiment. But he was sadly let down. On the day his cabinet went to Parliament for the traditional vote of confidence, the two Sunni Moslem ministers failed to appear and could not be contacted. They had been threatened that, if they appeared in Parliament, their lives would be at risk. Although the government commanded a respectable majority out of Parliament's ninety-nine votes, the vanishing act by our two Moslem colleagues left the Prime Minister no alternative but to resign. President Franjieh's experiment failed and the Sunni feudal lords continued to be the only leaders to speak for the Moslems in Lebanon.

As a minister during the confrontation with the Palestinians, I had first-hand knowledge of the dangers facing the country and its institutions. Middle East Airlines was especially vulnerable. The ineffective compromise forced on the Lebanese government merely provided a breathing-space during which the groups involved prepared themselves for ever bloodier confrontations. I was certain that serious troubles lay ahead and made contingency plans within MEA, knowing I could expect no financial assistance from the majority shareholders. Air France had formally notified us that it was the French government's policy not to contribute to any increase in the capital of Middle East Airlines, while Intra, with its four government shareholders, was equally negative. By withholding dividends in 1972 and the three following years, I added more than £L96 million to our liquidity and accumulated the largest amount of cash Middle East Airlines had ever held. The shareholders, especially Intra Investment, were hungry for dividends and pressed for payment. Their representatives on the board did not share my fears for the future and were prepared to use their majority power to overrule me. I threatened to resign, one of the very few times in my twenty-six years in MEA that I quietly used this ultimatum. However, I agreed to pay a token dividend distribution of £L5 million. When the troubles began in earnest in 1975, I asked the shareholders to repay this small amount, for I knew we would need all the money we could get and transferred our funds out of Beirut to Switzerland and converted them into Swiss francs and Deutschmarks – a precaution which incidentally produced substantial profits for Middle East Airlines on the exchange market. I also took a number of other precautions, all of which were to prove vital for the survival of MEA during the civil war of 1975–6.

One event of major importance was the decision by the board to sell 50,000 shares, or 5 per cent of the shareholding, to the employees. Because of legal formalities and red tape, the sale was not completed until 1973. It was voluntary, and shares were bought by 2,728 employees, representing 62 per cent of our total workforce and twenty-nine different nationalities. It was a project close to my heart as I had always regarded participation by the employees as proof of our progressive labour-relations policy in response to world-wide trends towards greater involvement of the workforce in corporation development. It was also a recognition of the contribution of the employees in helping the company to weather successive crises. I had hoped to see the percentage of employee participation increased gradually to reach 20 per cent, but it has stayed at 5 per cent ever since.

When, on 11 September 1974, Colonel Cyril Essely, former head of MEA's sales and traffic departments, died peacefully in his sleep, MEA lost one of its most able top executives and I a very dear friend and a most competent and trustworthy colleague. I had invited Cyril to join MEA nearly a month after I joined as general manager, asking him to organize and direct the sales and traffic departments. This he did most efficiently until he retired in August 1973 on reaching sixty-five. The board of MEA then decided, at my special request, that the chairman might appoint as personal adviser any employee who was past retirement age if he considered that appointment useful to MEA. This decision was necessary not only to retain Cyril but also to preserve the experience and knowledge of worthy executives after retiring-age. Cyril had been the first to qualify, and I had engaged him as my personal adviser for commercial affairs.

We could not have lost Cyril at a worse time as, within a month, we were facing the fourth Arab–Israeli conflict known as the Yom Kippur War. Although this lasted only from 6–26 October, its effect on traffic flow to the Middle East was considerable and its aftermath involved endless reverberations. Despite an earlier promise to freeze operations against Israel from south Lebanon, the Palestinians continued to harass the Israeli frontier. Lebanon was constantly blamed for failing to prevent these raids and for allowing them to train and base themselves inside its national territory. The Israelis counter-attacked throughout 1974, assaulting south Lebanon by land, sea and air. Villages were destroyed and their inhabitants fled to Beirut. Innocent victims of a quarrel not of their making, they crammed into the suburbs and lived in appalling conditions.

Radical forces in Lebanon grouped themselves into the National Movement, and Kamal Jumblatt was elected its leader and chief spokesman. The Palestinians promptly associated themselves with the National Movement, thus entangling their political disputes with domestic Lebanese problems. It was this which finally led to disaster.

By the summer of 1974, clashes and disturbances were happening everywhere. There were explosions in Beirut, a raid on the Bank of America by a group belonging to the Arab communist organization, strikes by students, night watchmen and firemen, and violent student demonstrations. Workers in Tripoli, Beirut, Sidon and Tyre took industrial action over the rising cost of living, and threats were heard of a general strike demanding changes in the Lebanese Labour Law. Political strikes against Henry Kissinger's visits to the Middle East degenerated into riots. The students of the American University in Beirut occupied the university buildings, demanding student participation in the running of the university and protesting against a proposed increase in tuition fees. The clashes, demonstrations and strikes were not accidental. They were motivated by political forces both inside and outside the country.

The country had become flooded with foreign secret agents who practised their trade to the detriment of Lebanon, recruiting Lebanese nationals. It became practically impossible, when talking to a foreigner, to know whether he was genuine or a spy working for one or more foreign powers. The Deuxième Bureau, the intelligence department of the Lebanese Army, which formerly supervised the activities of suspicious foreigners, had been disbanded in 1972 by the Prime Minister, Saeb Salaam, who resented its interference in Lebanese politics. It had been replaced by a new set-up which had yet to learn its trade.

The writing on the Lebanese wall was clear. A bloody battle was about to be waged on Lebanese territory and on the Lebanese people. Sophisticated weapons were pouring in and intensive preparations for a major confrontation were under way. In Middle East Airlines, I intensified preparations for a battle of survival, hoping against hope that, by the Grace of God, Lebanon and the airline could still be spared.

Tension increased when Rashid Karami, the hereditary Moslem political boss of Tripoli, announced he intended to present himself as a candidate for the Presidency of the Republic, the sacrosanct post reserved in the National Covenant for the Maronites. This caused immediate suspicion that the Moslems and their Palestinian allies were planning to destroy the delicately balanced Lebanese National Covenant to instal a Moslem leftist radical state. Civil war came one step closer.

Serious troubles started in Sidon on 28 February 1975. A demonstration of fishermen, joined by others, was staged against the Protein Company, which had been formed by the Christian leader, ex-President Camille Chamoun, with Lebanese and Kuwaiti capital. The fishermen claimed, despite assurances to the contrary, that this giant new company threatened their livelihood. The demonstration turned into a riot during which Marouf Sa'd, a Moslem political leader, was fatally shot, and a corporal of the Lebanese Army killed. The next day, Sidon organized another demonstration against the army and blocked the main road to south Lebanon. When the army was sent to free the road, armed civilians, both Lebanese and Palestinians, opened fire, killing five soldiers. The army retaliated and killed eleven civilians. Many were wounded on both sides.

The Sidon incidents were exploited by the leftists, who accused the Lebanese government of fascism and of being an ally to capitalists sucking the blood of the poor and suppressing any attempt at improving their standard of living. The Moslem establishment joined the leftists in their attack on the army, claiming it had no right to shoot at civilians, especially since it failed to protect south Lebanon from the Israeli raids. Christian political forces came out in support of army action and of the government's stand against anarchy.

The battle lines were drawn for a civil war which began on 13 April 1975. On that day the late Pierre Gemayel, head of the Maronite Phalangists (Kataeb), was on a visit to Ayn Al-Rummaneh, a Christian suburb of Beirut, to attend the consecration of a new church. A car with covered number plates drove towards the church and sprayed the crowd with automatic fire, killing four men, two of whom were members of the Kataeb — one a bodyguard of Pierre Gemayel himself. The killers got away.

On the same day, a bus full of Palestinian commandos, returning to their camp after attending a meeting in West Beirut, was passing through Ayn Al-Rummaneh when gunmen, presumed to be Christian, opened fire and shot dead thirty, of whom twenty-six were Palestinians. But these killers were not the Christian militia. So says Elias Khalil Zakharia, the Director-General of Justice in Lebanon in charge of investigating the incident. In an interview published in July 1983 in the Lebanese weekly *Al-Afkar*, he claimed that agents of a foreign power were responsible and that the shooting came from inside the bus, not from outside it. He also disclosed that the bus, which had all the evidence, disappeared from the municipality garage while in police custody and that it was never possible to find who was responsible for its disappearance. The shock of what happened to his investigation convinced the director-general that there was really no justice in Lebanon.

The war raged on and, despite incessant political activity, Lebanon failed to achieve more than short periods of calm which were invariably shattered by fresh clashes and attacks with rockets, cannon, missiles, bombs, explosive devices and the newly introduced tactics of terror — sniping and kidnapping. Government authority disintegrated and lawlessness prevailed.

The effect on Middle East Airlines was crippling. Political disturbances substantially cut the traffic to Lebanon while the fighting, and the consequent insecurity at the airport, gradually reduced our transit traffic. Throughout 1975, the airline maintained its operations under virtually impossible conditions. The employees volunteered to live on company premises at the airport, which ensured a continuous and smooth operation and enabled technical maintenance to be carried out to our usual high standards. I took an early decision to treat Beirut Airport as a transit station during the emergency, to allow our crews to be accommodated outside Lebanon and live under the relaxed conditions necessary for operational safety. But, like their colleagues in other departments, they suffered the hardship of being separated from their families for long periods.

It was a miracle that an airline could operate under the conditions which then prevailed. Nightmarish problems had to be faced each day, and it is difficult to find adequate words to describe the hardships. Some employees were killed coming to work, a far greater loss to MEA than any measured in money terms. Yet, despite the dangers, morale remained high and the staff's courage unequalled. During the last quarter of 1975 and up to the extended closure of the airport on 27 June 1976, more than 1,500 employees, men and women, were accommodated in our premises at the airport, while a few hundred 'commuters',

204

employees living in West Beirut, were still safely able to make their daily journeys to work.

The training-centre and other premises had been transformed by our engineers into what the employees called 'The Cedarjet Hotel', and thus it was possible to maintain an adequate workforce at the airport to ensure regular operation, even during the most difficult times. One thousand five hundred employees of different political affiliations, different religions and different social standards, cooped up for months in confined premises and living under constant stress, could easily have developed the political phobia then so contagious in Lebanon. But it did not happen. The employees decided to respect each other's opinions and to keep Middle East Airlines outside politics. They lived together as a true Lebanese family. It was a unique phenomenon in the Lebanon of 1975 and 1976, and one of which I shall always feel proud.

We faced shortages of every kind, the most serious being that of aviation fuel and diesel fuel for generators and other ground equipment. The first we remedied by using 'flying tankers'. Aircraft with empty tanks were flown to Amman, Damascus, Cyprus and Athens to fill up and return to Beirut where the fuel was pumped into the tanks of the operating aircraft. Diesel fuel came by road whenever possible, from Damascus, Amman and even Kuwait.

In the midst of this crisis I became deeply anxious for the health of my dear wife, Ida. During that year she had to go to London for two major cancer operations, having already undergone two, one in 1971 and one in 1973. Her health was an immense worry and I desperately wanted to be with her. During her critical illness I therefore suggested to the MEA board at its meeting of 17 October 1975 that I leave to be with my wife. They pressed me to stay on and granted me, once again, unlimited powers to do everything necessary to ensure the survival of the airline. I was in a dilemma, not knowing what to do for the best. It was Ida, ill though she was, who resolved the difficulty. She assured me she would feel better if I was doing everything possible to save MEA, for she knew how much that meant to me. In the end, I decided I must stay on and put aside any thought of leaving, and eventually I had the great dual happiness both of seeing Ida recover and of being able to enjoy with all the employees the satisfaction of successfully coming through what were then the most terrible days of the civil war.

We survived through 1975 without losses among our passengers and crew and with no serious damage to our aircraft. On the first day of 1976, however, the hand of fate struck again. A Boeing 707–720B on a scheduled flight from Beirut to Muscat exploded at 01.40 hours at an altitude of 37,000 feet over Qaysouma in the northern part of Saudi Arabia. All passengers and crew were killed. The official manifest showed sixty-seven passengers and fifteen crew, yet only eighty-one bodies were found in the wreckage and one passenger therefore remained unaccounted for. The aircraft scheduled for the flight was a Boeing 747 jumbo jet but, owing to a mechanical fault, the jumbo had been replaced by the 720B.

The ground staff of Middle East Airlines had counted the heads of passengers three times up to the moment of their transfer from the 747 jumbo to the 720B, when they had not considered it necessary to make a fourth count. Each of the three head counts had shown sixty-seven passengers which tallied with the plane's manifest. A theory was advanced that the sixty-seventh passenger, recorded on the manifest as Ahmad Said Salem – a false name – had boarded the jumbo jet with two suitcases, one of which contained a bomb set to explode after ten hours. The man concerned was suspected of being an Omani 'freedom fighter', and his plan was simple. The flight from Beirut to Muscat would have taken around five hours, giving Ahmad time to leave the suitcase containing the bomb as unclaimed baggage at Muscat Airport to explode at the set time. The plan misfired because of the mechnical delay at Beirut, and he must have sweated blood, sitting in the jumbo on top of his ticking bomb. His luck turned when it was decided to change aircraft, when he no doubt slipped away as passengers and baggage were transferred directly between aircraft. Because of the fighting, the airport aprons were in complete darkness, which helped Ahmad to leave unnoticed. Thus an hour and twenty-five minutes after take-off, the aircraft exploded, killing eighty-one innocent people who had nothing whatsoever to do with Oman and its political problems. The theory that the airport at Muscat was the target was accepted in the light of a similar incident in November 1975 when, because of aircraft delay, a bag full of explosives intended for Oman's capital exploded instead at Karachi Airport.

The Saudi Arabian authorities carried out a most thorough investigation, calling in British and American experts in addition to their own. Mr Eric Newton of the British Department of Trade, who had thirty-two years of experience in such investigations, was prominent among them. The conclusion they arrived at, after an exhaustive examination of all the available information, was that: 'An explosive device was detonated in the aft section of the forward cargo compartment splitting the fuselage in flight and causing complete loss of control. Aircraft occupants and control cabin crew sustained total and probably instantaneous incapacitation.'

The conclusion of the Royal Armament Research and Development Establishment in England, after examining materials taken from suitcases and the body of the aircraft, was that there had been a detonation of an explosive device containing RDX explosive and nitroglycerine in the forward baggage hold. The blast was so great that all the bodies scattered amid the wreckage in the desert were naked, completely stripped of their clothes. RDX is a military explosive of high performance, and extremely difficult to obtain except through official channels.

The fighting in Lebanon meanwhile followed a pattern of 'rounds', which flared up, then simmered down into periods of relative calm. These lulls gave Lebanese politicians, militia leaders, Palestinian commandos and involved parties from outside Lebanon opportunities for insincere dialogue and self-centred bargaining. There was time to review tactics of intrigue and for the recruiting of more mercenaries and agents. But, most important of all, these periods provided the necessary time for funds to reach Lebanon from Arab and foreign powers to finance the fighting and the purchase of arms in preparation for the next round. Funds were paid by instalments, round by round, for it was a proxy war. The interested parties were using surrogate armies to fight their battles in Lebanon rather than in their own countries.

The first round was set off by the Ayn Al-Rummaneh incident on 13 April 1975, and was followed by a second, a third, a fourth, a fifth and then by the sixth which started on 4 January 1976. After that, fighting became general. By 16 January, it threatened to engulf the airport, which had to be closed and to remain closed until the 24th. This was the first of three airport shutdowns in 1976. The second came during the first week in June and lasted until the 24th. In between the first and second closures, there were numerous shutdowns for hours at a time. The third closure was a nightmare, for the airport was besieged by gangs of armed men and completely cut off from the outside world.

Our engineering experts devised ingenious ways of communicating, which kept MEA stations everywhere informed of the welfare of the occupants of the 'Cedarjet Hotel' as well as the safety of installations at the airport.

While we were fighting for survival with rapidly diminishing revenues and escalating expenditure, the government issued a decree, dated 10 May 1976, authorizing the formation of LIBANAIR, a Lebanese public company for the transport of passengers and freight. Its founders were: L'Ordre des Moines Maronite, in the person of its

Superior General, Charbel Kassis, Dr Khairalleh Ghanem, and Michel Georges Mhanna. Granting this licence was directly countrary to the government's formal undertaking, when MEA took over the employees of LIA in 1969, not to issue such licences for a period of twenty years. Luckily, the company never got off the ground, though the licence remained valid and a theoretical threat.

On 27 June 1976, three days after the airport reopened, a Middle East Airlines Boeing 720B was loaded and about to start taxiing to take off for Amman, Jordan, when shells began to rain down on the airport from the hills. The passengers were taken off and moved to the comparative safety of the terminal building, but sadly, the crew were not so lucky. A shell hit the aircraft and the fuel tanks burst into flames. Captain Zouheir Mikati, a Moslem, was killed instantly. First Officer Louis Haddad, a Christian, and flight engineer Jonas Putna, an American, were able to jump out of the cockpit window but were badly burned. First Officer Haddad died later from his injuries and the flight engineer's life was saved. The reason for the shelling of this aircraft has remained a well-guarded secret. The airport was closed and the destruction of the MEA aircraft sparked off its conversion into a battlefield for all fighting parties.

The last quarter of 1975 and the six months leading up to the closure of the airport on 27 June 1976 saw, at that time, the worst of the fighting in Lebanon. Tens of thousands of innocent men, women and children were killed by indiscriminate shelling of residential areas by all the fighting factions. Rarely did the warring parties meet face to face in battle. Instead, they preferred shelling innocent people from safe positions and at safe distances. Such was their war of chivalry.

The commercial centre in Beirut was looted and destroyed. Factories were dynamited and reduced to rubble. Hotels were wrecked, hospitals were shelled. Banks, dock warehouses, commercial stores and depots were looted. Snipers became over-active and kidnappers overworked. Protection and extortion money became the daily taxes imposed by self-styled patriotic gangs. Our aircraft weaved in and out of the airport among mortar shells and rocket fire. But, thanks to God's mercy, MEA could claim to have had not one passenger killed or even wounded during those perilous days.

The Lebanese army split into factions, and this was the start of the degeneration of the fighting in Lebanon into full-scale civil war. There were countless ceasefires. None was respected. More and more mercenaries were imported and the inflow of spies became a torrent. Fighting spread throughout Lebanon. Politicians denounced each other and exalted their own lofty national principles, and even as they fought each other with declarations, the militia forces and street gangs were destroying Lebanon. There was even a military *coup d'état*, headed by General Aziz Al-Ahdab, but it fizzled out like all other attempts to stop the carnage.

Syria became actively involved when units of its army crossed the borders into Lebanon. These troops later became the major part of the Arab Deterrent Force. The Palestine Liberation Army, stationed in Syria, was allowed to join the fighting. Arab states were more than ever involved, and so were the United States and France. The USSR, as usual, supported the leftist movements. The Vatican prayed for peace, and heads of all the religious faiths in Lebanon did the same. The Lebanese used to claim hopefully that 'God is Lebanese', for he forgave their past mistakes and tolerated their faults. This time even the Almighty must have had more than he could stomach, for he shut his ears to all prayers for Lebanon and the insane Lebanese.

I had always feared that the airport would itself eventually become a hostage to fortune. It was obvious that certain fighting groups believed their enemies to be gaining an advantage from their airport positions. I anticipated that, sooner or later, the airport would be used as a pawn in games of political and other forms of blackmail. In preparation for the worst, I had given instructions to move spare engines, spare parts, spare seats, fabrics, aircraft carpets and various equipment out of Beirut to Paris-Orly, where Air France offered us the use of warehouses vacated when they moved to Charles de Gaulle Airport. We also transferred to Paris our supplies of items normally sold to passengers in flight, such as cigars, whisky and perfumes. These, I thought, could be irresistible items of temptation for the looters who surrounded headquarters at the airport.

When the banks were shut down in Lebanon, our funds, placed in Switzerland, helped to pay the salaries of employees and the bills of suppliers of goods and services. With money available in Europe, our creditors were paid, many before time. This action, when Lebanon was burning, gave a tremendous boost to MEA's prestige. The airline never defaulted on a payment or delayed meeting any of its financial obligations.

Being a realist, I had never believed in the magic of *boukra*, the Arabic word for tomorrow used by the lazy to postpone till tomorrow, or even for ever, something they do not feel like doing today. For a dozen years now, most Lebanese have been living in the hope that the fighting would end *boukra* – next week, and for sure next month. I was

209

certain that the airport closure of 27 June 1976 was going to be a long one, and therefore decided to move operations to Europe. The first priority was to try to obtain respective foreign governments' approval for scheduled operations overflying Beirut to the Arab states in the East and vice versa. If that was unsuccessful, I planned to convert operations to leasing and chartering services, and thereby earn as much revenue for the airline as possible.

London rather than Paris was first choice for a refuge base, since we had a pool agreement with British Airways for the London–Beirut and London–Gulf services and there seemed to be no possible objection to our services from London on the pooled routes overflying Beirut. No such pool agreement existed between Paris and the Gulf. We had not been able to persuade our partners Air France to agree to that, despite persistent efforts. London was also the centre for the aviation charter market, and we still needed charter work to augment our revenue. Furthermore, the Arabs preferred to travel to London rather than to Paris. Hundreds of thousands of Arabs from all over the Middle East continued to flock into London. In normal times, most of these would have been summer visitors to Lebanon, and Middle East Airlines would have carried the majority during the summer and returned them when the cooler weather arrived. With Beirut closed down, and MEA unable to fly its normal schedules, British Airways enjoyed a windfall and carried them to London and back. We felt we had an entitlement to some of this traffic.

Regrettably, it did not take long to discover that we were unwelcome in London. British Airways refused to allow us to fly out of London without passing through Beirut. No amount of argument or pleading could move them to change their attitude. Furthermore, we were told that, if our aircraft stayed in Britain more than six days, we would be required to pay customs duties! For one Boeing 747, that would have come to over $6 million. The British trade unions meanwhile refused to allow MEA technicians to do maintenance work on our own planes, and visas for employees were very difficult to get, took about fourteen days to obtain, and were only for single entry.

In all of this, I failed to detect the much-vaunted British sense of fair play or, indeed, their so-called friendship for the Arab world, an area that they at one time considered their own. MEA sadly packed and left for Paris, where things were different. Visas were given at the airport for any number of journeys; residence permits were granted to everyone; our technicians were welcomed by the unions and allowed to work on the maintenance of aircraft; work permits were given generously. The children of employees were admitted to schools and given admission priority even over French children. Their books and school equipment were supplied free. The use of the Air France warehouses at Orly was granted for six months without charge. The simulators of Air France were available for crew training, and its medical centre welcomed MEA employees. We were made to feel at home.

I remember, with gratitude, the gesture of Air France's pilots union when they went on strike because of a disagreement with their management. The pilots unions of all European carriers refused to allow their airlines to help Air France, and Air France could not charter any services from these airlines. To our surprise, the Air France pilots union made a special exception for Middle East Airlines. In sympathy with our plight, they allowed us to charter aircraft to Air France. In France, the Lebanese never felt like refugees, as they did everywhere else. The kind and compassionate treatment shown by the French authorities and Air France is something that MEA should never forget.

When MEA asked the French for permission to overfly Beirut on the Gulf run, however, our luck was no better than in London. First we had to produce written confirmation from the United Arab Emirates for permission to operate from Paris to Dubai. When this was done, a further condition was imposed by the French, that Gulf Air stopped its operation to Paris. This was obviously impossible and amounted to a polite refusal. As Lebanese, we were most welcome in Paris, but as competitors with Air France, we were not.

Chartering and leasing was the best hope. Two Boeing 747s and three Boeing 707s were leased to Saudi Arabian Airlines, complete with crews. The third 747 was leased, without crews, to Air France for use by Air Gabon. Some 707s with crews were based in Bahrain and Jeddah for *ad hoc* charters to the Middle and Far East, and for immediate dispatch to Beirut to resume normal operations the moment the airport reopened. Aircraft and crews were also stationed in Paris and were ready to fly anywhere in the world. We soon proved our efficiency and were able to guarantee any client an aircraft ready for take-off within three hours. The cedar tree of MEA was to be seen all over Europe, Africa and the Far East, and even in the West Indies. The workforce at Orly grew to more than a thousand. Many made the sea crossing to Cyprus and then flew on to Paris.

MEA earned over £L71 million in revenue from leasing and chartering and over £L27 million profit on the exchange market because of my foresight in converting liquid funds to Swiss francs and Deutschmarks. The combined leasing/charter and exchange revenues

211

were vital in MEA's fight for survival. Its ability to tighten its belt did the rest. First there was the contribution by employees of a reduction in salaries, and secondly a stringent control over expenditure in a united effort to save wherever possible. The year 1976 showed losses of only £L69 million, which were easily covered by available free reserves, retained profits and the profits made on exchange. It was not a bad result for a year in which a horrible civil war had raged and Beirut Airport been closed three times for a total of 171 days, latterly for 144 days. The airport finally reopened on 19 November to the delight of MEA, its employees and most Lebanese.

To describe the heroism and loyalty of the MEA employees in their fight to save their airline would require a book in itself. In fact, such a book, *Battle for Survival*, was written by Reginald Turnill, the well-known aerospace writer and broadcaster who was the BBC's Air and Defence Correspondent from 1958 to 1976. He started his research by having talks with me during which I told him all I knew. I appealed to him, however, not to mention any names, for in my opinion every employee in Middle East Airlines had done their part in saving the airline, so to mention some and not others would be unfair, and to mention all would be physically impossible. I also suggested that, whenever he wished to record anything I had done to help in our collective effort, he should write that it was the board rather than the chairman which had made the decision. Reginald Turnill agreed to my requests and the finished book gave a true and accurate account of our battle for survival.

Some time later, Reginald Turnill kindly turned over to me all the tapes of his interviews with the executives and employees of MEA. One day, when I had some spare time, I listened to them. Although I had learned never to be surprised at anything in Lebanon, I must admit that what I heard both startled and amused me. Nearly everyone interviewed claimed for himself alone the credit of saving Middle East Airlines. Of course, everyone played a part, but no one saved MEA single-handed. It was one of the most spectacular and praiseworthy collective efforts the employees of any airline can ever have achieved. It was the work of a team, or rather a family, where each gave of their best. Christians, Moslems, Druzes, people of every faith, and of the various political creeds in Lebanon, worked together in harmony in dire circumstances and saved the company.

As I look back on the unexpected reaction of British Airways and the British authorities to our request to operate from London, I am convinced they must have been influenced by the Dawson's Field

212

hijacking, the terror at the Olympic Games and most definitely by the sharp rise in oil prices, and the orchestrated, exaggerated blame which was heaped on the Arabs for that and all its consequences.

The hundreds of thousands of Arabs who flocked into London after the Lebanese troubles and the closure of Beirut Airport were happy to be in London, but their English hosts were not always happy to have them – although their money was welcome. The Arabs discovered, as quickly as we did in Middle East Airlines, that they were not really welcome. Some of the English press made no secret of the general hostility to them and their keenness to purchase properties in the United Kingdom. A campaign was mounted to tell the English public that the Arabs were 'buying up London'.

When a group of Arab businessmen bought the Dorchester Hotel in 1976, a well-known daily newspaper carried a short account of the sale under the heading 'Arab Threat to Our Heritage' and quoting a statement by a member of the British Parliament that 'quite frankly, Britain's heritage is at stake'. Another newspaper featured a caricature of a man sitting at table in the Dorchester grill, holding a Dorchester menu with a waiter telling him, 'Sirloin is off, sir. I recommend sheep's eyes or date pâté.' In front of the main entrance to the Dorchester Hotel, someone added to the sign: 'Please do not park cars', the words – 'OR CAMELS!'

Not all the British press published anti-Arab news and stories. As proof of the English sense of fair play, many took the side of the Arabs. Rather late in the day, *Punch*, on 20 September 1978, wrote under the headline 'Sheik-down': 'Native Londoners may be surprised to learn that most of our Arab visitors come here not to kill, maim or shoplift but, quite properly, to be robbed, ripped off and exploited by our hotels, shopkeepers, taxi-drivers, casinos and, of course, by the medical profession.'

The anti-Arab campaign produced few effective results in the property market. The Arabs were buying and the English were selling, and both sides were satisfied – although the former are no longer such an easy touch. Perhaps the same could be said of the Arab rush to buy race-horses!

However, the most venomous campaign against the Arabs had been unleashed after the dramatic rise in the price of oil in 1974 – before the outbreak of fighting in Lebanon in 1975 and the subsequent Arab *razzia* of London. The Arabs were then singled out as the greedy culprits responsible for all the evils of the rocketing oil prices. Very little was said against the non-Arab oil-producing countries, or against

213

those who had initiated the move to increase oil prices. The Arabs were portrayed as inhuman, freezing pensioners to death in the severe winter and closing schools and even hospitals which could not afford the exorbitant new price of oil. They were also accused of being responsible for inflation and for the economic crises in every country in the world, rich and poor alike.

One of the most widely circulated English newspapers asserted in 1974 that: 'The Arabs could buy all our banks with 11 days of surplus cash, ICI (Imperial Chemical Industries) could be bought in 15 days and British Leyland in 18.4 hours.' And, the newspaper emphasized, 'that's just using surplus cash'. The French magazine *L'Express*, quoting from the English press and converting the 'horror oil wealth statistics' to apply to France, fantasized by telling its readers that it would take the 'surplus of the oil-producing countries (OPEC) only 15.6 years to buy all the companies quoted in the stock exchanges of the world and 3.2 years to buy all the gold of the central banks at 850 francs the ounce. It could buy all the Champs-Élysées in ten days and the Société Tour Eiffel in only eight minutes!'

I did my best to explain, especially to the British public, the real facts, and to put before them some true statistics which should have quickly dispelled their misconceptions of grotesque Arab oil wealth and dismissed the accusations of its ruthless use against the West. I spoke in many symposia and societies which showed a willingness to listen. I stressed how, by comparison with the prices of other commodities, the price of oil was not unrealistically high. The price of a gallon of petrol in London was £1.57 while the price of a gallon of English bottled water was £2.52 and that of a gallon of foreign imported bottled water £3.52. Water is practically inexhaustible and cheap to extract and process, while oil is exhaustible and very costly to extract and process.

Moreover, I pointed out, the price paid by the British consumer for a gallon of petrol did not all go to the oil-producing countries. Sixty per cent of it represented taxes to the British government, 32 per cent to the oil companies, leaving only 8 per cent for the oil-producing countries. If 8 per cent produced enormous wealth for the Arabs, owners of the oil, then surely the West was not doing badly with its share of 92 per cent?

The problems and economic ills of the West were not all to be blamed on the price of oil and on the Arabs. The increase in the price of oil was not the only cause of inflation, of currency depreciation, of unemployment or of political, social and economic unrest. It certainly played a part, but only a small part. While the ailments of the West

214

and the price of oil were undoubtedly inter-related, little mention was made of all the other basic causes — industrial instability and falling production, soaring food prices (which have the biggest effect of all), speculation in raw materials, currency instability, political unrest and the lack of co-operation between the countries of the West.

According to the *OECD Economic Perspectives*, the direct incidence of the increase in crude oil prices on internal prices for most of OECD countries was 0.5 per cent, while, when the secondary effects of higher oil prices were taken into consideration, this incidence became 1 per cent. In the United Kingdom, the direct incidence of higher oil prices on the price level was 0.6 per cent; with secondary effects added this became 1.2 per cent. On the other hand, and according to estimates by OECD, food prices emerged as the single most important cause of increases in both consumer and wholesale prices.

In 1979, the total gross oil revenue of the Arab Middle East amounted to $98 billion, the gross revenues for the same year of the five largest multi-national corporations came to $287 billion, and the gross revenue of the seven international and largest oil companies, better known as the 'Seven Sisters', was $314 billion — over three times the oil revenue of all the Arab Middle East. If the oil revenue, in 1979, of the Arab Middle East — twenty-one countries with a total population of over 141 million — was less than a third of the revenue of the 'Seven Sisters', what was the basis for all the agitation and exaggeration about Arab wealth?

The Arab oil-producing countries had never had the slightest desire to weaken or damage the economy of the West. After all, the West remained the best and most important client for Arab oil. Similarly, since most of the Arab wealth was recycled to the West, it could not be in the interests of the West for that wealth to be diminished drastically or to fall into the hands of people who would not be so readily and naïvely interdependent with the West as the Arabs.

My arguments, reported in the English press, had little effect on the English public, and none whatever on the Arabs whom I was trying so hard to defend — with one exception. Nather Bey Al-Omari, of the Ministry of Foreign Affairs of the United Arab Emirates, wrote me a letter of appreciation and congratulation for what I had tried to achieve. He was only one out of 141 million Arabs, and the Arabs themselves continued to contribute to the widely publicized image of the 'Ugly Arab'. Stories of the Arabs' contempt for that 'undeserved' wealth and their love of throwing it around were being told everywhere — of Arabs losing millions in gambling (one was reported to have lost in London's casinos £26 million in two weeks), of Arabs distributing half-million-dollar diamond necklaces to 'call girls'. Thousands of similar stories portrayed the Arabs' love for displaying their wealth as well as their insensitivity to foreign reactions to their extravagant antics.

One of the most amusing stories was told to me by the director-general of Air France. After a dentist friend had attended to the teeth of an Arab oil sheikh, he sent a bill for $6,000 for his work and promptly received a cheque of $60,000 in settlement. Naturally he thought there was an error of one zero. He went to see the sheikh and pointed out the mistake through the sheikh's interpreter, only to be disturbed by the sheikh's apparent angry reaction. He was told, 'The sheikh never makes mistakes. The cheque is correct.' The dentist was shown out, bemused but happy at his patient's arrogant stupidity and contempt for the value of money.

17
Farewell to MEA

By the end of 1976, fighting had ceased, the airport was reopened and Lebanon had agreed to the presence of an Arab Deterrent Force to keep law and order. It looked as though there was a reasonable chance of the ordeal being over. The Lebanese heaved a sigh of relief and proceeded to repair the destruction and ravages of war. Middle East Airlines licked its wounds, resumed regular operations and in record time was back to normal. By the end of 1977, we had carried over a million passengers, nearly as many as in 1974. We had also made substantial profits.

The airline's problems appeared to be over, but sadly not mine. For several years, Ida, my wife, had been suffering from cancer and been forced to undergo a number of serious operations, which began with the removal of her right kidney in 1971. In the summer of 1973, part of her left lung was removed. In the summer of 1975, she underwent major intestinal surgery and, at the end of that year, a large tumour of the left adrenal gland was taken out. In September 1977, all the left lung was removed. After this operation, the doctors said Ida should not travel for at least six months. They were also afraid that, if the disease struck again, I would have to take her to the United States for chemotherapy since no further surgery was possible.

I was told that her life expectation was limited. Clearly, my duty was to be at her side. The doctors had, however, been wrong about surgery, for Ida did undergo another operation in London in 1978, when a tumour, together with the remaining adrenal gland, was removed. She again pulled through, thanks to Almighty God and her great courage.

Despite the severity of her illness, Ida had always urged me not to leave Middle East Airlines, especially in the years 1975 and 1976. But in 1977 I was determined to leave everything and be with her. I owed it to her, my life-partner, who had, for twenty-six years, patiently and uncomplainingly made endless sacrifices to enable me to attend to

217

Middle East Airlines and its everlasting problems. She both loved and hated MEA: loved it because she was well aware of my devotion to it and because she believed it was in the interests of Lebanon; hating it because of the amount of time I devoted to the airline at the cost of neglecting my family. More than once Ida had said, 'You have two wives, me and MEA, and sometimes I wonder which of us you love most.'

In deciding that the time had come when I should retire, I was also influenced by a number of other factors. I was getting tired of having to manage an airline that was constantly undercapitalized and with a shareholding circus deliberately refusing to come up with the much-needed support. It had been a long, hard twenty-six-year struggle, and the constant intrigues against the airline, especially intense in Lebanon itself, and the underhand fighting of unprincipled opponents had taken their toll. I was over sixty-eight years old, and the time had come when I thought it right to make way for the younger generation. I was also convinced that it is far better to leave when everybody wants you to stay than hold on until they want you to go.

There was, moreover, the election of Elias Sarkis as President of Lebanon in the wake of the 1975–6 fighting. Sarkis had first appeared on the public scene when chosen as chief aid to President Chehab. In no time at all, he had become the *éminence grise* of the Chehabist régime. Pierre Sadiq, the cartoonist of the newspaper *An-Nahar*, once portrayed him as the Sun King of France above the caption 'Ilyas XIV', the monarch who proclaimed, *'L'état, c'est moi.'* He was not a man with whom I could get along. He had strongly opposed the Air Liban merger and we did not see eye to eye over the take-over of LIA by MEA. We had other disagreements while I was a minister in 1965, and I resented the role he had played in the downfall of Intra. There was no love lost between us and the dislike was mutual.

Soon after he took office as President of Lebanon, we clashed over Hamat Airport, which had, during the civil war, been constructed in the Christian enclave of Lebanon. He wanted MEA also to operate out of that airport to ensure the safe air transport of Christians. He said that he could not allow their air transport to be subjected to the whims of the Palestinians who controlled the roads to the Beirut International Airport. Fully sympathetic to his point of view, I nevertheless told him that I strongly opposed his proposal since what he suggested was, in fact, partition. The pilots, engineers, traffic officers, caterers, porters and other personnel required for the Hamat operation would have to be

218

Christian, and it followed that those serving Beirut International Airport would be Mohammedans.

MEA had always been not only non-sectarian but one well-knitted Lebanese family. God willing, so long as I was head of the airline, I would do my best to keep it as such. I suggested we should do our utmost to convince all fighting factions to maintain Beirut International Airport as neutral and open. In addition, he could order the security forces to keep the access roads protected and safe. I said I would fight to my maximum ability any attempt to partition the airline.

'Why should you do so?' he asked. 'We have always had two airlines in the past, MEA and Air Liban.'

'True,' I replied, 'but you know better than anybody else my struggle to unite the Lebanese airlines. They have been merged for fourteen years already.'

'Quite right,' commented His Excellency, 'but we have Liban Air, which could be used.'

'That would be even worse,' I replied. 'To have Middle East Airlines operate from two airports would still give it a cloak of unity. To introduce Liban Air with its powerful politically religious owners would be final partition.'

As a possible solution, I suggested that we open negotiations with Cyprus Airways for a twice-weekly charter operation between Larnaca and Hamat, to continue until the end of the sectarian fighting in Lebanon. President Sarkis was unconvinced and insisted that, in his opinion, the only solution was to have two airlines, one serving East Beirut and the other West Beirut. I left the Presidential Palace certain that there would soon be trouble and MEA would suffer the consequences. This, in itself, was no adequate reason for me to retire. I had never worried at the prospect of clashes, even with the Presidents of Lebanon, and it would not have been the first time in the history of MEA that I had stood up to them. My first concern was my ailing wife, beside which all other considerations were secondary. As it happened, 'Operation Hamat' was thwarted by the Syrian forces, who occupied the airport to prevent its possible military use by the Israelis, and so MEA was spared partition.

After informing the management of MEA and the major shareholders of my intention to retire, I felt I should, out of courtesy, also inform the President of the Republic and the Prime Minister. I therefore went to the Presidential Palace to inform Elias Sarkis in person. I had always disliked the place. It had been designed by a firm of Swiss architects, commissioned by President Camille Chamoun, and I considered it the ugliest building in Lebanon. Its entrance looked like a European railway station. None of Chamoun's successors liked it either, and attempts were made to find another use for it, but although it was ostentatious, it was none the less too small to be used for anything else. Just to enter this modern monstrosity, so out of place in the beautiful Lebanese countryside, was depressing, and I used to wonder whether the ugliness of the building actually imposed itself on the ugly decisions taken by presidents living inside.

When I informed President Sarkis of my intention to retire, he made no comment, but I had a strong feeling that His Excellency was pleased. It was clear that, as a bachelor himself, he was totally incapable of understanding the family reasons that prompted the decision and was far more interested in the question of who should succeed me as head of MEA. He asked me to propose someone, and while I politely thanked him for asking my advice, I pointed out that it would be improper for an outgoing chairman to name his successor. That was a task for the board and shareholders.

The President then asked in particular about Asad Nasr. Anxious not to give the impression that I was playing the traditional Lebanese faction game by recommending a fellow Druze, I emphasized that Asad was a Greek Orthodox Lebanese, and not a member of the Druze Nasr family from Kfar Faqoud. Asked about his ability, I told His Excellency that unless Asad Nasr had been qualified I would never have kept him as my number two for the past sixteen years. The President then asked me to delay the election of my successor to give him time to think of a suitable candidate.

When I then called on the Prime Minister, Salim El-Hoss, the nephew of Fawzi El-Hoss, our old friend from the early days of MEA, the announcement was also received with indifference, albeit with the usual Lebanese courtesy. Prime Minister El-Hoss tried, but not very hard, to dissuade me, but I had the impression that he firmly believed no one was indispensable and that, as a Moslem, he believed the saying that, 'The Prophet Mohammed died but the Moslems did not die.'

I had built up Middle East Airlines from a small 'bazaar' company with a capital of one and a quarter million Lebanese pounds, hardly any assets, an annual revenue of only £L5 million and employing a handful of people, into one of the most prosperous and efficiently managed airlines in the world. I had set the pace in progressive labour relations and demonstrated what could be achieved, industrially and socially, in Lebanon. We were an example to follow, not only in Lebanon, but in the rest of the Arab world. At the time of my retirement, MEA had a capital of £L90 million, only £L15 million of which was actually paid up by the shareholders (the rest being converted profits), an annual revenue of £L509 million, 4,462 employees, and assets valued at over $1,000 million. During my time, the airline brought in a total revenue of nearly £L4 billion, more than half of which was spent in Lebanon.

In view of this, I found it strange that neither the President nor the Prime Minister thought fit to commemorate my departure with some official gesture. They did not even award me the kind of honour the Lebanese government customarily offered the departing regional manager of a foreign airline after a few years in Beirut, who would, as a matter of course, be decorated in an official ceremony for his services to Lebanese civil aviation.

It was not that I needed public honours. Many had already been heaped upon me, and I had been amply decorated for my contribution to civil aviation. President Suleiman Franjieh had honoured me with the 'Lebanese Ordre National du Cèdre, Grand Officier' and I had received highly distinguished decorations from many European, African and Arab countries. But the decoration of greatest significance to me, as a Druze, had been that of the Great Cross of the Order of Saint Sylvester conferred on me by His Holiness Pope Paul VI. I was the first Druze to be so honoured, and the ceremony took place at Bkerke, seat of the Maronite Patriarchate, in the presence of my friend, the late Patriarch Pierre-Paul Méhouchi.

Other recognitions included being elected Aviation Man of the Year 1974 by the Academy of Aviation and Space Medicine, receiving the Golden Medal of the European Travel Writers Union and the Pioneer Chain of the Windrose (Academica Cosmologica Nova), and being awarded the Golden Star, the highest decoration of the Association of Arab Tourist and Travel Agencies (AATTA). With such testimonials, I had more public honours than I possibly deserved. Nevertheless, it would be dishonest to say that I was not hurt by the Lebanese government deliberately ignoring all I had done for Middle East Airlines and Lebanese civil aviation.

The truth was that I had never been popular with politicians, nor had I courted their popularity by bestowing favours at the expense of the airline. It is always easy to become popular by giving people whatever they ask and never saying no. This was not my policy. The welfare of Middle East Airlines and its employees meant far more than personal popularity.

In Lebanon, favouritism, nepotism and back-scratching, colourfully known as 'bottom-pushing', has become part of the way of life.

221

Politicians used to crowd my office, my house in Shimlan, and even our farm in the country, begging for promotion and choice jobs for their relations and protégés among many other favours. I always refused such requests, explaining that ability and qualification were the only paths to success in MEA. This they would not understand, and some threatened dire reprisals.

Yet, while refusing the requests of the parasites and leeches, we did much for those who genuinely needed help. Genuine charitable organizations were generously aided. Deserving pilgrims were carried free to Rome and Mecca. Schools, sports clubs, sporting events and deserving sportsmen were assisted. And numerous other contributions and services were freely given, provided they were fully justifiable and in the interests of Lebanon and of Middle East Airlines. But in Lebanon, more than in most countries, politicians appreciate and applaud those who do them favours rather than those who serve the national interest. In view of the resentments I must have caused by always putting the interests of the airline first, it did not surprise me that the politicians should treat my decision to retire with such indifference.

Any disappointments I may have felt were more than compensated for by the sincere regrets at my departure and expressions of praise for my achievements that arrived in the great quantity of letters I received. These came not only from MEA staff, but also from Lebanese friends and from all over the Arab world, as well as from business executives and leading personalities in the sphere of aviation. The Beirut press also joined with the aviation specialist press to acknowledge my work. But the tribute I cherished most was a pledge signed by MEA employees in Lebanon promising, as a sign of affection and appreciation, to continue the good work we had done together for the country and the airline.

I called a board meeting on 2 December 1977, four weeks after my meeting with the President, and submitted my resignation. Fellow board members in the company urged me to stay in office, but when I insisted on retiring to spend more time with my suffering wife, they reluctantly accepted and, as a mark of their feelings, unanimously voted me honorary chairman for life. The majority shareholders, Intra Investment and Air France, made their acceptance of my resignation conditional on my remaining a board adviser. I agreed in the belief that my presence in this capacity would offer a shield of political protection for my successor, Asad Nasr, a man with no Lebanese political roots.

Asad Nasr had been elected chairman of MEA as planned. I was subsequently told that President Sarkis was displeased as I had not allowed him adequate time to choose his candidate. One month in the

Lebanese political game was, it seems, hardly enough. Moreover, many people believed, and some still believe, that I arranged the succession. That I did and the fact that Asad Nasr had served under me as general manager for a long time, and that I had earlier recommended him for election to the board, and later to the post of deputy chairman, must have given credence to this belief. Restricting the period of politicking for the post to four weeks no doubt also helped.

Electing Asad Nasr, although justified at the time, was greatly resented by the hopefuls for the job in MEA, in Intra and in Lebanon at large. A phenomenon, possibly unique to Lebanon, is the belief of any person with secondary education or higher that he is qualified to fill any post in the country if he plays his political cards well. Electing Asad Nasr, the number two in the airline, had been a victory over the hopefuls and a precedent in MEA which I hoped would be followed in electing future chairmen from within the airline's qualified executives. I was also happy to continue my life with MEA as a board adviser to assist Asad Nasr in dealing with the complex problems of the chairmanship.

In this I was mistaken. Before long Asad Nasr told me he had no need for my assistance and that he was determined to prove, both to himself and to everybody else, that he could run the company successfully without the help of Sheikh Najib Alamuddin. I wished him the best of Lebanese luck, which I felt sure he would need far sooner than he imagined, and felt deeply disappointed and saddened by his behaviour. My first impulse was to resign immediately as board adviser, but I decided, on further consideration, to wait so as not to destabilize the airline and the employees, who had, when the news of my retirement as chairman spread, come to me individually, in groups and as a union, to plead with me not to leave. They had been greatly relieved when I had told them that I would, as board adviser, remain with them and MEA. Therefore I stayed on, but distanced myself from the new chairman.

I sometimes regret, for the sake of MEA, that there never seemed to be an opportunity to pass on the benefit of my long experience as chairman in the extraordinary business of running an airline in faction-torn Lebanon and the aviation jungle of the Arab world. I had had to learn the hard way, starting from scratch, and it seemed a pity not to be able to transmit that valuable knowledge of the quirks of human behaviour. Asad Nasr was, during his sixteen years as general manager, kept busy in the day-to-day operation of the airline and never aware of the complex functions of the chairman. Also he had frequently told me that he hated to deal with politicians. He preferred to learn the

معالي الشيخ نجيب علم الدين الجزيل الأحـترام

شيخنا العـزيز

إذا نحن حاولنا أن نجمع ما نكنّه لك من حبّ وتقدير وعرفان بالجميل
في هـذه الكلمات القصيرة ، نكون مثل من يحاول أن يجمع ماء البحر في
كوب صغـير .

التاريخ وحده قادرٌ على رسم الأمور بأحجامها ، فبين يديك البيضاء ترعرع
طيران الشرق الأوسط ، وبصدرك احتمى وبحكمتك وهداك اشتـدّ
ساعده ، وصار يضاهي الأحسن ، بل وإنّه أصبح الأحسن بالنسبة للبنان
ولنا نفخـر به ونلوذ بحماه .

هـذا كان الماضي الذي رسمتهُ لنا فبنيناه ، والآن كما علمتنا ننظـر
الى المستقبل حاملين الامانة التي تركتها لنا على الدرب الطويل وكلنا
تفاؤلٌ وثقةٌ بوجودك معـنا دائمًا مرشـدًا وموجّهًا تشـدّ من أزرنا
وتوجّـه خطـانا .

كلمتنا هـذه ليست وداعًا ، بل انتقال الأمن مرحلةٍ مرّت الى
مرحلةٍ نريد ان نبدأها بعهـدٍ امام الله وامامك بان نقوم بواجبنا
الكامـل نجـاه وطننا وشركتنا ، طالبين من المولى تعالى ان
يبقيك معنا وان يديم لك الصحة والسعادة ، ولشـركتنا
الازدهار .

التواقيع ـــ

Figure 2. The pledge presented to Sheikh Najib on his retirement from MEA, signed by all the airline's employees in Lebanon. This translation attempts to capture the flavour of the emotional aspect of the Arabic language:

'We cannot attempt, in only a few words, to express all the love we feel for you, or our appreciation and gratitude. To do so would be like trying to contain the waters of the sea in a small cup.

'Only history is able to portray deeds in their right perspective. To you goes the credit for the development and growth of Middle East Airlines, and the guarding of its interests. Your wisdom and unerring judgement have contributed to its strength and its position among the world's best airlines. In fact, it is in our eyes the best for ourselves and for Lebanon, for which we are proud, and we look to it for protection.

'This was the past you planned for us and which we built together, and now, as you taught us, we look to the future with the faith you left us to carry on along the road ahead. We are full of optimism and confidence that you will continue to be with us, a constant adviser and teacher, supporting and guiding us.

'Therefore these words are no farewell, but only a step from the past to the future. We pledge before God and you that we will carry out our full duties to our country and to our company, praying to God Almighty to keep you with us and grant to you health and happiness, and to our company success and prosperity.'

hard way, and soon after his election became deeply enmeshed with the politicians he so disliked.

It became clear the following year, 1978, that those who were intent on destroying Lebanon had no wish for the hopes of peace in the country to bear fruit. The situation was deteriorating rapidly, and before long fighting broke out with renewed intensity. Against this backdrop of violence and suffering, fresh troubles began for MEA. A new chairman of Intra made his appearance when Chafic Mouharram replaced Lucien Dahdah.

Lucien had known how to delegate authority and had intelligently supervised and supported the management of all the Intra companies under his wing. On the board of MEA, he was helpful and co-operative, though alert and constructively critical when necessary. His departure was a loss to the airline.

Chafic Mouharram, a product of the French Polytechnic in civil engineering, had acted as President Chehab's technical adviser, and when the General decided not to run for a second term, had been appointed deputy governor of the Central Bank. After the election of Elias Sarkis, governor of the Central Bank, to the presidency in 1976, Chafic Mouharram was, on the basis of seniority, the most likely candidate to become governor. It was not to be and he had to step aside for a co-religionist friend of the President. The governor of the Central Bank had to be a Christian, and Mouharram was a Moslem. To make amends, and because he was also a close friend of Elias Sarkis, he was appointed chairman of Intra over the heads of senior Intra hopefuls.

Chafic Mouharram and I had a cool acquaintance. Nevertheless, I was pleased for MEA's sake that he and Asad Nasr were known to be good friends. But, for reasons I could not fathom at the time, he surprised everyone by starting a quarrel with Asad Nasr at his first board meeting. This hostility soon developed into a positive feud and board discussions were transformed into a running battle between the chairmen of MEA and Intra.

In my capacity as board adviser, I took the initiative in trying to prevent the paralysis of the company as a result of these rows. I suggested to Mouharram that, before each meeting, I should meet him and go through the agenda to explain its subjects and so narrow any areas of misunderstanding between him and Asad Nasr. He politely declined my offer, preferring confrontation to peace at board meetings. He was suspicious of every decision and appeared to have little faith in either the board or the management of MEA. I hoped that, given time and a greater understanding of the airline business, his attitude might

226

change. But it was not to be, and arguments between the chairmen grew more personal and acrimonious. Chafic Mouharram seemed determined to fight Asad Nasr and to act as if Intra and Middle East Airlines were his own to do what he liked with.

The position of board adviser does not exist in Lebanese Commercial Law, nor in the Articles of Association of Middle East Airlines. It was a very special case conceived by the majority shareholders since they were convinced of the importance of my assistance to the new chairman and my stabilizing influence on the airline and its employees. The functions of the position were not defined because the board and I assumed that, after the long, successful collaboration between me and Asad Nasr, no definition would be really necessary. Unfortunately, matters turned out otherwise. Asad Nasr declined my assistance and even resented it. And, without a close collaboration with the chairman, the position of board adviser became practically impossible. Should the chairman submit a recommendation to the board with which the adviser disagreed, it placed the latter in a difficult position. He had either to oppose the recommendation and undermine the authority of the chairman or else support the recommendation against his better judgement – something I would never have done.

The first serious trouble between myself and Asad Nasr began early in 1978, soon after his election, when I opposed an over-ambitious seven-year plan to purchase an additional five Boeing 747 jumbo jets or their equivalent. With war having erupted again in Lebanon, I firmly believed the time was inopportune for such a costly expansion. Things finally came to a head when a request was made by MEA on 4 June 1979 to the US Export-Import Bank (Eximbank) for a huge loan to finance the purchase of new aircraft. MEA's letter to Eximbank was a formal application for a loan to finance an initial purchase of up to eight aircraft of US manufacture at a total price of $403,915,000 and an option for a further eleven aircraft at an additional cost of $718,403,000. Eximbank approved credits for the entire transaction of eight plus eleven option aircraft as one package, making MEA's total borrowing the colossal sum of $1,222,318,000.

The management of MEA requested Eximbank for this loan without the approval or knowledge of the board. I likewise was not consulted, or even informed, perhaps for fear of my opposition to such a foolhardy proposal. A company operating out of war-torn Lebanon, with a capital of less than $30 million and its financial resources stretched to the limit, would, to say the least, be most unwise even to think of committing itself to a loan of nearly one and a quarter billion dollars.

I felt, having been the builder of the airline and the new chairman's boss for over twenty-two years, that keeping me in the dark was a deliberate insult that violated my functions as board adviser. I also knew that my advice on various other important matters had gone unheeded, and even on occasions been deliberately removed from the board minutes. In such circumstances, I could not conceivably continue to serve the airline. The choice facing me was either to denounce the chairman publicly and make a fight of it, or simply to resign. It was not an easy decision, for I was deeply disturbed by the untimely request for such a large financial commitment and the on-going battle between Asad Nasr and Chafic Mouharram, and was reluctant to make matters worse by introducing a new dimension.

Finally, and out of consideration for the stability of MEA, I decided to resign quietly on 5 July 1979, without voicing misgivings or making any public declaration. I had not spent all those years building a successful company to play a part in damaging it now I was in retirement. I remained as honorary chairman, watching from a distance and very conscious that, although I had built the airline, I ceased being responsible for it at the moment when I resigned in December 1977.

Nevertheless, many believed I was still advising the board of MEA and its chairman, for they had no reason to think otherwise. They could not believe that my relationship with Asad Nasr could ever turn sour. I can truly say, however, that, apart from opposing the seven-year plan, and later the so-called 'Deal of the Century' (the story of which is told in the following chapter), I played no part in whatever happened in Middle East Airlines after my resignation in December 1977. Asad Nasr, who replaced me in that office, deliberately chose to bear full responsibility. To him must go the credit for any successes of MEA between then and his departure in 1982; on his shoulders, too, must lie the responsibility for any setbacks and failures.

18

The Boeing Affair

It is quite customary for airlines to have a special secret fund for use in safeguarding the company's interests when out-of-the-ordinary payments need to be made. Some airlines call the fund a *caisse noire*, others call it a 'special fund', 'slush fund' or 'development costs'.

As far back as 1956, the MEA board had delegated to me, as chairman, annual authority to make certain essential payments under the heading of 'development costs'. In 1973, Asad Nasr also received from the board a similar authority as general manager. No restrictions were placed on the sums spent or on the purposes of expenditure. Theoretically, the general manager and I were separately empowered, under development costs, to pay any amount of money, provided we considered that such payments were in the interest of the company. In practice, because of the accounting procedures used, such payments had to be both small and unobtrusive. Any disbursement of a large sum without supporting documentation could have led to wild speculation which might have damaged the company.

What we needed to face the political turmoil in the 1970s was a really secret *caisse noire*, so that essential payments might be made in the strictest confidence. This became an essential with MEA especially at risk as its headquarters at Beirut International Airport became surrounded by the bases and camps of militant and heavily armed organizations. The factor, however, that made the operation of such a special fund by normal board decision quite impossible was the board's composition. First, there was the presence of the representatives of four different countries, who, in the explosive situation prevailing in Lebanon, would never have approved the establishment of a *caisse noire* without the prior approval of their respective governments. And would all these governments have approved the payment of cash subsidies to any of the political factions involved in the fighting in Lebanon? And who knew what governments were in fact already supporting which faction?

Secondly, the Lebanese members of the board were Christians, Moslems and Druzes. Each one of them was prominent in his religious community. Two of the Maronite Christian members were serious contenders for the presidency of Lebanon and, with the other members, were directly or indirectly involved in factional Lebanese politics. All were closely associated with their own communities' political feudal lords, who seemed, at the time, to be busy preparing for civil war. Consequently, there was a universal demand for financial assistance for the cause — their particular cause. Had we asked these members to approve a *caisse noire* and the subsequent payments from it, the resulting political tug-of-war, not to mention possible confrontations within the board, would have been most embarrassing to everyone and could have put an end to the *caisse noire* and its benefits. There was also the risk of sectarian split in the board, which could overflow into the company as a whole and destroy its Lebanese unity of which we were so proud.

The dilemma became more acute after the 1973 confrontation between the Lebanese Army and the Palestinians. The ostrich-like fiasco compromise imposed on the Lebanese government triggered an arms race between all political parties, religious factions, militias and neo-militias. All were preparing for war and needed funds badly. Urgent requests for financial assistance poured in from all sides, especially as war funds from outside Lebanon had only begun to trickle in. They only became a torrent much later, after universal fighting broke out.

Some requests were accompanied by hints about what might happen if MEA failed to comply; in other cases, the threats were more explicit and left little doubt they would be carried out. Without going into details, I can say now that every faction in Lebanon at one time or another made demands. Acutely conscious of the lack of any secret fund to meet such demands, we had to grant services in kind to those who threatened the airline. But, as it began to be clear that Lebanon was moving towards civil war, MEA's need for a real *caisse noire* was increasingly urgent. It was quite obvious that we would not be able to talk our way out of pressing demands for ever.

An opportunity presented itself to put things right as a result of MEA's negotiations in 1974 to purchase three 747 jumbo jets from Boeing. Asad Nasr, then general manager, who was conducting the negotiations, sensed that there was within this deal a chance at last to set up an emergency secret fund for MEA. Boeing had no official agent in Lebanon, which made it possible to arrange for the commission on the sale of three aircraft, that would normally have gone to such an agent, to be paid instead to MEA.

Asad Nasr discussed the proposal with me, and I authorized him to negotiate the deal, provided that Boeing was told clearly that the agent's commission money was to be used to serve the interests of MEA and would not benefit anyone in the company. He was also to make sure that Boeing, to recover the payment, did not increase the price of the aircraft, spares and equipment under the current agreement, or those which might be bought in the future. To this end, two contractual letters were obtained from Boeing as an integral part of the purchase contract. In the first, Boeing gave an assurance that their prices, terms and conditions were no less favourable than to other purchasers. In the second, they assured us of most-favoured customer treatment and stated that they would not increase the price of future MEA purchases to cover extraordinary items on the present purchase — a clear reference to the commission paid to MEA. Finally, Asad Nasr told me he had assured Boeing, leaving no possible doubt, that this money would not benefit any airline employee, but would be used to protect MEA's interests.

Having obtained these letters, an agreement was concluded between the Boeing Company, our MEA bankers (the Swiss Bank Corporation) and Resora, a Lichtenstein establishment wholly owned by the Swiss Bank Corporation. Resora was paid by Boeing the sum of $3.6 million, negotiations being conducted by Asad Nasr at the highest levels of management in Boeing and the Swiss Bank Corporation. The chairman of Boeing, its treasurer and the joint general-managers of the Swiss Bank Corporation in Geneva were all party to the agreement. The Swiss Bank Corporation confirmed that the arrangement was legal and proper in Switzerland, and it was confirmed that such an arrangement was also legal and proper in American law. Resora was then asked to place $2.4 million at my disposal for the *caisse noire* and $1.2 million at the disposal of Asad Nasr. This arrangement was arrived at so that he could meet all 'serious demands' promptly in the event of them being made while I was out of the country. During this period, I was spending as much time as I could by the side of my wife, who was seriously ill in Europe.

We were happy with the deal and congratulated ourselves on having taken prudent measures to safeguard the airline. The long-awaited *caisse noire* had thus been finally established with funds obtained from outside the company. Without it, the airline would never have survived. It was used with the utmost care and secrecy, and the results spoke for themselves. MEA's fleet, stores, workshops and installations, worth over $1,000 million, survived the civil war of 1975–76 intact, while everything else around the airport, whether privately or government-owned, was looted or destroyed. At times the very lives of our staff were at stake and could be saved only by paying up. MEA was by no means the only organization to resort to such unsavoury methods to survive those lawless years. In Beirut, no single commercial or industrial group, no building or shop, remained intact unless it had paid for its survival.

It may puzzle readers that, at this time of great danger in Lebanon and even as we were taking emergency measures to protect the very existence of the airline, we should none the less have taken the bold step, in 1974, of approving the purchase of these costly Boeing jumbo airliners. I can explain the paradox by recalling that, despite the political instability in Lebanon and in the Middle East as a whole, traffic both in passengers and freight was booming. Business was so good that MEA had introduced a second daily flight on the Beirut–London service. It was as clear as daylight that the service could be made much more profitable by operating one large-capacity aircraft instead of two smaller ones at a time of high fuel costs. Studies of air traffic trends confirmed the need for large-capacity aircraft, and the Boeing 747 was the best available on the market.

But this commercial need had to be balanced against our fears about the political situation in Lebanon. Forward planning was necessary, and, anxious as we were about the future, it was still not totally certain that large-scale civil war would break out. In any event, we considered the purchase of the 747s to be a good investment – a judgement that proved well justified, for ownership of those three aircraft actually saved MEA after civil war closed down Beirut International Airport for nearly six months in 1976, when, unable to operate them ourselves, we leased two to Saudia, the Saudi Arabian airline, and the third to Air France for use by Air Gabon, the African airline. This arrangement was possible because the 747 combis – a combination of passenger and cargo capability – were greatly in demand. Our ability to lease them provided not only badly needed revenue but also employment for more than 500 MEA personnel. It continued until 1979, when the management of MEA terminated the lease with Saudia as a show of confidence in the country and the government of the day.

When, during the 1980s, MEA considered selling one or more of the 747s, offers were received from the Boeing Company and a few other purchasers of $30 million per aircraft. Considering that MEA had originally paid a little over $30 million for each, the price offered after more than seven years of useful and hard service proved what an excellent choice and wise purchase these aircraft had been. It was not the undoubted success of our purchase of these aircraft which attracted public attention and comment, however, but the creation of the *caisse noire* which arose out of the deal. While the establishment of a *caisse noire* should have been an item of normal business – especially in the circumstances prevailing in Lebanon – a number of strange events turned the affair into a *cause célèbre*.

The affair began when the American authority which supervises public companies, the Securities and Exchange Commission (SEC), filed a complaint against Boeing with respect to payments by the company in connection with its foreign sales. It was reported that the commission specifically wanted information on sales to the following fourteen airlines: Air Canada, Air France, Air India, Air Nippon, Egyptair, Middle East Airlines, New Zealand Airlines, Olympic Airways, Royal Air Maroc, Sabena, Syrian Arab Airlines, TAP, Varig and Iberia.

Boeing opted for a settlement with SEC and, as part of that settlement, filed its report No. 8–K, dated 28 July 1978, describing some payments they had made and identifying some of the countries concerned, but leaving out the names of the people involved. Boeing picked out only Egyptair, Syrian Arab Airlines, Middle East Airlines and Olympic Airways of the aforementioned fourteen airlines on which SEC had asked for specific information, and added to these four the sale to airlines of Saudi Arabia, Kuwait, United Arab Emirates, Iran, Korea, Nepal, and a mysterious country and airline which Boeing refrained from naming or identifying, simply calling it 'another country'. This made eleven airlines in all, seven being Arab airlines, and an eighth, Sudan Airways, also being mentioned in connection with payments made to a general consultant.

Boeing stated in its report that, as part of the settlement, SEC had required the company to describe transactions with the aforementioned eleven airlines, including the seven Arab. No reason was given for SEC's selection of these particular customers of Boeing. The Arabs, it seems, merited SEC's special attention. But the most mysterious information supplied by Boeing concerned a transaction described on page 8 in the following manner: 'In another country the Company engaged as consultant an individual who was a member of the ruling political party and who, after the initial sales were made, became a Government official. This individual was paid commissions of $3.3 million on aircraft sales to a government-owned airline of such country.'

What was the name of that country and its airline, and why did it enjoy immunity from being named like the others? Why was it spared the smear of suspicion? Why should its name be withheld, and not that of Saudi Arabia, for example, a staunch friend of the United States that has given billions of dollars of business to the Boeing Company? The cover-up for the favoured country emerged loud and clear, but Boeing's coyness about it was followed in the report by the case of the deal that never was: 'In connection with a proposal to sell aircraft to an airline in the United Arab Emirates an individual, whom a company salesman believed to be an official of one of the states which owned the airline and influential as to any decision to purchase the aircraft, demanded and the Company agreed to pay such individual a commission if a sale were consummated. The sale was not consummated and no payments were made by the Company to that individual.' Why was it necessary to mention a case that never happened? Could it have been simply to add one more Arab country to the other six as part of an attempt to implicate and vilify the Arabs?

The most detailed description of all the transactions was the payment made to a 'privately owned airline in Lebanon'. The account ended with the statement: 'The airline official who advised the Company of the requirement has assured the Company that the money did not benefit any airline employee.' Those involved with the deal in the Boeing Company knew very well that the money did not benefit any employee and was meant to serve only the interests of MEA. Boeing confirmed this later to Chafic Mouharram, then chairman of Intra, in a letter of 12 July 1979 which stated: 'interrogation of all involved company employees by Boeing and by several United States Government agencies had produced no evidence of improper use of funds'.

With such positive evidence at its disposal, it seems extraordinary that Boeing should include the MEA purchase of the three 747s in its report to the SEC. Boeing, however, explained the reason for its action in the same letter to Mouharram: 'The second paragraph beginning on page 9 of the Form 8–K report refers to the transaction involving the sale of three 747 aircraft to MEA. This paragraph was included in the report at the insistence of SEC lawyers as a condition of settlement.'

It seems curious that the Middle East Airlines transaction should be considered of such special importance that the lawyers of SEC made its inclusion in the Boeing report a mandatory condition of the settlement. It is difficult to see what MEA could possibly have done to excite the interest of these American lawyers, especially since MEA was a foreign private company with no government connection, and as such fell under no US legislation, which forbids the payment of 'incentives' only to officials of foreign governments. Was there a special reason, known only to the SEC lawyers, why MEA should be punished?

The answer came loud and clear when President Reagan and his administration gave retaliation instructions for a more recent hijacking to Beirut of a TWA flight on its way from Athens to Rome, with over forty Americans taken as hostages. The punishment was directed not at the hijackers nor at the Lebanese government, which was responsible for the security (or lack of it) at Beirut International Airport, but at Middle East Airlines, the privately owned company and an innocent bystander in the affair. MEA's traffic rights to the United States were arbitrarily cancelled and America's allies were asked to do the same. It was reminiscent of how, in the 1968 Israeli raid on Beirut International Airport, the innocent MEA was similarly singled out for punishment and destruction.

Even as the Security Exchange Commission was probing the sales transactions of Boeing, so the US Department of Justice initiated an investigation of the Boeing Company for fraud against the United States, involving possible false statements made by Boeing to the Export-Import Bank to enable MEA to obtain financing for the purchase of the three Boeing 747s. The banks now accused Boeing of signing a false certificate that no improper commissions were paid, and claimed it would not have granted the loan had it known of any improper payments. The Department of Justice listed the names of minor executives of Boeing (omitting the important ones), executives of the Swiss Bank Corporation and Asad Nasr, general manager of MEA, as the persons involved in this possible fraud.

'It is extremely odd that the Department of Justice should have named the General Manager of Middle East Airlines. There was no precedent for a Department of Justice prosecution based on nothing more than a suspicion of kick-backs to officials of a foreign private company, such as Middle East Airlines.' This was the opinion of the well-known Washington lawyers, Arnold and Porter, conveyed in their letter of 8 January 1979 to the lawyers of the Swiss Bank Corporation. There must have been a special reason for the Department of Justice taking this unprecedented action, but, distressing as the American commotion over the international aircraft sales of the Boeing Company was to MEA, it made no great impact on public opinion in Lebanon itself at the time.

Far more excitement was generated nearly a year later by Asad Nasr's announcement that Middle East Airlines had embarked on a fleet replacement plan involving the purchase of nineteen modern aircraft at a cost of over $1 billion. He also announced that he had warned aircraft manufacturers not to employ agents, representatives, consultants or any other intermediaries for this deal unless they had been in the service of the manufacturers for at least the previous five consecutive years. It was a ruling that excluded practically everybody in Lebanon.

The media hailed the news of the fleet replacement as the 'Deal of the Century', for it was by far the biggest purchase contract ever to be concluded in Lebanon by a private concern, or even by the Lebanese government. It was sensational news which, in the circumstances prevailing in Lebanon, demonstrated the sort of panache which appealed to popular imagination. However, Asad Nasr's restrictions on intermediaries aroused anger and controversy, Lebanon's economy being largely based on the sale of services — any services. Name what you want to buy or sell, and many Lebanese will step forward as agents to help you with the deal. There are no limits to the nature of the services that may be bought and sold.

The news of a deal in the making for $1 billion brought with it an expectation of glittering financial prizes for scores of influential Lebanese intermediaries. The announcement of the 'Deal of the Century' was followed by news that finance was available for the whole deal. Would-be intermediaries were thus convinced that fortunes lay within their reach, anticipating a minimum commission of between $50 and $60 million. There was also the possibility of more rich pickings on further aircraft sales in the region, should the inter-mediaries' services to the lucky manufacturer be successful in Lebanon.

Small wonder, therefore, that Asad Nasr's restrictions on those who might act as agents brought the most venomous reaction from the would-be intermediaries, who saw themselves deprived of the opportunity of a lifetime. They declared war against the restrictions and against the man who had dared to impose them. A ferocious battle also began among the manufacturers, for, apart from the important sale to Middle East Airlines, the manufacturers knew, from past experience, that the aircraft chosen by MEA would also be bought by other Arab airlines.

The competition was fiercest between the Americans and the European Airbus Industries, as was demonstrated when the US Export-Import Bank approved a loan to MEA of $953, 970,300, nearly a billion dollars, to buy American-built aircraft for Asad Nasr's 'Deal of the Century'. Eximbank did not this time ask MEA for a guarantor, despite Lebanon being in a horrific and destructive civil war, a most generous commitment in sharp contrast to the bank's attitude of

November 1974, when it had insisted on a guarantee from a consortium of international banks for a small loan of only $43 million to enable MEA to buy the three Boeing 747s at a time when Lebanon and MEA were basking in the sunshine of economic and financial prosperity. In its letter of 8 November 1979, informing the House of Representatives of its massive credit to MEA, Eximbank claimed that it was motivated by the 'intense competition from Airbus Industries and its subsidized credits from government sources'.

The manufacturers were well aware of Asad Nasr's computerized formula, known as ASNA, which is supposed to determine quickly the type of aircraft most suitable for an airline's operation, thus saving months of manual calculation. They must therefore have known, long before the date of the official submission of offers, which aircraft had been chosen by Asad Nasr and MEA. In actual fact, a particular American aircraft was named as MEA's choice in pre-purchasing gossip and it was therefore not surprising that some of the unlucky manufacturers became just as angry with Asad Nasr as were the intermediaries. It was reported that one manufacturer in particular was furious at being let down.

Rumours quickly spread that Asad Nasr had lost favour because of his opposition to intermediaries and might, as a result, be removed. This started an unseemly scramble among dozens of hopeful candidates to replace him, the MEA chairmanship being the most coveted position in Lebanon. So it was no wonder that practically all the Lebanese MEA board members, and most of those on the Intra board, joined the campaign against Asad Nasr and began offering themselves and manoeuvring for the appointment. They were soon joined in the rush by scores of Lebanese outsiders.

The wolf-pack hunting the chairmanship joined the angry aircraft manufacturers and the intermediaries in an unholy alliance. Their interests, although basically different, would, in their opinion, best be served by the removal of Asad Nasr. It was not that any of the parties wished harm to Middle East Airlines. On the contrary, their interests, though different and separate, were best served by a prosperous airline. They were, however, manipulated by the enemies of Lebanon, and ruthlessly used, as eventually emerged.

It was against this background, hardly a month after Asad Nasr's announcement of the 'Deal of the Century', that what came to be known as the 'Boeing Affair' exploded in the Lebanese press — four years after the purchase of the three jumbos and one after it had first been unobtrusively reported in the Beirut newspapers. Now things were different, and the story was presented in a maliciously contrived campaign of scandal. It derived from an article which had appeared in the Swiss newspaper *Tages-Anzeiger*, providing details of payments made by Boeing to Resora through the Swiss Bank Corporation. Significantly, the only person to be mentioned by name was Asad Nasr, a man little known in Switzerland. There was absolutely no mention of Swiss executives or of the top men in Boeing, all of whom, being much more prominent internationally, should have merited inclusion in a sensational article. The story was being processed solely for Lebanese consumption.

My own inquiries produced indications that it had been a representative of an aircraft manufacturer who provided the story to the Swiss paper and then masterminded a press campaign against Asad Nasr which was taken up in Lebanon. As the proprietor-editor of a Lebanese magazine told me, the same manufacturer provided him with the Swiss-launched story, together with a heavily subsidized request to make the best possible use of it – which he did! The effect, of course, was to revive and draw public attention to the arrangement with Boeing, not through a true and honest story, but one shrouded in insinuations and hints of questionable dealings. The press campaign was stepped up and strengthened by a whispering campaign.

The MEA board now had to be told the true story. At the request of Asad Nasr, the board decided at its 25 May 1979 meeting to appoint a committee to carry out an administrative investigation of the Boeing affair, consisting of Air France, represented by Gilbert Pérol, its director-general, and Intra, represented by Chafic Mouharram, its chairman. By limiting the committee to two who, between them, controlled most of the shareholding of MEA, Asad Nasr no doubt hoped that the matter could remain confidential so that the *caisse noire* might continue to be used in the interests of the airline. He knew that Air France, in particular, had extensive knowledge of the use of such funds in the aviation industry, and no doubt felt its director-general would properly appreciate the need for them. He also must have been encouraged by the fact that he had told Chafic Mouharram, as early as July 1978, of Boeing's statement to the SEC about MEA, and had given him a copy sent by Boeing, who expressed regrets at being coerced into including it in their report. Chafic Mouharram seemed not unduly concerned at the time, and raised no questions.

Asad Nasr and I sought to arrange a meeting with the two-man committee to brief them on the whole affair and its origin. This was arranged to take place on 12 June 1979, and we were confident that as

238

soon as the committee was aware of the facts, it would issue a statement to the board to put an end to harmful gossip and rumours. That meeting never took place. It was pre-empted by letters dated 9 June, sent to Asad Nasr and each board member, one also being addressed to me in my capacity as chairman at the time of the Boeing purchase in 1974. The letters, couched in legal terms and signed by Chafic Mouharram on behalf of the investigation committee, requested a written reply detailing all available information on the purchase of the three Boeing 747s. We were also asked to comment on the SEC report and the press reaction.

In the case of Asad Nasr, who had conducted all technical, economic and financial studies and subsequent negotiations for the purchase of the Boeing 747s, the committee did not insist on a reply to their letter. Instead, they asked him to forward to Intra all files relevant to the purchase together with related board minutes.

Chafic Mouharram also wrote to the Boeing Company on 14 June, asking for more information on their disclosure to the SEC in connection with 'aircraft sales to a privately owned airline based in Lebanon'. In addition, he asked Boeing about the disclosures in the *Tages-Anzeiger* newspaper. When Boeing replied on 12 July, they emphasized the following points. First, 'Interrogation of all involved Boeing Company employees by Boeing and by several United States Agencies has produced no evidence of improper use of funds.' Secondly, 'The price and terms of this sale were highly favourable to MEA and concessions were made to MEA in the negotiations that were not made available to other 747 customers during the comparable period.' Thirdly, 'Boeing records reflected that MEA was represented by Mr Asad Nasr, who was responsible for all aspects of the transaction from detailed technical specifications to financial terms and conditions.'

In the same letter, Boeing went on to say: 'The newspaper report referred to in your letter quotes from a report filed by Boeing with the United States Securities and Exchange Commission on July 28, 1978 in connection with its settlement with SEC.' Boeing enclosed a copy of that report.

It seemed mystifying that, whereas the *Tages-Anzeiger* article named Asad Nasr as the MEA official implicated in the affair, the Boeing report to SEC mentioned only 'an airline official' and named no one. Someone must therefore have supplied *Tages-Anzeiger* with the name.

In due course, the replies from board members, together with Boeing's letter and its enclosures and the files and documents supplied by Asad Nasr, were passed to a retired judge, Boutros Nujaim, who was covertly appointed to assist the committee in its investigation. The choice of Judge Nujaim awakened suspicion, since he knew nothing about aviation. He seemed an odd choice to assess such matters, especially as the mandate of the committee was to carry out an administrative not a judicial investigation. The committee would have done better to call in an aviation expert from Air France. Judge Nujaim's appointment seemed to provide the first sign that Chafic Mouharram of Intra really intended to use the business of the *caisse noire* in his vendetta against Asad Nasr, and at the time it never crossed my mind that the implications were anything more sinister.

The meeting we were anxious to have with the committee, although of vital importance, was repeatedly delayed despite reminders. They did not meet with me until 17 August, a few days after Asad Nasr. At least we were now able to explain why MEA needed a *caisse noire*, how it was established, and how administered for the protection of the company and its employees. We could point out how every effort had been made to minimize payments and keep the situation under control, and how, as a result, more than $2.4 million out of the original $3.6 million were still in the *caisse noire*.

The committee was fully satisfied with these explanations. The only comment directed at me came from Chafic Mouharram, when he said: 'Had I been in your place, I would not have exposed myself to possible criticism in order to save Middle East Airlines.'

'Of course not,' I replied, 'because you could never be in my place. Middle East Airlines is my company. I nurtured it from a small local airline to one of the most efficient and profitable international airlines. You do not have the same relationship with MEA that I have, and you never will. Of course you would not do what I have done. MEA means little to you but much to me. And what was there to criticize?' I continued. 'My only concern at the time was to save Middle East Airlines, and I acted without any thought of possible criticism or of praise and gratitude.'

With this exchange of personal views, my meeting with the committee was concluded. It now had all the facts, and we felt sure it would report its findings to the MEA board at once. But now there were further numerous pretexts and excuses for delay, the most plausible being Air France's rejection of a draft report by the Intra representative, Mouharram, who claimed he must consult his board, which met only once a month, as well as the Lebanese authorities, before he could agree to any change in it. Words, phrases, sentences and even question marks became the subject of long debates. Exasperated, Air France threatened

240

to issue its separate and independent report, only to be told that the President of Lebanon wished to see a joint report submitted. When Pérol was asked to pay a special visit to Beirut to see President Elias Sarkis, Air France backed down. The committee's joint report then took seven months and ten days to produce, so giving plenty of time for the conspiracy to continue.

First on the list of dirty tricks came the notorious Nujaim Report, completed on 20 August 1979, three days after my meeting with the committee, but then kept secret for months, except when slyly leaked to various ill-intentioned people and later to the press. In due course, it became clear that Boutros Nujaim had been deliberately manipulated and provided with false information, so that a completely fraudulent report could emerge. Its most deceitful feature was that it was so worded as to give an impression of being the work of the investigation committee, as illustrated by the statement on page 50 that 'these are the conclusions of the investigation committee based upon foreign sources and upon the dossiers and documents of MEA . . .' Although the report was dated, it was not signed, the absence of any signature reinforcing the impression that it was the committee's work.

To refute all the Nujaim Report's errors, misconceptions and deviations from the truth, even in summary form, would itself fill a book. It takes a little time to tell a lie, but much longer to disprove it. I shall therefore deal only with two accusations which lay at the core of the report.

The first accusation ran that the choice and purchase of the three Boeing 747s was imposed on the board of MEA by its management, for no valid reason except to enable them to pocket a commission from Boeing. To support this accusation and deprive the purchase of the 747s of any merit other than the desire of MEA management to net the commission, the report stated on page 44 that the investigation committee did not consider it part of its task to pronounce on whether or not the purchase and choice of the 747s was sound, since this would require technical, economic and financial studies. Yet the studies already existed. They had been made in 1974 by MEA experts, and those of Air France, before the decision to purchase the Boeing 747s was taken. They were on the files Asad Nasr was asked to send to the committee, and also on the files of Air France and Intra. The truth was there for the authors of the report to uncover had that been what they were truly searching for.

It seemed an incredible abnegation of responsibility that Gilbert Pérol and Chafic Mouharram should allow such a statement to be attributed to them. It was the more remarkable in that both had been present on the MEA board in 1978 which approved the revaluation, by three independent international assessors, of the three Boeing 747s concerned – a revaluation that brought the airline, after four profitable years of service from these aircraft, a profit of £L143 million ($40 million at the time) duly incorporated in the MEA accounts for that year. It was even more remarkable in the light of Pérol's declaration recorded in the board minutes for 3 September 1976: 'Monsieur Pérol also praised MEA's decision to have acquired the combi 747 aircraft and confirmed that Air France is following MEA's wise decision in adding combi 747 aircraft to its fleet.' And now here they were, in August 1979, apparently declaring that they were unable to judge whether the choice and purchase of these aircraft were favourable to MEA.

The second accusation was that, to net the commission, the management of MEA deliberately disregarded normal commercial practice by not including a clause in the purchase contract to prohibit the Boeing Company from paying any commission on the deal, and claimed the inclusion of such a clause to be normal commercial practice. This was utter nonsense! The very opposite is customary commercial practice. Manufacturers all over the world promote the sale of their products by paying sales commissions to their accredited agents, and since there were no intermediaries or agents involved in the purchase of the Boeing 747s, MEA rightfully claimed for its own use in the *caisse noire* the commission which would have been paid to a Boeing accredited representative had Boeing had one in Lebanon. Boeing had no such representative and was therefore enabled to pay MEA instead.

Judge Nujaim had forgotten that Boeing, on the subject of commissions, refused to accede to the American authorities' wish, and declared on page 2 of its report No. 8–K, dated 28 July 1978, to SEC, that 'the company intends to continue to make use of consultants when doing so is in the best interests of the company and its stockholders'. Judge Nujaim was fully aware of this declaration and reproduced its exact French and Arabic translations on page 10 of his report. Furthermore, he could not have been unaware that, in Lebanon, Decree Law No. 34, promulgated on 5 August 1967, protects commercial representation and therefore prohibits the inclusion of such a clause. Both Boeing and MEA would have been liable to substantial damages if such a clause had been included in the purchase contract, and if, as a consequence, an accredited Boeing representative, should there have been one in Lebanon, then lost his commission or his fees.

Asad Nasr's vain attempt in his 'Deal of the Century', not to banish

242

but to restrict the use of intermediaries, sparked a storm that nearly cost him the chairmanship and, at the end of which, the intermediaries won and collected millions of dollars from the deal.

Every time in the past when Middle East Airlines had bought equipment, vultures calling themselves intermediaries, who had no connection whatsoever with MEA, would take advantage of the occasion and extort commissions from manufacturers by fooling them into believing that they were in a position to influence the deal in their favour. Such people never rendered any service to the manufacturers or to MEA. We never even knew of their existence until a long time after we had purchased the aircraft, and then only from the manufacturers, who naturally were furious at discovering they had been so shamelessly deceived. These people's ill-earned commissions were invariably added to the price of the aircraft, which meant we had to work even harder while the vultures feathered their nests at the expense of MEA. We had tried to stop them when we bought the Caravelles, and I insisted then that we include in the purchase contract a clause stating that no commissions would be paid to anyone in MEA or outside MEA, and that the contract would become null and void should it ever be found that such commissions had been paid. This was possible because Special Law No. 34 of 5 August 1967 was not then in existence.

Despite this clause, however, it emerged years later that two Lebanese businessmen, unconnected with MEA or anyone in MEA, did in fact receive a substantial commission on the deal. We were advised that there was nothing we could do against the manufacturers of Caravelle, for they had found a legal loophole to pay the commission. We had to suffer our frustration in silence.

The Viscounts had been no exception, as these were bought by BOAC and resold to MEA at a fair-sized profit. At the time BOAC owned 100 per cent of the shareholding of MEA, and must have had a good reason for making a profit on the deal. But it was a different story when we bought the Comet fleet. We learned, very much later, that a businessman, who was one of the founders of Intra, exploited his friendship with Bedas and extorted a commission from the manufacturers of the Comets. This personage had no connection whatsoever with MEA, or with anyone in MEA, and at the time he was not even any longer connected with Intra.

With the Boeing 320Cs, bought in 1968, the list of the so-called intermediaries, which I heard about a couple of years after the purchase of the aircraft, came to be as long as one's arm. It included a minister, a deputy, two officially appointed intermediaries by Boeing, a number of other Lebanese businessmen and even an intermediary in the United States. None of these people had any connection with MEA or its people, and it was after this experience that Boeing refused to appoint any intermediaries or representatives in Lebanon. The purchase of the three 747s was the first time that we successfully arranged for the commission to be paid to MEA.

The committee was legally and duty bound to refer the Nujaim Report immediately to Chairman Asad Nasr and the MEA board for comment. It should have given those falsely attacked the chance to rebut accusations. It did nothing of the kind. On the contrary, the board of Intra, without, I am told, being shown the Nujaim Report and acting on the briefing of its chairman, Chafic Mouharram, decided on 25 October to ask Chairman Mouharram to request Asad Nasr to resign from MEA, adding that, if he refused to do so, steps should be taken to dismiss him. Mouharram reported to the next Intra board meeting in December that Asad Nasr had flatly refused to resign, and so the Intra board reconfirmed its unconditional request to Asad Nasr to step down.

This decision met with the same response as the first. In both cases, the MEA board, the legally responsible body, was not informed and so was contemptuously ignored. Yet five of the Intra board members were also on the board of MEA which had appointed the investigation committee and instructed it to report back only to that board. The same five were on the MEA board which had in 1974 approved and praised the choice and purchase of the Boeing 747s. For more than fourteen years, they had been Asad Nasr's friends and colleagues. Nevertheless they were quick to convict him and ask for his resignation without granting him the right or courtesy of being able to tell his side of the story. They had not even waited for the genuine report of the investigation committee they appointed!

The Nujaim Report was finally sent to MEA board members nearly four months after being written and only three days before being leaked to the press, misleadingly disguised as the report of the committee. Even then, it was not sent for comment, but only to implicate the board in the planned leak to the press by making them possible sources for the leak.

When I read the Nujaim Report in the newspaper *As-Safir*, I at once denounced it publicly, pointing out that it was full of errors, distortions and deliberate omissions, and that, moreover, it was not the report of the investigation committee. I beat the censorship, which did not dare to suppress my denunciation, and my angry onslaught forced Mouharram to declare to the Lebanese press, in the name of the committee, that the Nujaim Report was not that of the committee and its own report would be submitted shortly to the board of MEA – a 'shortly' that took a further three months and eight days to materialize.

The press reported President Sarkis as saying he would not allow another 'Intra catastrophe', and that the Council of Ministers wanted an urgent investigation into the leak of the committee's documents to the press to discover those responsible. Similarly, it was reported that the Prime Minister, Salim El-Hoss, had summoned Mouharram and inquired how the leak could have occurred and who was behind it. Yet no investigation was carried out to find those responsible, and their names were never disclosed. Official noises were considered an adequate smoke screen and there was no real desire to go further. In other words, those to blame had enough political power to protect themselves from exposure. My personal inquiries met with such a complete and stubborn silence as to lead me to suspect that the source of the leak was politically invulnerable. Only after President Sarkis stepped down from office was I reliably informed that the report and its related documents were leaked to *As-Safir* by the Presidential Palace. Knowledge of the presidential involvement in the Boeing Affair came as no surprise for I had long suspected who was really behind it.

Despite the obvious government decision to cover up the leak and the names of those responsible, the Nujaim Report and its welter of distortions had quite the opposite effect to the one envisaged. The Lebanese public could recognize the smell of conspiracy without any prompting. Members of Parliament sent telegrams to President Sarkis and Prime Minister El-Hoss, voicing their concern. The Federation of Lebanese Trade Unions expressed its anxiety. Most of the Lebanese press sounded the alarm in one way or another. Everyone feared that the plot was part of a bigger and more ominous conspiracy to destroy MEA and with it the Lebanese economy. Everyone remembered what had happened to Intra.

Ike, an English-language newspaper published in Lebanon, called the delay in publishing the report of the investigation committee a 'conspiracy of silence' and was puzzled at the real reasons, 'unless one falls back on the theory that Lebanon's only passenger airline, like the bank that was once Lebanon's largest, has become the target'. *Ike* was not far off the mark, for the attack on Middle East Airlines was an almost exact replica of the conspiracy against Intra. Both were propagated, sponsored and exploited by the highest authority in the country. Similar tactics were used, with matching professional skills. The production of a forged report, the intimidation of board members

245

to ensure their silence, the spreading of insidious rumours, delaying tactics, misleading press statements, the abuse of the services of a retired judge, the leaking of forged reports to the press and the whispering campaign all followed an identical sinister pattern.

The late Riad Taha, who was then president of the Lebanese Press Syndicate, held a special conference on 26 December 1979, at which, using strong language, he openly accused the government of involvement: 'To save our country we should require honesty from those who govern. Those in authority, who are entrusted with our destiny, must be above reproach.' Then he lashed out at Intra, 'which received instructions from the government and had activated the Boeing affair'. He went on to say that publication of the committee's documents appeared to have been prompted 'not by honourable motives but by motives of an opposite nature'. He also called for an investigation of Intra itself. Riad Taha was always courageously outspoken — too outspoken in lawless Lebanon. He was assassinated on 23 July 1980.

Leaking the report to the press made it imperative for the investigation committee to submit its report to MEA's board without further delay. But, despite repeated and urgent demands and promises that submission was imminent, nothing happened. Plainly a great deal of wheeler-dealing was in progress. There were agreements to be clinched, bargains to be struck, deals to be fixed. The so-called administrative investigation was evidently transformed into an arena for the 'Sporty Game', which was the latest name for aircraft cut-throat selling, and for bargaining as to who got what from the commissions expected from 'The Deal of the Century'.

But when all arrangements were agreed and such problems settled, then things moved swiftly. The committee submitted its final report to the board of MEA on 28 March 1980. It had taken the committee ten months and four days to achieve a Caesarean birth for its two-page report, and after all its labour it gave birth to a mouse. It said that the Boeing Company paid a commission of $3.6 million to Resora, which we had used for the affairs of the company, that written statements had been submitted giving the reasons for the action, and that, on our own initiative, the unused balance of $2,431,939 was transferred to the official company's accounts. The report further stressed that the Nujaim Report of 20 August 1979, prepared by an expert under instructions of the committee, did not constitute a report but an 'analysis of facts', and that it had been outdated (dépassé) by our explanations. So the committee admitted at last that the Nujaim Report was prepared under its own instructions by an expert — a very peculiar kind of expert!

246

Finally, the committee considered that we should have submitted the *caisse noire* arrangement to the board of MEA for approval and that our act ought not to constitute a precedent for the future. In this they showed a deliberate disregard for the truth. In my August meeting with the committee, I had stressed that we had all the powers enabling us to authorize the *caisse noire* arrangement and to effect payments when required. I had confirmed all this in writing, enumerating for the committee's benefit the numerous board resolutions, the legal provisions and other relevant facts which showed beyond doubt that we had the necessary powers. The committee never questioned these facts, but nevertheless, for reasons of its own, included its incorrect and misleading opinion. The report also omitted any reference to the leak to the press of its confidential documents. It has become widely recognized that leaking confidential information is a commonly used political tool. But when such information is published at a time of the strictest government censorship — such as prevailed in Lebanon in 1979 — it takes on more sinister tones.

The board adopted the report in its entirety. The Nujaim Report, the leaking of documents to the press and all other irregularities and improprieties were never even discussed or queried. The board members acted like programmed robots. Nevertheless, before the end of the meeting, Jean de Gennes, speaking for Gilbert Pérol, who, significantly, did not attend, had made a formal declaration stating: 'The terms obtained by Middle East Airlines–Air Liban SAL for the acquisition of three Boeing 747/200 in 1974 compared favourably with the best market conditions at the time.' Satisfying as it was to me to know that this authoritative judgement had been made, I found it preposterous that it should be left to Air France to make a point that ought to have been included in the official report. It was also strange that Air France, as a member of the investigation committee, should have accepted the non-inclusion of its opinion. Stranger still was the fact that the MEA board, aware of Intra's abysmal ignorance of aviation, did not question this abnormal incident and freely and unprotestingly accepted the glaring evidence of Intra's bias and prejudice.

I was shocked at the inadequacy and worthlessness of this miserable document, consisting of only two meagre pages. It seemed a puny response to an affair that had caused grave crises in MEA for almost a year and that had rocked Lebanon. Certainly it was unworthy of a committee that had included Air France. I vigorously attacked the committee, its sham investigation and its petty report, and especially for saying that the affair of the *caisse noire* should have been submitted to the board for approval when the committee was well aware that this had been unnecessary. The press release represented an instantaneous outburst of my anger and disgust. But perhaps it served to enlighten the Lebanese — although, by then, most Lebanese needed little or no further enlightenment on the affair.

I never doubted that I had all the powers and legal authority necessary to authorize the setting up of the *caisse noire* and to approve its source of funding without reference to the board of directors. As this was the only point raised by the investigation committee, however, I wanted to have my convictions legally confirmed and so called on a capable Lebanese lawyer, commissioning him to study all available documents and give his advice. His study was thorough and irrefutable and needed no amplification. Yet we both felt that it would, in the circumstances, be advisable to make doubly sure and also seek the opinion of a top French jurist. My Lebanese lawyer friend, after consultation in Paris, was referred to Professor Barthélémy Mercadal, one of France's most eminent jurists, who was knowledgeable in Lebanese law, which is largely based on French law.

After a study of the case, its related documentation and the relevant board minutes, Professor Mercadal confirmed that I had all the powers granted by the board as well as the legal authorities provided by Lebanese commercial law to authorize the establishment of the *caisse noire* and the payments made therefrom. In addition, he stressed that, from the day I was appointed chairman, in 1956, the board of directors had delegated to me all powers, with the exception of the purchase and sale of aircraft, mergers, and the acquisition of holdings, when its authorization was required. Besides this general power of management, the board had even relinquished to me its own limited powers in cases of crises (the Intra crash and the civil war), and granted me the absolute power to take 'all necessary measures to ensure the continued operation of the company, the protection of its interests and the safety of its employees and passengers'.

Professor Mercadal further confirmed that, as well as the powers and legal authority vested in me, there was a well-founded justification for the action I authorized in the exceptional nature of the circumstances in which the company was placed as a result of the civil war and its consequences. He declared that French courts had ruled on the principle that companies are under no obligation to comply with their rules of procedure when exceptional circumstances supervene. Finally, the Professor was scathing about the irresponsible behaviour of the investigation committee and its bogus Nujaim Report. He condemned the committee for having wilfully set out to mislead the board of directors of MEA with regard to events it was set up to clarify. He was equally contemptuous of the irresponsible behaviour of the MEA board.

Armed with these forceful opinions by my distinguished legal advisers, I gave serious thought to taking those responsible for the conspiracy to law. Not only was I indignant about the manner in which the whole plot had been conducted, but the idea that wrong-doers in Lebanon might once again get away scot-free was repugnant. Yet, knowing by now who the real culprits were in the affair, I realized how impossible it would be ever to see justice done. Justice had fled, in utter disgust, from demented Lebanon, leaving the law of the jungle behind. And this was hardly the kind of law to allow anyone to take to task the predators of that jungle.

This plot against Middle East Airlines failed, as had all previous ones. The difference was, however, that we had managed to fight and crush the earlier ones with as little public noise as possible. I had always tried to keep the fighting very quiet, and in most cases succeeded in keeping it secret from everyone, including the board and management of MEA and even my own family. The many ugly divisive details were therefore never disclosed. Given the delicately balanced factional compromise in Lebanon, I feared that the details of the fighting and the many confrontations we continuously had to face would, if divulged, destabilize the airline. There were some incidents, like the Israeli raid, the Lebanonization of MEA and the acquisition of Air Liban and its shareholding, which could not be concealed, but nevertheless even these were kept on as low a key as possible.

The Boeing affair was quite another matter. It was deliberately exploded with the loudest bang, nationally and internationally. Then, because of the circumstances of war in Lebanon, the conspirators had gone straight for the kill. In this they misjudged the courage, tenacity and immunity that had developed at MEA to plots and conspiracies. For there is no doubt that it was a conspiracy against the airline and Lebanon. In his book, *I Speak for Lebanon*, the late Kamal Jumblatt wrote that Dr Edmond Rabbath, a well-known Lebanese jurist and Air France's legal adviser in Lebanon, warned him how, when he was in Switzerland, American friends had told him, 'You will shortly witness the destruction of the economic structures and institutions in Lebanon. An international conspiracy is under way.' Dr Lucien Dahdah, at one time Minister of Foreign Affairs, a member and former chairman of the Intra board and one of the people most informed about what really happens in Lebanon, was among the first to cry conspiracy against

Lebanon and its economy, and to do so publicly after a visit to President Sarkis to discuss the Boeing affair. It was linked, in his view, with the destruction of the hotels and the mysterious looting of the banks.

The fact was that Middle East Airlines had, from the first day of its creation, met resistance, hostility and intrigues which grew stronger as the airline spread its wings and battled for survival. It encroached on civil aviation preserves consecrated, by divine right, for powerful countries and not for tiny Lebanon. As it fought for a living, it had to tread on too many toes, Lebanese and non-Lebanese. There were those who did not like Pan-Am pulling out of MEA; others resented BOAC doing likewise; and many hated our acquisition of Air Liban from Air France, although all these airlines had acted of their own free will. MEA walked on prohibited ground by participating in the conception and establishment of Masco, which was destroyed before it even started to achieve its objectives. And then MEA had the temerity to dream of a united Arab airline. In its excitement, it had forgotten that the Arabs are never to be permitted to unite in anything, not even in their worship of Almighty God.

Our determination to keep politics and politicians out of MEA had been resented and made many enemies. But the deadliest of Lebanese sins was MEA's refusal to be sectarian. Moslem politicians hated us because we were not exclusively Moslem; Christian politicians hated us because we were not all Christian; and most politicians hated us because we were non-sectarian Lebanese. From this there sprang our biggest crime of all when Middle East Airlines, during the civil war, remained Lebanese, acted Lebanese and worked as one Lebanese family, serving no particular community except Lebanon and all its citizens. We forcefully resisted efforts to partition the airline, and thus became a threat to plans to fragment and destroy Lebanon. For this we were to be wiped out, but it proved wishful thinking on the part of the conspirators. Their latest attempt, the Boeing affair, finally ended in the dustbin where it belonged.

Yet the vultures who scrambled for rich pickings from the 'Deal of the Century' won in the end as all aircraft manufacturers concluded agreements with intermediaries whom they believed could assist them to get the MEA business they so desired. The competitive fight for the new aircraft MEA was to buy was, most deservedly, not won by the manufacturer who had exploded the Boeing affair and sponsored its scurrilous press campaign. The consequential developments unfolded in the following way.

On 30 May 1980, the ordinary general assembly of shareholders of

Middle East Airlines re-elected the entire board of directors, including Asad Nasr, for a period of three years. Then the new board re-elected Asad Nasr as chairman.

Fuel prices had been escalating since 1974, but, curiously enough, it was only on 19 June 1980 that Middle East Airlines suddenly became uncomfortably aware of the rising cost of fuel and decided to eliminate from their fleet replacement plan three-engined aircraft types. They decided to choose instead between the more economical twin-engined Airbus A310 and the Boeing 767. Aircraft offered by Lockheed and Douglas were, for the first time, eliminated from the bidding for MEA fleet requirements.

Air France had always assisted MEA in its choice of aircraft, and remains one of the biggest customers of Boeing in Europe. It was itself currently purchasing their aircraft, and for this reason it seemed more than likely that it was in a position to secure more co-operation and understanding from Boeing than from the other two American manufacturers. In August 1980, Air France undertook to buy twelve 737s from Boeing, the first of which was delivered on 18 December 1982. This purchase, of course, had no effect on the choice of aircraft to be made by Middle East Airlines.

Later in 1980, on 28 November, the board of MEA decided to buy nineteen Airbus A310 aircraft, five on firm order at a cost of $70 million each, for a total of $350 million. The airline took options on the remaining fourteen at a total basic cost of $980 million, which, with escalations over the planned ten-year delivery period, would have become at least $2,000 million. The 'Deal of the Century' would ultimately have cost Middle East Airlines around $2,350 million, a gigantic financial burden at a time when the airline, operating in Lebanon in the midst of a destructive civil war, could not even afford the initial $350 million.

I had earlier warned each member of the board, in a detailed report dated 20 June 1980, against any fresh financial commitment without due consideration to the political instability in Lebanon and the financial position of the company. I felt strongly against the timing of the fleet replacement plan, and this was the only occasion, after my resignation as board adviser, that I felt the need to intervene. The proposal was of the utmost importance and going ahead would have had, in my opinion, the most damaging effect. Chairman Asad Nasr was upset, considering that my report amounted to sabotaging his 'Deal of the Century'. Air France was unhappy and thought my report jeopardized MEA's chance of buying the Airbus. The rest of the board members paid not the slightest heed to my views.

In the event, the sealed-envelope method of adjudicating between the Airbus 310 and the Boeing 767 was chosen – so far as I know, the first time in the history of aircraft purchase that this method has been used. I could not imagine that Asad Nasr, a firm believer in his own computer techniques for evaluating the merits and suitability of new aircraft, would ever have resorted to this absurd and unusual method unless pressured and coerced into doing so. It seemed most surprising that Boeing and Airbus Industries should also have agreed to such a novel and exceptional procedure in the aviation industry without apparent protest or comment. To my way of thinking, it was shameful and humiliating that the MEA board should have consented to sealed-envelope bids, which amounted to a public confession of their doubts about the honesty and integrity of the MEA management and, indeed, of the board itself. The board, it seemed, could not trust its members to evaluate honestly and choose disinterestedly which aircraft to buy according to the recommendation of the management and the tried methods used by other airlines.

As it happened, the sanctimonious halo cast over the 'sealed envelope' affair failed miserably to prevent widespread gossip about large commissions being paid to middle-men by Airbus Industries. Ironically, the gossip was confirmed by none other than Chafic Mouharram, chairman of Intra, in a letter to Asad Nasr, as chairman of MEA, dated 15 December 1981, in which he stated that commissions amounting to tens of millions of dollars were being shared out among those responsible for the purchase of the Airbus. He must have been in a position to know!

The board of MEA also introduced a novel concept of an isolation penalty in favour of Airbus and against Boeing. This was based on the pretext that none of the countries to which MEA flew had purchased Boeing 767s, but that Airbus had sold to some of them. It was claimed that this would, if MEA chose to equip with Boeing 767s, force it to bear the expense of providing its own stock of spare parts and engineering services at many foreign airports. The cost of doing this was estimated at $2.6 million per aircraft, and for this reason the isolation penalty, equal to this amount, was to be added to the price of each Boeing aircraft under offer. This was, indeed, curiously odd, for Boeing had sent a letter on 25 August 1980 to Chairman Asad Nasr, three months prior to the sealed-envelope grand opening, offering a comprehensive special programme of product support, at no charge to MEA, for at least three years after the delivery of the first 767. This programme comprised technical assistance, spares support on consignment, insurance parts, a main base store for spares, maintenance tools and ramp equipment, line station parts and technical training as well as technical assistance by Boeing personnel in Lebanon and in countries served by Middle East Airlines.

In the light of Boeing's detailed undertakings, it is difficult to believe there was any need or justification for the isolation penalty. Nevertheless, the MEA board disregarded Boeing's undertakings and applied the isolation penalty. As a result, the Airbus price per aircraft was $132,000 less than each Boeing 767, and Airbus was declared the winner of the sales contest. The surprising feature was that Boeing accepted the isolation penalty, despite the fact that its application cost it the whole deal. As soon as the result was declared, the Boeing Company sent a gracious letter of congratulation to the chairman of MEA for the fair manner in which the adjudication had been carried out. In other words, Boeing thanked MEA for the 'isolation penalty' and for its application, which led MEA to buy the rival Airbus A310 instead of the Boeing 767.

The Airbus contract was finally signed after lengthy bargaining, and financing was made available when President Sarkis instructed the Board of Development and Reconstruction to loan MEA £L150 million. It was the first time that a Lebanese government had given financial assistance to the airline. The gesture was most welcome, no matter what reasons lay behind it, especially since this money was later used to pay salaries and other expenses and not to buy the Airbus!

Having brought the 'Deal of the Century' to a conclusion, Asad Nasr resigned on 6 May 1982, a few months before the end of his three-year term of office. On his recommendation, the managing director, Salim Salaam, was elected chairman of MEA for the remaining months of Asad Nasr's term, and then, on 26 August 1983, Salim Salaam was re-elected chairman to serve a three-year term with a board consisting of a mixture of new and old members.

By this time, MEA's losses had risen so dramatically that they exceeded by many times the company's paid-up capital. Salim Salaam declared on 31 October 1983 that the much-trumpeted plan to buy the Airbus had been abandoned since the airline could not afford it. This declaration was later withdrawn. The Airbus contract was therefore placed in limbo, as a reminder of the 'Sporty Game' and MEA's kamikazi jump into the dark.

For MEA, this wound up the saga of the Boeing affair and its *caisse noire*. For Boeing, however, it all took longer. On 30 June 1984, it was reported that Boeing had been fined $400,000 by a United States Federal Court for failing to make proper disclosures to Eximbank concerning its sales of aircraft. Boeing said that this settlement ended the five-year investigation by the Department of Justice into its sales transactions and stressed that it had not been charged with making improper payments by the Department of Justice, nor by the Securities Exchange Commission, nor by the Federal Trade Commission in the investigations now concluded by these government agencies. Yet if Boeing had not been charged with making improper payments by all the US departments concerned, why had it been necessary to drag friendly countries and Boeing's client airlines into four years of 'scandal suspicion' publicity, damaging not only to the airlines concerned but also to Boeing's future aircraft sales?

The fine of $400,000 was trivial beside the damage done to the Boeing Civil Airplane Company by the harmful and pointed publicity that followed its report to SEC. Boeing paid heavily in loss of sales. The Middle East had been Boeing's market. All its airlines were equipped with Boeing aircraft, and future sales should have normally gone to Boeing. But the situation was overturned by politics, and by the commotion of puritanism, if that is what it really was.

Boeing lost many orders in the Middle East market to Airbus Industries. On 27 May 1980, Kuwait Airways announced a substantial Airbus order. Subsequently it changed its mind and bought the 767 — although, to achieve the sale, Boeing had to take over the Airbus aircraft already bought, which were later sold on to Pan-Am. After MEA decided on its 'Deal of the Century' on 24 November 1980, and ordered nineteen Airbus aircraft, Saudi Arabian Airlines followed suit with a big Airbus order, as did other airlines. Boeing may well have lost more than $4,000 million and the control of a lucrative market which had been its undisputed preserve. The most important factor was the temporary loss of its dominant prestige as a Middle East aircraft supplier, which it has since been fighting strenuously to win back.

It all makes a curious tale, full of national and international intrigues, human greed and unscrupulous behaviour. Meanwhile, the original acquisition of the three Boeing 747 combis in 1974 continued to prove to have been an extremely wise buy. Out on lease to other airlines, or available for *ad hoc* charters, they have been MEA's main currency earners and, indeed, have kept the airline alive.

19
Goodbye Lebanon

When fighting broke out in Lebanon at the start of a civil war which has now lasted more than a decade, I began considering how, as a patriot, I might best help to restore peace. It seemed to me that, as chairman and president of MEA, my first duty was to remain neutral in the factional strife to ensure the safety of the airline, to preserve it as a truly national institution and keep it out of the fighting. The most important consideration was to provide a life-line between Beirut and the outside world. That was my clear duty, and to the best of my ability I carried it out during the early stages of the fighting.

But when the fighting recommenced in 1978, a few months after my retirement from MEA, I felt free from such obligations and began to consider a more active role. Even though my wife was in poor health and in need of my support and company, she again demonstrated, as she had before, her love for Lebanon, and urged me to try to do something for my country. For me, it was encouragement enough. I set about trying to represent sanity in an increasingly manic situation. But it soon became clear that, if I was to make my voice heard over the gunfire, I would need the support of a private army of at least several thousand fighting men. Such is the paradox of the peacemaker in Lebanon. I should have had to pay this force regularly and supply it with weapons and the copious amounts of ammunition nowadays expected.

As the Alamuddins do not possess a sufficiently large fortune for such a purpose, I would have been forced to sell myself into the control of an Arab power, or of a foreign country, to raise the money. There were, in fact, a number of powers eager to buy my services and conscience, and one in particular became incensed by my refusal and considered it an affront. Yet I was not prepared to trade patriotism for patronage. And so there was nothing to be done except to watch with mounting horror the destruction of my country.

255

Hundreds of books and thousands of articles have already been written about the war in Lebanon, its causes and atrocities, the ruthless killings and systematic destruction. Nevertheless, in writing this book, I feel I have to put down my own feelings as to what happened and, more importantly, give my own assessment as to why the Lebanese allowed themselves to be manipulated into fighting an insane civil war.

It all really began in September 1970 with the incursion into Lebanon of thousands of armed Palestinians, chased out of Jordan by King Hussein's army. Shortly after settling in their new host country, they began to act with an arrogant disregard for the Lebanese government's authority. In 1973, this behaviour provoked a confrontation with the Lebanese Army that lasted fourteen days. After two weeks of intermittent shooting, both sides came to an arrangement. By the standards of only two years later, it was a modest affair, but even so both sides were by then running short of ammunition.

During the autumn of the same year, the war, known in the West as the Yom Kippur War, broke out between Israel and the Arab countries of Egypt and Syria. It lasted only three weeks, but, despite the large stocks of arms and ammunition built up by all three countries, their arsenals were so depleted after two weeks of fighting that the Americans had to mount a massive airlift to Israel and the Russians needed to do the same to Cairo and Damascus.

Since that time, shortages of ammunition have seemingly been no problem in Lebanon. During the eleven years of civil war, there has been continual shooting, the waste of ammunition, especially in Beirut and later in the mountains, being truly profligate. Nor do the men with the guns confine their shooting to the serious business of war. They pull the triggers with their rifles set at automatic at the least excuse, military or otherwise. It was always a Lebanese custom to fire a *feu de joie* to commemorate a special occasion, but these used to amount to nothing more than a few volleys of carefully hoarded bullets, too precious to waste. From 1975 onwards, apart from the fighting, all hell would break loose at the slightest pretext: weddings, funerals, feasts, circumcisions, returns from pilgrimage, recovery from illness, election to office – all would be celebrated by automatic weapons pumping thousands of rounds into the sky. Even personal quarrels, which would have been settled with a knife or a single pistol shot a few years before, erupted into full-scale battles. And sometimes the bullets would start to fly for no clear reason whatsoever.

Not only rifles are used in such a spendthrift fashion. Machine-guns, cannon, rockets, anti-tank missiles and anti-aircraft guns all add their

256

expensive clamour to the celebrations. The gunmen never seem to run short of bullets, shells and missiles, however many they fire, and it is not merely a matter of the amounts of weapons and ammunition that have flooded into Lebanon. There is also the question of the quality of the weaponry making its début in that unhappy country. Sophisticated weapons systems, some not even issued to the armed forces of the manufacturing countries, have been supplied to the warring factions in Lebanon and made freely available, regardless of their devastating effect on people and property. Like Spain during its civil war in the 1930s, Lebanon has become a testing-ground for new weapons as well as for new methods of psychological warfare, which are, in their own way, as deadly as the bullet and which will probably, in the long run, have an even more devastating effect.

The arsenals of the world's greatest powers have been opened to Lebanon, which has been showered with weapons as if from some deadly cornucopia. Yet such weaponry is not supplied free. It is purchased expensively, and the funds seem to be inexhaustible. So who pays for this obscene extravagance? Certainly not the Lebanese, who cannot possibly afford it.

Elias Sarkis, President of Lebanon for six years during some of the darkest days, had no doubts. On 31 January 1982, the Lebanese journal *An-Nahar* quoted him as saying: 'The solution of the Lebanese crisis is not in the hands of the Lebanese but in the hands of Brezhnev, Reagan and Begin.' Chafic Wazzan, then Prime Minister of Lebanon, was even more specific. In a speech reported by *L'Orient-Le Jour* on 12 March 1982, he said: 'Les États-Unis sont responsables de nos malheurs' ('The United States is responsible for our misfortunes').

The United States may or may not be responsible. What is certain is that the United States has the power to end the destructive madness which reigns in Lebanon at any time it cares to exert its authority. Yet successive American presidents have found themselves unable to do so for a number of reasons — not least the power of Jewish voters in the United States. It is a chilling thought for the free world, which depends so much upon the United States for protection, that such a great power finds itself incapacitated from stopping the destruction of tiny Lebanon.

When Prime Minister Wazzan blamed the Americans alone for what was being done to Lebanon, he forgot the others: the Russians, the Europeans, the Arab countries, the Israelis and the Palestinians. All these bear their share of guilt for what has happened, not only in Lebanon but throughout the Middle East. All have pursued their own

257

interests and, separately and collectively, have brought death and destruction to a beautiful country by doing so.

The United States sought to support Israel, fight international communism and protect the Arabian oil fields in which it holds an interest. It has repeatedly assured the Lebanese of its support for their continued independence, sovereignty and geographic integrity, and has displayed its readiness to lend a powerful hand to those who were fighting leftist influence. The USSR wants to fight imperialism, support the Palestinians, destabilize the region and support the Arab socialist states. Israel, in the short term, wants to annex south Lebanon and fragment Syria, and as many other Arab countries as possible, into numerous small mini-states, hopefully as Israeli satellites. In the long term, the Israelis still hope to realize their dream of a Greater Israel.

Syria wants to regain the districts it claims were taken from it under the 'Grand Liban' settlement of 1920 and to help the Palestinians and convert Lebanon to its own, Baathist, version of socialism. The Palestinians, supposed to fight Israel from Lebanon, were sucked into the plot to destroy Lebanon and came to believe they have the right to play a dominant role in the situation as the militia forces of the Moslems. They claimed the road to Jerusalem lay through Jounieh, but Jounieh is a town in the heart of Maronite Christian land, north of Beirut and in the opposite direction to Jerusalem!

As for the Arab oil-producing countries, they have supplied funds and arms to almost all the fighting parties under various pretexts — aiding the Palestine cause; helping rightists against leftists, leftists against rightists; protecting Moslems from Christians, Christians from Moslems. In reality, all they want to do is to make sure that the Palestinians and their problems are confined to Lebanon and kept as far away from themselves as possible, even as they continue to swear in public that they are helping the Palestinians in their just cause.

France, for its part, supports Lebanon, and proclaims its sympathy for the Lebanese, especially the Maronites, so long as its lucrative trade with the Arab oil-producing countries is not harmed and it is able to continue supplying arms, aircraft and military equipment. The English, too, play a part, presumably to assist the United States, but no one knows for certain what this is in reality. Certainly they wish to preserve their Middle East markets. No one understands what the other European states really want, or what they are doing in Lebanon, yet nearly all of them maintain a presence there.

All countries with arms industries sell their wares to the various factions, either directly or through the arms merchants who descended upon Lebanon like jackals round a carcass. Yet, even though all these countries must take their share of the blame, we, the Lebanese, cannot escape our own responsibility for what has happened. Other countries certainly played vital roles in the devastation, but they could not have succeeded had we not been more than willing partners for their schemes. The truth of the death of Lebanon is that it was not murdered; it committed suicide.

No less than 160,000 of my Lebanese compatriots have been killed since 1975 in the two Israeli invasions and the never-ending factional strife, which has also left hundreds of thousands badly injured. For the most part, these were innocent victims, trapped through no fault of their own in conflicts nurtured by international intrigue. The outside world accepted these man-made disasters as though they were acts of God, like hurricanes and earthquakes. Lebanese resentment at the world's indifference was expressed in a letter Madame Farid Chehab, wife of a former Lebanese Ambassador, wrote to her friend, Madame Charles Dubois, whose husband had been the Swiss Ambassador in Beirut. Published in *Le Monde* on 20 April 1976, it said: 'Qu'on ne me parle plus de civilisation Européenne, ni de l'Onu, ni du pape . . . Le silence a propos du Liban est une honte . . . Nous vivons un cauchemar . . .' ('Let no one talk to me of European civilization, nor of the United Nations, nor of the Pope . . . The silence over Lebanon is shameful – we live a nightmare . . .')

At the root of the Lebanese vulnerability to outside manipulation lies religious discord, feudal political domination, corrupt government and social injustice, as demonstrated by the huge gap between rich and poor. To understand fully how these eventually destructive shortcomings came about, we must look back over the last 145 years. For centuries prior to the 1840s, fighting in the Lebanon had been fairly frequent, with Druze fighting against Druze and Maronite against Maronite. The alignment was feudal and partisan rather than religious or sectarian. Travellers and observers repeatedly commented on the spirit of friendship that characterized Druze–Maronite relations.

As late as 1840, Druzes and Maronites were standing together against aggressors, and eight years earlier Lamartine had written: 'Scotland, Savoy and Switzerland do not exhibit to the traveller a busier scene of life, with more contentment and peace, than the foot of these mountains of Lebanon, where we expected to meet only barbarians.' After 1840, there were three outbursts of fighting between Maronites and Druzes, in 1841, 1845 and 1860. The last was the fiercest and escalated into a bloody civil war which had many similarities to that of

259

1975. Then, as today, the fighting was started by the Lebanese themselves but fostered by outside powers. One of its main causes, as in 1975, was the disgraceful gap between rich and poor and an oppressive domination of feudal power.

The 1860 fighting was sparked off by the successful rising, in January 1859, of the Maronite peasants of Kisrwan against their rich co-religionists who owned the land over which they sweated for so little. Led by Tanious Shahin, the first Lebanese socialist leader, the peasants drove the Maronite feudal lords from their homes and took over the land. News of this successful Maronite rebellion spread throughout the countryside and raised the hopes of all the peasants, including the Druze peasants, who suffered just as much as the impoverished Maronites. To counteract this, the Druze feudal lords stirred religious fanaticism among their peasants, even as the Maronite feudal lords did the same among their Maronite peasants, in an attempt to nip in the bud the challenge to their authority. Families who had lived in amity for generations were turned against one another by carefully spread rumours and tales of atrocity.

Sectarian strife was further encouraged by the Turkish authorities to curb the Maronites, who had been causing problems for them by seeking help from their Christian brethren in Europe and become a thorn in the side of the Ottoman Islamic Empire. Christian missionaries fanned the flames of religious hatred between Maronite and Druze, and the French, British and Austrian Consuls were no mere innocent bystanders. In these circumstances, it was inevitable that fighting should break out, and the Druzes and Maronites went at each other's throats with great ferocity. Many died on both sides, but the Druzes were victors.

The European powers vigorously intervened with the Turkish government to stop the fighting, and the French landed troops to protect the defeated Maronites as the warships of the British Royal Navy and other European navies cruised, ready for action, off the Lebanese coast. Various international solutions to the problem were discussed before, on 9 June 1861, a protocol was signed, making Lebanon an autonomous province of the Ottoman Empire under the guarantee of the six signatory powers, Turkey, France, Britain, Russia, Prussia and Austria. In 1867, Italy joined the guarantors. And so it had taken a civil war for Lebanon officially to become a political entity for the first time. Geographically speaking, it was an emasculated entity, stripped of the districts of Beirut, Beqa', Tripoli and Sidon.

Autonomy brought peace, happiness and distinct privileges, the

260

most attractive of which was exemption from military service in the Ottoman army. All of this helped to coin the saying: 'Happy is he who possesses a piece of land in Lebanon even if small enough for a goat to sleep in.' Ironically, almost 130 years later, the saying could be inverted into: 'Happy is he who possesses such a piece of land outside Lebanon.'

The agreement stipulated that Lebanon was to be governed not by a Lebanese, but by a Christian Ottoman whose appointment was to be approved by the Turkish government and the European guarantors. The first to fill the post was — of course! — nominated by the French. The governor was to be assisted by a twelve-member council, representing the religious communities: four Maronites, three Druzes, two Greek Orthodox, one Greek Catholic, one Sunni Moslem and one Shi'ite Moslem. This was how sectarian representation was introduced into Lebanese administration.

Feudalism was to be abolished — at least, so the protocol said. In practice, the Ottoman governor, to keep the feudal lords happy, made their traditional feudalism official, appointing them to leading government positions. Thus began the political feudalism in government administration which has plagued Lebanese politics ever since.

The Druzes were content with the establishment of an autonomous Lebanon and settled down to live peaceably, as a respected minority, alongside the Christians. But although the protocol was particularly beneficial to them, the Maronites came, with the passage of time, to resent the Ottoman administration. They felt moreover that the agreement had robbed Lebanon of its most fertile districts, and most of all they resented the loss of the port of Beirut. They wanted the lost districts to be returned and the old frontiers restored. Their ambitions seemed doomed to failure when Turkey joined in the First World War on the side of Germany, and in 1915 suspended the protocol and stripped Lebanon of its autonomous status. There was therefore much rejoicing among the Christians when, with the Allies victorious, France occupied Lebanon in 1918. Two years later, France was given a Mandate over Lebanon and Syria by the Allied Supreme Council meeting at San Remo.

Just four months later, on 1 September 1920, the French High Commissioner proclaimed the creation of Greater Lebanon (Grand Liban), giving back to Lebanon everything the protocol of 1861 had taken away. The Maronites seemed to have achieved all their ambitions. Today many of them believe that the creation of Grand Liban was a grave mistake. In the first place, it brought within Lebanon's borders large numbers of Moslems who eventually demanded a more equitable share in the running of the country. In the second, it caused great bitterness among the Syrians, from whom the 'lost districts' were taken and who had come to regard them as their own.

Syria has never accepted the frontiers imposed by the French in 1920, nor acknowledged Lebanon's sovereignty over Grand Liban. Because of this, no official diplomatic relations have ever been established between the two countries.

On 23 May 1926, Greater Lebanon became the Republic of Lebanon and was given a constitution which provided for an 'equitable' distribution of government posts between the religious communities. It did not specify the ratios of distribution, nor did it assign specific government posts to each community. These decisions were left in the hands of the French High Commissioner. It came as no surprise that he gave the best jobs to the Maronites. Nevertheless while the French Mandate remained in force, the problems of power sharing caused no serious trouble. Naturally the Maronites co-operated fully with the French and looked on them as the guarantors of Lebanon's independence. Franco-Maronite relations became strained, however, in 1943, when, in a bid for independence, the Maronites joined all the other communities and, with the help of the British, ousted the French – then Vichy-controlled – from Lebanon. The French never forgave either the Maronites or the British.

After the departure of the French, power sharing was supposed to be equitably distributed among the communities in Lebanon by the unwritten National Covenant of 1943. The President of the Republic was to be a Maronite Christian; the President of the Chamber of Deputies, a Shi'ite Moslem; the Prime Minister, a Sunni Moslem. The Greek Orthodox were to have the deputy premiership and the vice-presidency of the Chamber of Deputies. Although it was not clearly stipulated, the Druzes were to have the prestigious but in practice ineffective Ministry of Defence, for the Maronite commander-in-chief of the army held all the powers and the minister none. The Director-General of Security was a Maronite Christian. A ratio of six Christian deputies in Parliament to every five Moslems was stipulated. This distribution of power according to religious persuasion permeated all the executive branches of government.

The National Covenant thus endowed Lebanon with a hybrid democratic style of government, based on feudalism and religious representation. The feudal lords partitioned Lebanon into spheres of influence and controlled elections to Parliament. Each made his own list, and most of them sold the privilege of being on the list to candidates willing to contribute to what they called the election fund. It was a Parliament of feudal stars, each with his human satellites. There were, however, two genuine political parties, although these had, at the time, neither the numbers nor power to be effective, and even they were feudal in their leadership, which passed from father to son.

Parliament was divided into two groups: those with the government and those against. Being with the government depended on the number of privileges and favours allowed a political feudal lord. If he was denied the privileges that he felt were his due, he joined the Opposition, and thus would change his position at the same frequency as those privileges were granted or denied. Ministers were appointed not for their qualifications to manage a specific ministry, but to please the feudal lords and assure the newly appointed government of an adequate vote of confidence in Parliament.

A feudal lord's popularity depended on his ability to help his supporters flout the law and get unqualified members of his clan appointed to positions in the government and in Lebanese business organizations. The government's administrative services suffered most from this type of interference, and business organizations only slightly less. Reforming Lebanese society and the Lebanese system of government, and ridding it of the weaknesses of the confessional distribution of posts, proved consistently impossible, and thus did dual political and economic systems evolve in Lebanon. Political feudalism continued mostly along the lines established by the French during the Mandate, while by its side there flourished a monopolistic system of financial control and exploitation by a handful of chosen traders. The ignorance of most of the political feudal lords of economic and financial matters, and their disregard for the national interest in favour of their own, encouraged the growth of what might be called a mafia of Lebanese traders, composed of merchants, bankers and traders who co-operated, regardless of religion, to exploit the country at the expense of the deprived Lebanese.

There was an unwritten understanding that the misdeeds of the political barons would be tolerated and never prosecuted. Article 80 of the Lebanese Constitution stipulates that a Supreme Court be formed with the power to prosecute the President of the Republic and the ministers should they be charged with treason, abuse of power or dereliction of duty. That court was never formed. Conversely, a tradition developed which allows the incoming president to close the file on any misdeeds perpetrated by the outgoing president or his entourage. It also became the custom for a number of aides of an outgoing president to be appointed to positions of immunity as ambassadors or promoted to important positions in the government. Naturally such a tradition, which guarantees heads of government safety from retribution, encourages mismanagement and corruption throughout the administration.

When corruption in government became endemic and too obvious, a few political leaders, headed by Kamal Jumblatt and Raymond Eddé, forced through a law, passed by Parliament on 14 April 1954, requiring all public servants to submit a declaration detailing their families' assets to enable the authorities to verify additional sources of revenue. It was known as 'The law of where did you get this'. It came as no surprise when it was filed and never applied, and no one objected. In Lebanon, there is no civil or national public opinion, because even that is sectarian. Occasions are almost unknown when all the religious communities agree to act as Lebanese. But it is not only sectarian differences which are responsible for the subservience of the Lebanese public. Through resistance to every invasion in the past, the Lebanese have mastered the art of survival, whose first axiom is to look after oneself. In order of priorities, a Lebanese puts his personal interests first, then the interests of his family, then those of the religion he belongs to, and finally the interests of the particular political feudal lord whom he expects to protect his personal interests. Traditional attachment to a feudal political system and religion played a major part in bringing about the civil war.

The National Covenant was intended to be a national policy, but the Lebanese never really and honestly believed in it. It worked for some time because it served the purpose of the political feudal lords. It crumbled in the face of the first real political crisis. I can add little to what the late President Beshir Gemayel said in a speech on the day he was assassinated in 1982:

Seule la vérité nou sauvera aujourd'hui. Seule la vérité nous permettra de persévérer et de garder la tête haute. C'est parce que nous nous sommes moqués du monde pendant quarante ans que le monde s'est moqué de nous. C'est parce que nous avons menti au monde pendant quarante ans que le monde nous a menti à son tour. C'est parce que nous nous traitions nous-mêmes en quantité négligeable que le monde nous a négligés (see Appendix for translation).

The world never took Lebanese sovereignty seriously because it was not, in reality, a country with national unity. Ambassadors of foreign nations habitually intervened ostentatiously in internal national politics. After their frequent visits to political leaders to exchange views, these diplomats make political declarations which not only abuse Lebanese hospitality but mock normal diplomatic practice and even violate the sovereignty of Lebanon. They appear to believe that their letters of accreditation give them authority to meddle in Lebanese affairs. Attachés, counsellors, intelligence officers and spies from the embassies then assume the same rights. These odd patterns of behaviour were first established by the ambassadors of the super-powers, but a diplomatic free-for-all soon followed. It made it extremely easy for those powers to play an active part in fomenting and fanning the flames of the civil war.

The Lebanese weaknesses, imperfections and faults contributed greatly to the war which transformed Lebanon from a beautiful showcase of efficient trade and attractive tourism into a monstrous human slaughterhouse. But Lebanese imperfections alone could not have led to the bloodbath in such a dramatic fashion. The situation could have been solved by a few skirmishes, even a short-lived civil war speedily ended by the usual Lebanese compromise, had it not been for two formidable underlying forces.

The first is Israel, with its expansionist desire to expand into Arab lands and its plans to fragment the Arab countries to protect its expansionist policy. To Israel, Lebanon seemed the easiest country to fragment. The second is oil, a commercial necessity at the root of modern civilization. Those who desire it and covet the power it brings, as well as those who already have it and abuse the power it has given them, are constantly engaged in catch-as-catch can.

Unluckily for Lebanon, it was ideally placed to serve the objectives of these two powerful forces. The West resented having to pay a realistic price for oil and were jealous that the Arabs had their hands on the fortunes it previously reserved for itself. It was determined to get the money back, the easiest way being to foment trouble in or near the countries which produce the oil — especially in the Third World — and then stand by to sell them all the arms needed to enable the dissension to go on. This process has been cynically called the recycling of petro-dollars. The Arab–Israeli conflict was encouraged and used for that purpose. What proof is needed beyond the terms of the Camp David Agreement between Egypt and Israel in 1978? Through the fiction of 'arms for peace', the United States promised the two countries $4,500 million in military grants and loans, and by contrast very little in economic aid.

The civil war in Lebanon provided an additional market for the arms trade, not only within its own confines but in Syria, Israel, Jordan and other Middle East countries further afield. But greed knows no limits, and the Arab–Israeli wars and events in Lebanon were not considered adequate stimulants for the arms bazaar. Therefore the endless Iraq–Iran war started, with arms vendors busily selling their wares to both sides. Before the war, Iraq had three arms suppliers, now it has eighteen. Iran used to have five, now it has seventeen. In all of this, the West and the Soviet Bloc co-operate.

The *Financial Times* in London, in December 1974, shortly before the flames of war were kindled in Lebanon, condemned what was happening and predicted what might happen further in the oil-rich Middle East. There could have been no truer judgement and no more accurate forecast where Lebanon was concerned:

There can be no more distasteful aspect of the contemporary world scene than the way in which the industrialized countries of the West and the Soviet Bloc are effectively collaborating to enable the Arab oil-producing countries to devote a sizeable part of their increased wealth to financing massive armament programmes. And it is surely high time that all advanced countries recognized that they have a collective duty to stop getting profit for themselves by providing the bullets for small countries – rich and poor – to fire at one another. It is a sombre fact that all the major armed conflicts since World War II have taken place in the Third World. No doubt the willingness of so many advanced countries to pour arms into this major theatre of war can be set down to their wish to ensure that their respective 'spheres of influence' are suitably supported and rewarded. But it is difficult to escape the impression that the current determination to reduce oil deficits by hook or by crook is playing a major part in seeing that the Middle East gets all the arms it needs to enable its dissensions to go on flourishing. Whatever the reasons, it is abundantly clear that, if the Middle East does go up in flames once again, it will be because the advanced countries have effectively 'willed' it to do so by furnishing it with the fuel to support another massive conflagration.

The United Nations, in its 1985 report on the world social situation, confirmed the *Financial Times*'s earlier premonition for the Middle East and further revealed that, since the end of the Second World War, about 150 armed conflicts, big and small, had killed about 16 million people, perhaps as many as 20 million, and that the majority of the dead and injured were mostly civilians from the developing countries, better known as the Third World. 'Implements for killing people in the Third World are the most lucrative of all commodities,' wrote the late Kamal Jumblatt in his book, *I Speak for Lebanon*.

The Stockholm International Peace Research Institute (SIPRI) published the following relevant statistics on military expenditure in its 1983 *World Armament and Disarmament Yearbook*:

> Total military expenditure in 1982 in the Middle East amounted to 53.3 billion US dollars of which over 43 billion was spent by the Arab countries. By contrast, the figures for 1974 were only 28.4 billion dollars. More significant were the sums spent by OPEC countries in 1982 which amounted to 52.9 billion dollars compared with only 9 billion dollars spent by non-oil developing countries. Among the biggest importers of weapons were the Middle East countries with Syria, Libya, Saudi Arabia and Israel at the top of the list.

Not content with the major role it played in stoking the fires of the civil war by supplying arms, ammunition, military training and expertise to the Maronites in Lebanon, Israel invaded Lebanon on 6 June 1982, naming its operation 'Peace for Galilee', or, as others in Israel called it, 'Litani II', 'Litani I' having been the invasion of Lebanon in 1978. The full account of the invasion of Lebanon has already filled several books, the most accurate and best documented being *Error and Betrayal in Lebanon* by George Ball, an Under-Secretary of State during the Kennedy and Johnson administrations. If I repeated less than half of what George Ball wrote, I would be accused of being anti-American and anti-Semitic, neither of which would be true. Here I will therefore only give a résumé of events that many Israelis themselves consider to be outrageous and inhuman.

When the invasion started, Israel announced that its aim was to drive the PLO beyond a line forty kilometres from its northern border, so 'that Israel would no longer be within PLO artillery range'. In actual fact, the Israeli Army pushed its way to Beirut, destroying everything in its path. When I read that Israel's Prime Minister, Menachem Begin, had declared that Israel did not 'covet one single square inch of Lebanese soil', I shuddered, remembering the words of Levi Eshkol, a previous Israeli Prime Minister, on the first day of the Israeli–Arab war in June 1967: 'Israel has no intention of annexing even one foot of Arab territory.' Nevertheless, within fifteen years of that declaration, Israel had annexed Arab Jerusalem, the Golan Heights and much of the West Bank, which remains on the verge of total annexation.

By October 1982, according to the *Guardian*, Begin was saying 'Arab lands will never be surrendered,' and so Israeli troops have continued to occupy south Lebanon. In March 1984, Prime Minister Yitzhak Shamir stated: 'Israeli troops are likely to stay in Lebanon for all time'; and, according to a report in the *Jerusalem Post* for 16 August 1986, Brigadier-General Tat-Aluf Danny Rothschild, Commander of the Israeli liaison unit in Lebanon, had declared there was 'no choice but to stay' in south Lebanon.

It was claimed that the invasion was sparked off by the attempted assassination of the Israeli Ambassador in London, but this was soon dropped even as a pretext, to be replaced by an allegation that the ceasefire of July 1981 between the Palestine Liberation Organization and Israel had been violated 150 times. Yet the British Foreign Secretary told the House of Commons on 9 June 1982, three days after the invasion, that there had been no attacks by the PLO across Israel's northern border between the ceasefire of July 1981 and May 1982 when the Israelis broke the ceasefire themselves and attacked Palestinian positions in Lebanon. This was confirmed from within Israel on 5 July 1982 by *Haeretz* publishing a letter from Ya'kov Guterman, the son of the Zionist Simha Guterman, who fell in the Warsaw ghetto rising, and the father of Raz, one of the first Israeli casualties in the attack on Beaufort Castle in south Lebanon. Ya'kov castigated the Begin government by writing: 'Cynically and shamelessly you declared the "Peace for Galilee" operation when not one shot had been fired across the northern frontier for a year.'

Israel's eminent historian, Professor Yehoshua Porath, has declared that the decision to invade Lebanon

resulted from the fact that the ceasefire had held . . . Yassir Arafat had succeeded in doing the impossible. He managed an indirect agreement, through American mediation, with Israel and even managed to keep it for a whole year . . . this was a disaster for Israel. If the PLO agreed upon and maintained a ceasefire they may in the future agree to a more far-reaching settlement and maintain that too.

The implication of Professor Porath's statement is that Lebanon was invaded, not because the PLO was attacking Israel and the Israelis, but, strangely enough, because it was not. It seems curious that Arafat's ability to maintain the ceasefire was considered a disaster for Israel, when that ceasefire meant the security of the northern borders so frequently claimed as Israel's main concern. And why should Israel fear that the PLO might, in the future, agree to maintain a more far-reaching settlement? Could it be that what Professor Porath means is a solution to the Palestine problem?

The trumped-up pretext that the 1982 invasion was necessary to safeguard the security of Israel's northern borders was used to camouflage a long-planned invasion, the real objective of which was later announced by Menachem Begin in the Knesset: 'To establish in Lebanon an independent and sovereign state friendly to Israel and to push the PLO out of Beirut.' Or was this perhaps a manifestation of Begin's 'divinely ordained war', as reported in *The Times* on 16 July 1982: 'More than five weeks after the Israeli forces launched their massive invasion, the resulting war has been officially described as being divinely ordained by Mr Begin. Until now, he has preferred to rely on the argument of self-defence to justify Israel's widely criticized tactics.'

There was nothing divine about the invasion of Lebanon. By 14 June, the Israeli Army had encircled Beirut and laid siege to its western sector where the PLO fighters were dug in. The siege was fierce and lasted until 12 August. Electricity and water were cut off. Food supplies were not allowed through and medical and other forms of aid were barred.

West Beirut was shelled and bombed to pieces, some 60,000 shells being fired into the city. Cluster bombs were used, each one of which could destroy an area the size of a football pitch, tearing to shreds any human being within range. The United States had first provided cluster bombs to Israel during the 1973 Yom Kippur War, but, because of their barbarously inhuman effects, their use was curtailed, not only by the law limiting American-supplied weapons to self-defence, but also by specific special restrictions. Israel had signed an agreement, pledging not to use these bombs unless attacked by two or more of the countries Israel fought in 1967 and 1973. Even then, cluster bombs were to be used only against fortified military targets and never 'against any areas where civilians were exposed'.

This last restriction was introduced when the American Central Intelligence Agency (CIA) reported that Israel violated the agreement when, in 1978, it 'saturated south Lebanon with United States cluster bombs — mainly against civilian refugee camps'. During the 1982 invasion of Lebanon, Israel used cluster bombs widely and indiscriminately against civilians. According to authentic American reports, Israel used nine types of cluster bombs in Lebanon in nineteen locations in

West Beirut as well as in fifty-one others throughout Lebanon. In the face of such indisputable evidence of wanton misuse, the United States suspended further supplies of cluster bombs to Israel, but only temporarily. President Reagan lifted the suspension during Prime Minister Shamir's visit to Washington in 1983 – not surprisingly since the Pentagon confirmed that the United States was itself using cluster bombs against Syrian positions in Lebanon.

Eventually, the PLO forces were evacuated on 21 August under the supervision of an International Peace Keeping Force made up of American marines and French and Italian troops. There was an undertaking that this force would also protect civilian Palestinians left behind after the departure of the PLO fighters. Israel, however, showed no real desire to destroy the PLO. The invasion only forced the PLO fighters in West Beirut to quit the city, leaving the rest of their forces in the mountains, in the Beqa' valley and in north Lebanon. Even before the PLO left West Beirut, Eric Silver reported in the *Guardian* of 30 June 1982 that 'Prime Minister Begin offered to let the Palestinian guerrillas leave Beirut with their personal weapons.' And so they did, to reappear shortly after in north Lebanon and the Beqa' valley. Before long, Arafat's PLO fighters were chased from the Beqa' valley and north Lebanon, not by Israel but by Palestinian dissidents. Israel, in fact, tried to prevent the PLO's departure.

The media all over the world reported fully on the invasion, its killing of tens of thousands of innocent people, the destruction of Tyre, Sidon, West Beirut and scores of Lebanese villages, the ruthless bombing and shelling, and the use of cluster bombs, phosphorous bombs, vacuum or suction bombs and other American-made instruments of destruction, probably being tested in Lebanon for their effective killing capacity. The world condemned the invasion, but in words only. The UN Security Council produced on 9 June 1982 a resolution condemning and threatening Israel with sanctions unless it agreed to a ceasefire and unconditional withdrawal from Lebanon. The United States vetoed the resolution as not being 'sufficiently balanced'. It emerged later that the invasion had had the United States' approval, or at least that of Reagan's Secretary of State, Alexander Haig.

At the outset, President Reagan was reported as being angered and outraged, but this did not stop him, according to the *International Herald Tribune* of 3 August 1982, sending birthday greetings to Menachem Begin on 2 August at the very time when Israel was conducting 'the heaviest Israeli shelling and bombing of the war'. Other Western heads of state, equally enraged, presumably sent no birthday greetings. The Soviet Union, apart from blaming the United States, made low-pitched noises of protest. The US Secretary of State, Alexander Haig, described the Soviet Union's attitude as 'encouragingly cautious'. Even in the Arab world, voices were muted. Perhaps there were secret hopes that at last they would be rid of the Palestinians and their problems, and that Israel would be blamed.

According to Lebanese government casualty figures, the human cost of the invasion at the end of August 1982 was 18,000 dead and 30,000 wounded, 90 per cent of whom were civilians. Beshir Gemayel, Israel's ally, during the seven years of Lebanese fighting which preceded the invasion, was elected on 23 August 1982 President of what was left of the Lebanese Republic. Only twenty-three days later, he was assassinated in a huge bomb explosion at the Phalangist party headquarters in East Beirut, before he had officially assumed his post as President. No one ever knew who was responsible for his murder.

During the years of civil war in Lebanon, only those who plan and execute assassinations really knew who has done them and why. Kamal Jumblatt, Beshir Gemayel, Riad Taha, Salim Lawzi, the CIA regional officers in the American Embassy car explosion, the American marines in their Beirut International Airport headquarters, the French soldiers and officers in theirs, are only some of the victims of mysterious assassinations. Hundreds of other lives have been terminated in the same way, and assassinations breed further assassinations. Two days after Beshir Gemayel's killing, the brutal massacres of the Sabra and Chatilla camps took place. The Peace Keeping Force, which was to guarantee the protection of civilian Palestinians after the departure of the PLO, had itself departed suddenly and inexplicably a few days before the massacre and before the end of its mandate. Nobody knew why, and no one asked the reason, but the slaughter of over 2,000 innocent civilians, including many women and children, sent waves of shock and revulsion throughout the world, especially in Israel itself.

The Israelis and their Phalangist allies at once accused each other of committing this atrocity. The world's official reaction was confined to verbal condemnation, but the Israeli people's extremely critical reaction compelled their government to appoint a Commission of Inquiry. When the true facts were revealed, the government was forced by Israeli public opinion to admit its responsibility for the massacres and take disciplinary measures it would have preferred to avoid. The resignation of Colonel Eli Geva because of the invasion, and that of the Energy Minister, Yitzhak Berman, because of the Israeli government's initial refusal to hold a public inquiry into the massacres, together with the

Israeli people's sincere reaction to the crime, should have given the Arabs some real hope that peace with the Israelis might be possible despite their Zionist hawks.

Beshir Gemayel was succeeded by his brother Amin, elected with universal Lebanese support. The Lebanese were fed up with the civil war, its fighting, killings and destruction, and hoped the new President and the much-publicized United States support would at last save them from their endless misery. The Peace Keeping Force was ordered to return to Beirut, and its reappearance gave the Lebanese hope and confidence that the mighty United States and its European allies, France, the United Kingdom and Italy, with their troops and an armada of more than forty warships off the shores of Lebanon, would surely put an end to the nightmare they had endured for seven long years.

American envoys, special and not so special, shuttled between the United States, Europe, the Middle East, and especially between Lebanon, Israel and Saudi Arabia. As a result, a tripartite treaty was hammered out and signed on 17 May 1983 by the United States, Israel and Lebanon. The treaty stipulated, among other things, the total withdrawal of Israeli troops from Lebanon, in return for which the Lebanese made many concessions. Nevertheless the United States and Israel, a few days after the signature of the treaty and apparently without Lebanon's knowledge, secretly signed an addendum that gave Israel the right to stay in Lebanon as long as Syrian troops remained on Lebanese soil. Since it was certain that Syria, who had been ignored in the negotiations, would reject the treaty and not withdraw its troops, the addendum not only abrogated the treaty but guaranteed American approval for Israel's continued occupation.

As anticipated, Syria rejected the treaty outright on the grounds that it threatened its national security and flatly refused to withdraw its peace-keeping troops, which had been in Lebanon since 1977 at the invitation of the Lebanese government and with the approval of the Arab countries. Syria called on its allies in Lebanon to support its position and promptly supplied them with the necessary arms and ammunition to intensify the fighting everywhere and convince the Lebanese government, the United States and Israel that Syria was an interested party to be reckoned with.

The Lebanese, aware of Syria's firm stand against the treaty, expected trouble from that quarter, but Lebanon was still relying on the special relationship between the United States and Israel to pressure the Israelis into withdrawing from Lebanon and to use American influence to give Lebanon and the Lebanese the long-awaited peace. They were unaware, as it emerged, that the United States had blundered into allowing Israel to continue its aggressive policies. The *New York Times* put it neatly when it commented: 'Our problem lies in those "Dear Menachem" letters that "your friend, Ron" kept sending. In Israeli politics they have been blank cheques, unwitting endorsements of the whole range of Begin policies.'

Faced with Syria's rejection of the treaty, its refusal to withdraw troops and the consequential internal fighting on many fronts, Lebanon postponed its ratification of the treaty and later revoked it altogether. Israel retaliated by provoking the mountain war between the Druzes and the Maronites. By supporting both sides, it fanned the flames of a fratricidal conflict which it alone controlled. But when Israel suddenly decided to pull back its troops to the Awali river, north of Sidon, the fighting blossomed into a full-scale war. In no time the Druzes had cleared and controlled the mountains.

Personally, I was able to derive hope and reassurance from the knowledge that, even as the Druzes and Maronites were locked in bitter battles only a few kilometres from the airport, within Middle East Airlines Druzes and Maronites still worked amicably side by side, seeing themselves not as members of rival factions, but as members of MEA — the same team, the same family. In the madhouse of Lebanon, MEA continued as a beacon of sanity and hope for a return to sense. The airline had, alone among the country's institutions, managed through the long civil war to preserve Lebanese unity by keeping factionism at bay and maintaining a true national character. In a country torn apart by its own folly, encouraged by the greed of outside forces conspiring to destroy it in a time of national disorder, MEA was unique in that it managed, against apparently impossible odds, to continue operating with remarkable reliability. I feel immensely proud of MEA and of my contribution to the collective effort of all who worked for it and made it what it is — the cedar tree airline which managed to defy and weather all turbulence.

Meanwhile the fighting and the war went on all over Lebanon, encouraged and provisioned by the supporters of the different factions and by the arms merchants who hoped the fighting might go on for ever. In the midst of it all, the International Peace Keeping Force, headed by the United States marines, with no clear definition of their role, dug in and became sitting ducks, to be killed and massacred in suicidal explosive attacks by fanatics whom nobody could identify with certainty.

The Lebanese feudal war lords agreed, under pressure, to meet for

273

reconciliation in Geneva in November 1983. The meeting was a farce, and whatever they seemed to have agreed on in Geneva they denounced as soon as they returned to Beirut. The killing and the destruction went on, and so did the meetings, the pressures, the declarations, the counter-declarations and the shuttles in search of support by all leaders of the fighting factions.

Then orders were given to the United States marines and the US naval ships to support the Lebanese Army. Intensive shelling of Lebanese Druze villages and civilians became a daily sport, and in this the Shi'ites were not spared. It was a grave mistake, for it transformed the Peace Keeping Force into yet another fighting faction in Lebanon after the United States had publicly pledged that its troops would fight back to protect themselves only if attacked. In the wake of the confusion about the objectives of the Peace Keeping Force and the resulting mess, the countries which had supplied the troops, led by the United States, decided to pull them out of Lebanon.

The Lebanese Army, as it had in 1976, then split apart, each sectarian part joining the respective fighting militias. It was impossible to persuade officers and soldiers to shoot and kill people from within their own communities. President Amin Gemayel therefore turned to Syria for help, and Syria responded with enthusiasm. A reconciliation conference was arranged in Lausanne, Switzerland, for March 1984.

The conference, after ten days of talking and arguing, ended, like the one in Geneva a year earlier, in failure, it being claimed that the war lords had disagreed on power sharing in the Lebanese government. Where the Mohammedans sought a revision of the National Covenant to guarantee a more equitable and effective sharing of power between them and the Christians, the Christians firmly opposed any such revision. Neither side could bring themselves to accept the truth that it is not important who wields power in Lebanon, but how that power is used, and to what ends. The question is not one of a revision of the National Covenant, or whether such a formal arrangement even exists. The truly important consideration is that power should be properly exercised to serve, not the interests of any one faction, but those of Lebanon and the Lebanese as a whole. By contrast, the great majority of Lebanese — those incredible, wonderful people who have stoically survived more than eleven years of a ruthlessly murderous civil war — will, if given the chance to speak freely, tell you they do not wish to see a return of the power sharing that authorized the Cairo Agreement, the acquisition of Fath Land in the south by the PLO, the butchering of Intra, the Reform Law, the intentional burial of Article 80 of the

274

Constitution and a widespread corruption in government administration. They do not want the kind of power that emasculated the Litani project, preventing its use for much-needed irrigation in Lebanon and badly needed water supplies in Beirut, and confining it to the minor role of producing seasonal and unreliable hydro-electricity. They do not want the kind of power which appoints unqualified co-religionist friends to posts of national importance, as has happened in the Central Bank, which controls the country's economy, ever since its creation.

But, in the last resort, it was not power sharing that scuttled the reconciliation attempts in Switzerland. That only provided an excuse. The fact is that the Lebanese have lost control over their own destiny. It is time for all the parties concerned to realize that there can be no peace in Lebanon unless Syria and Israel agree to it, with the approval and blessing of the United States and the Soviet Union. But does Israel really want peace? It has come to seem that its survival depends more and more on its continued war with its Arab neighbours than on making peace. For one thing, the huge subsidies essential for sustaining Israel's ambitious economy keep pouring in as long as that war is alive and active. For another, war is essential to unite the oddly heterogeneous population of Israel, consisting of more than twenty nationalities from different cultures and with different languages. It is said that Israel radio broadcasts in twelve languages besides Hebrew.

Of course, Israel continually talks of peace, its own kind of peace, which the Arabs cannot and will not accept since they are convinced that Israel's peace would mean denying the Palestinians their rights and be based on the fragmentation of the Arab nation into many satellites, dominated militarily, commercially and financially by Israel. In any case, Zionist expansionist plans for a Greater Israel are still far from being realized, and Israel shows not the slightest hesitation or weakening in its determination to implement those plans.

Israel's essential need for war, its unacceptable plans for peace, the greed of the arms manufacturers to sell their wares in the Middle East — the only region of the Third World which has ready cash to pay for arms purchases — and the deeply rooted illogical sectarianism of the Lebanese, all make the road to peace in Lebanon look still very long and agonizingly rough. Whatever happens, however, Lebanon can never be the same as it was. The golden days of the Land of Milk and Honey are gone for ever, to be replaced by a divided and mutilated country with possibly an 'Arab face'.

275

Appendix

From p. 168:
In the power struggle which engulfed Middle East Airlines–Airliban after the crash of Intra Bank in October 1966, Air France, which held 30 per cent of the shareholding, was unable to ensure for itself the control of the company (MEAL) which passed to the new Intra, which now belongs to the Credit Commodity Group of America.

From p. 264:
Only the truth will save us today. Only the truth will allow us to persevere and to keep our heads high. It is because we have taken the world lightly for forty years that the world is now taking us lightly. It is because we have lied to the world for forty years that now the world lies to us. It is because we have treated ourselves as of little account that the world now ignores us.

Index

278

Armenia, 26
Arnold and Porter, 235
Arslan family, 2
As-Safir, 244, 245
Asfour, Dr Hanna, 166
Association of Arab Tourist and Travel
    Agencies (AATTA), 221
Association of the Baalbeck
    International Festival, 8
Association of Intra Depositors, 156
Athenaeum Court Hotel, 49, 68
Athens, 56, 135, 173, 177, 191, 193,
    205, 235
El-Atrash, Sultan Pasha, 86–7
Austria, 260
Awali river, 273
Ayn Al-Rummaneh, 203–4, 207
Ayn Dara, 3

Baalbeck Festival, 116
Baalbeck studios, 144
Baaqline, 6–7, 8
Baathism, 258
Baghdad, 39, 56, 173, 187, 188
Bahamas, 141
Bahrain, 211
Balfour, Arthur, 21–2
Balfour Declaration, 21–3, 73
Ball, George, 267
Bank of America, 137
Banque de France, 159
Banque d'Indochine, 180
Banque de Syrie et du Liban, 135–6,
    147
Banque Sabbagh, 180–1
Barclay's Bank, 90, 140
Bath, 29
Beaufort Castle, 185, 268
Bedas, Yousif, 52, 130, 243; helps
    MEA buy out BOAC shareholding,
    66–7, 72, 73, 75; and MEA's
    purchase of Comets, 69; and MEA's
    merger with Air Liban, 86, 90; and
    the destruction of Intra Bank, 135–
    40, 145–62, 163–4; background,
    140–1; Lebanonization plan, 142–5
Bedouins, 16, 25, 26
Begin, Menachem, 257, 267, 268, 269,

270, 273
Beirut: air services, 39; 1958 civil war,
    59; Palestinian resistance movement
    in, 198; origins of civil war, 202; in
    civil war, 208; protection money,
    232; Israeli siege, 267, 269–70; PLO
    evacuation, 270; Peace Keeping Force
    in, 272
Beirut International Airport, 31, 198,
    229; *hajjis*, 46; MEA buys land at,
    57; Israeli raid on, 171–8, 191, 235;
    Israeli threat to, 188; in civil war,
    204–5, 207–8, 209–10, 212, 218–
    19, 232; TWA hijack, 235
Beit-Eddine, palace of, 7
Belgium, 190
Bell, Robert, 41, 53
Benghazi, 190
Beqa' valley, 260, 270
Berman, Yitzhak, 271
Bern, 192
Bkerke, 221
Black Forest, 105
Black September Organization, 194–5
Blake, Norman, 40, 45–6
BOAC, 130, 164, 250; and formation
    of MEA, 37–8, 39; majority interest
    in MEA, 49, 50–3, 55–9, 61; ends
    partnership with MEA, 61–3, 65–75,
    77–80; MEA repays loans, 95; sells
    Viscounts to MEA, 243
Board of Development and
    Reconstruction, 253
'Boeing Affair', 237–54
Boeing Company, 230–5, 237–54
Boeing 320Cs, 172, 243–4
Boeing 707s, 129, 173, 190, 211
Boeing 720Bs, 173, 205–6, 208
Boeing 747s, 210, 211, 227, 232–3,
    234, 237–9, 241–2, 244, 254
Boeing 767s, 251, 252–3, 254
Bolsheviks, 15
Bombay, 191
Bourj el-Barajneh, 10
Boutros, Fouad, 166
Brake, Sir Francis, 49, 51, 53, 65
Brazil, 141
Brezhnev, Leonid, 257

279

Britain, 105; Sykes-Picot agreement, 15–16; NA at Exeter University, 17–18; Round Table Conference on Palestine, 18–23; and establishment of Jewish National Home, 22; MEA service to, 57–8; Suez crisis, 59; support for King Hussein, 60; television concession in Lebanon, 120–1; aircraft sales to MEA, 129–30; Intra Bank investments in, 141; Palestinians hijack aircraft over, 191; reactions to Palestinian hijacks, 192; refusal to help MEA during civil war, 210, 212–13; anti-Arab feelings, 213–16; oil price rises, 213–15; and the Lebanese civil war, 258, 272; and Lebanon's autonomy, 260; and the Israeli invasion of Lebanon, 268

British Air Registration Board, 111

British Aircraft Corporation (BAC), Super VC-10, 129–30

British Airways, 210, 212–13

British Army, 31

British Associated Companies Ltd (BOAC-AC), 61–3, 65–6, 69–71

British Council, 17

British European Airways, 172

British Leyland, 214

Cairo, 39, 56, 81, 97, 191, 193, 197

Cairo Agreement, 185, 274

Cambridge University, 105

Camp David Agreement (1978), 194, 265

Canada, 100, 141

Canadian Air Line Pilots Association (CALPA), 189

Caravelles, 88, 91–5, 172, 173, 176–7, 243

Casino du Liban, 144

Catholic Church, 261

'Cedarjet Hotel', 205, 207

Central Bank of Lebanon, 121, 135–8, 146–7, 153, 154, 158, 226, 275

Central Intelligence Agency (CIA), 134, 269, 271

Chamberlain, Neville, 20

Chamoun, Camille, 36, 37, 59, 60,

115, 203, 219

Charles de Gaulle Airport, Paris, 209

Chase Manhattan, 145

Chatilla camp, 192, 271

Chehab (radio operator), 43

Chehab, Madame Farid, 259

Chehab, General Fouad, 87–94, 116, 143, 179, 218, 226

Chicago Conference (1944), 37, 61

Chobanian, Aprine, 102

Chouf Artisanat, 116

Christians, 203, 204, 250, 274; see also Maronite Christians

La Ciotat, 153

Civil Aviation Department, 57, 109, 111–12, 179, 182

Colonial Office (Britain), 18–19

Comet 4Cs, 69–70, 71, 72, 73–4, 172, 173, 243

Commercial Code, 154, 168

Commodity Credit Corporation (CCC), 159, 160, 169

communism, 131–2, 133–4

Compagnie Générale de Transport (CGT), 38–9

Concorde, 95

Congressional Record, 134

Constitution, 153, 157, 160, 168, 262, 263, 275

Contracting and Trading Company (CAT), 73

Convair Coronados, 180, 181

Cooper Brothers, 149–53, 155–6, 160, 161

Copeland, Miles, 134

Coronados, 172

Council for the Advancement of Arab-British Understanding, 192

Council for External Trade, 117

Council of Ministers, 119, 124–5, 127, 147, 148, 153, 180, 182, 245

Court of Appeal, 10, 155

Cox, Sir Henry, 17, 26

Crédit-Suisse, 159

Cribbett, Sir George, 37, 59, 61–3, 66, 70

Cribbett–Alamuddin agreement, 69

Crusaders, 3

Cunard, 49
Cyprus, 135, 188, 190, 198, 205, 211
Cyprus Airways, 219

Dagher, Pierre, 160, 164–5
Dahdah, Dr Lucien, 226, 249–50
Daily Express, 174
Daily Mail, 174, 189
Daily Telegraph, 9
d'Albiac, Air Marshal Sir John, 58
Damascus, 81, 205
Damour, 188
Darwish, Abdallah, 152
Darwish, Jasim, 152
Dawson, Air Chief Marshal Sir Walter, 190
Dawson's Field, 190, 191, 192–3, 194, 196, 212–13
Dayan, General Moshe, 172, 188, 190
Dayr Al-Qammar, 7
De Gaulle, General, 88, 94, 159
De Havillands, 69–70, 73–4
'Deal of the Century', 228, 236–54
Dennett, Dan, 17
Department of Civil Aviation (Jordan), 82
Department of Justice (US), 235, 254
Department of Posts, Telegraphs and Telephones (Syria), 31
Department of Trade (Britain), 206–7
d'Erlanger, Sir Gerard, 59, 67–8, 70
Desert Force, 26
Deuxième Bureau, 118, 202
Dhahran, 56, 111–12, 173
Diab, Aboudi, 28, 29
Diab, Karim, 28, 29
Diab, Salim, 28
Djebel Druze, 86–7
Doha, 81
Dorchester Hotel, London, 213
Douglas, 251
Douglas Aircraft Corporation, 167
Douglas DC-4, 172
Douglas DC-6, 172
Douglas DC-7, 172
Douglas DC-8, 129, 130, 167
Druze Supreme Council, 115
Druzes, 122, 123; divisions, 1–2;

history, 1–5; beliefs, 4, 5–7; persecution, 4–5; position of women, 9–10; fatalism, 106; employed by MEA, 132–3; wars against Maronites, 259–60; sectarian representation, 261, 262; mountain war, 273; in civil war, 273, 274
Dubai, 211
Dubois, Madame Charles, 259

Eddé, Raymond, 264
Egypt, 189, 193, 256, 265
Egyptair, 233
El-Al, 177, 190–1, 197
Elazar, David, 190
Empress of the Skies, 49–50
Eshkol, Levi, 267
Essely, Colonel Cyril, 201
Essex, 191
Ethiopian Airlines, 173
Europe, and the Lebanese civil war, 257, 258, 272
European Airbus, 236–7, 251–3, 254
European Travel Writers Union, 221
Exeter University, 17
Eximbank (US Export–Import Bank), 167, 227–8, 235, 236–7, 254
L'Express, 214

Fadel, Mounir Abu, 141
Fahoum, Badr, 141, 153
Faisal, King of Iraq, 15, 59, 152
Faisal, King of Saudi Arabia, 19, 21, 194, 197
Fakhruddin II, Emir, 1, 3, 7, 10
Far East, 211
Farah, Samir, 105–6
Faris, Laila, 28
Faris, Dr Nabih, 28
Farouk, King of Egypt, 20–1
Fath land, 185, 274
Federal Bureau of Investigation (FBI), 191
Federal Trade Commission (US), 254
Federation of Lebanese Trade Unions, 245
El-Feyez, Mithqal, 25
Field Aircraft Services, 57

Iberia, 233
Ike, 245
Imperial Chemical Industries (ICI),
145, 214
Institute of Air Transport (ITA), 91–2
Intercontinental Hotel, Amman, 192–3
International Air Transport Association
(IATA), 38, 56, 63, 97–100, 102,
112, 189, 191–2
International Bank for Reconstruction
and Development, 116
International Civil Aviation Conference,
37
International Civil Aviation
Organization (ICAO), 101–2, 111,
189
International Conference on Land
Tenure and Related Problems in
World Agriculture (1951), 31–4
International Herald Tribune, 270
International Peace Keeping Force, 270,
271, 272, 273–4
International Red Cross, 191–2
International Telephone and Telegraph
Corporation (ITT), 31, 49
International Traders, 140–1
Intra Bank, 28, 52, 130, 200;
formation of, 141; support for Masco,
61; buys shares in MEA, 67–8, 69,
73; and the merger of Air Liban and
MEA, 89–94; destruction of, 135–
40, 145–62, 163–9, 245–6, 274;
Arab shareholders, 141–2; Bedas's
Lebanonization plan, 142–5; NA
buys shares in, 163–4
Intra Investment Company, 140;
formation of, 161, 164–5; and MEA's
civil war contingency plans, 200; and
NA's resignation, 222; Mouharram's
disagreements with Asad, 226–7; and
the 'Boeing Affair', 238–40, 244,
246, 247
Iran, 45, 233, 266
Iraq, 26, 50, 59–60, 192, 193, 266
Iraq Petroleum Corporation, 59
Iraqi Airways, 188
Iskandar, Marwan, 161
Israel: Suez crisis, 59; rumours about

Bedas, 143–4; Arab–Israeli wars,
145; raid on Beirut airport, 171–8,
191, 235; El-Al aircraft attacked in
Athens, 177, 191; invasion of
Lebanon, 185, 267–71; intercepts
MEA aircraft, 188–9; MEA aircraft
hijacked to, 190; reactions to
Palestinian hijacks, 192, 193;
Palestinian guerrilla campaign
against, 194; hostages taken at
Olympic Games, 194–5; raids
Palestinian refugee camps in Lebanon,
195; Johannesburg consulate
attacked, 196; Yom Kippur War,
201–2, 256, 269; and the Lebanese
civil war, 257–8, 265–6, 272–3,
275; Camp David Agreement, 265;
use of cluster bombs, 269–70; and the
massacre in the refugee camps, 271–2
Israeli Air Force, 188, 189, 195
Israeli Army, 193, 267, 269
Israeli Pilots Association, 189
Italy, 56–7, 260, 270, 272

Jabal-ad-Duruz, 1
Jalloul, Mohammed, 10
Japan, 100
Jeddah, 47, 81, 211
Jerusalem, 81, 258, 268
Jerusalem Post, 268
Jews, Balfour Declaration, 21–3
Johannesburg, 196
John Paul II, Pope, 73
Johnson, Lyndon B., 130
Jordan, 50, 59, 86, 141; coup foiled,
59–60; MEA operations in, 80–3;
Palestinian hijack threats to MEA,
185, 186–8; Palestinians hijack
aircraft to, 190, 192–4, 196–7;
expels Palestinians, 193, 194, 256;
and the Lebanese civil war, 266; *see
also* Transjordan
Jordan Airways, 81–3
Jordanian Army, 192, 193, 194
Jounieh, 258
Juhhal (the Ignorant), 5
Jumblatt, Kamal, 2, 137, 267; invites
NA to join list of parliamentary

283

candidates, 3; and the beginning of the civil war, 59; friendship with NA, 131, 132; and the destruction of Intra Bank, 147, 166; formation of National Movement, 202; and the Boeing Affair, 249; attempts to stop government corruption, 264; assassination, 133, 271

Jumblatt, Walid, 2

Jumblatt family, 2, 132

Jumblatti Druzes, 2

Karachi, 206

Karam, Milhem, 118

Karami, Rashid, 117, 203

Kassis, General Charbel, 208

Kawas, Captain Adel, 190

Keesing's Contemporary Archives, 197

Kfar Faqoud, 220

KGB, 134

Khaled, Leila, 187, 191, 197

Khan, Kamal, 167

Khoury, Abdallah, 73, 75, 112, 164

El-Khoury, Sheikh Bishara, 34–5, 36

Khoury, Nadia, 112–13, 165

El-Khrisha, Haditha, 25

Kidder Peabody, 159

Kisrwan, 260

Kissinger, Henry, 202

Kitchen, Miss, 6–7

Korea, 197, 233

Kuenzler, 'Papa and Mama', 26

Kuwait, 50, 81, 141, 159, 160–1, 173, 205, 233

Kuwaiti Investment Company, 160–1

Labour Party (Britain), 66

Lahoud, Salim, 115

Laker Airways, 172

Lamartine, A.M.L. de, 259

Larnaca, 219

Lausanne, 274

Lawzi, Salim, 271

Lebanese Air Force, 43

Lebanese Army, 88, 202; and Israeli raids on Lebanon, 172, 177–8; clashes with Palestinians, 194, 198, 230, 256; in civil war, 203, 208; sectarian

split, 274; American support for, 274

Lebanese Bankers Association, 148

Lebanese International Airways (LIA), 83, 91, 163, 166, 167, 172, 178, 180–2, 218

Lebanese Penal Code, 43

Lebanese Press Syndicate, 246

Lebanese Stock Exchange, 28

Lebanon: French occupation, 261–2, 263; Round Table Conference on Palestine, 19; and the Balfour Declaration, 22; land-tenure problems, 32–3; American aid programme, 33–4; Saeb Salaam's government, 35–6; growth of civil aviation, 36–9; 1958 civil war, 59–61; tourism, 116, 121–2; mass media, 120–1; National Covenant, 122, 142, 203, 262, 264, 274; sectarian discrimination, 122–3, 125; Reform Law, 124–6, 129, 274; Constitution, 125, 153, 157, 160, 168, 262, 263, 275; destruction of Intra Bank, 135–40, 145–62; Bedas's Lebanonization plan, 142–5; Israeli raid on Beirut airport, 171–8, 191; lack of civil aviation policy, 179–80; Cairo Agreement, 185; Israeli invasion, 185, 267–71; and the Israeli interception of MEA aircraft, 188–9; Palestinian resistance movement, 194, 197–9, 202, 256; Israeli raids on refugee camps in, 195, 271–2; origins of civil war, 199–203, 259–65; civil war, 203–5, 207–12, 250, 255–9, 265–75; favouritism and nepotism, 221–2; weaponry used in civil war, 256–7, 258–9; autonomy granted, 260–1; sectarian representation, 261, 262

Liban Air, 207–8

Liberia, 141

Libya, 46, 189, 190, 195

Lichtenstein, 231

'Litani II', 267

Litani project, 275

Litani River, 115–16, 185

Lloyd's, 102, 111, 174

Lockheed, 251
Loedel, Liselotte, 103
London, 18–23, 57–8, 129, 141, 149, 173, 174, 191, 205, 210, 213, 217
Londonderry Hotel, London, 149, 150–1
Lucerne, 162
Ludwig, Daniel, 163, 166
Lufthansa, 166, 195
Lydda Airport, 190

Ma'ans, 7
McCrindle, Robert, 37
MacDonald, Malcolm, 18–21, 23
MacMahon, Sir Henry, 21, 23
McMillan, Eric, 148–9
Madison, Wisconsin, 31–2
Mallat, Wajdi, 125
Maronite Christians, 7, 106, 122, 123, 230; sectarian representation, 203, 261, 262; French support for, 258; wars against Druzes, 259–60; and the creation of Greater Lebanon, 261–2; mountain war, 273
Martínez, Maria (Leila Khaled), 191
Marxism, 131–2
Masco *see* Mideast Aircraft Service Company
Mecca, 46, 81, 222
Méhouchi, Patriarch Pierre-Paul, 221
Meir, Golda, 189
Mekawi, Jamil, 56
Mercadal, Professor Barthélémy, 248–9
Mhanna, Michel Georges, 208
Middle East Airlines (MEA): formation of, 36–9; NA becomes general manager, 35–6, 40–4; expansion, 39, 55, 56–7, 105, 129–30, 135; NA's programme for, 42–3; strike, 43–4; deteriorating relations with Pan-Am, 45–6, 48–53, Hajj crisis, 46–8; BOAC takes majority interest in, 49, 50–3; Viscounts, 55, 56–7, 72, 73–4; association with BOAC, 55–9, 61; Salaam-Hoss quarrel, 39–41, 49, 53–4, 58–9; NA becomes chairman, 59; during the 1958 civil war, 60–1, 62; ends partnership with BOAC, 61–3,

65–75, 77–80; Intra Bank buys shares in, 67–8, 69, 73; buys Comet 4Cs, 69–70, 71, 72, 73–4; buys Masco, 74; independence, 77–80; Jordanian operations, 80–3; merger with Air Liban, 86–95; employees' religions, 88–9; and IATA, 100; Ankara crash, 101–3; commercial pool agreements, 107; engineering department, 107–8; training-centre, 108; hostesses, 108–9; pilots, 109–11; Dhahran crash, 111–12; tourist publicity, 116; coffee drinking forbidden, 118–19; social revolution, 130–2; Druze guards, 132–3; and the destruction of Intra Bank, 140, 161, 163–9; and the Israeli raid on Beirut airport, 171–8; takes over LIA, 181–2; Palestinian hijack threats, 185–8; Israel intercepts aircraft, 188–9; aircraft hijacked to Israel, 190; airbridge to Saudi Arabia, 199; contingency plans, 200–1, 203; Yom Kippur War, 201–2; in civil war, 204–5, 207–12, 232, 250; aircraft bombed over Saudi Arabia, 206–7; leasing and chartering activities, 211–12, 232; recovers from civil war, 217; NA retires from, 217–28; Sarkis proposes separate Christian airport, 218–19; Mouharram's disagreements with Asad, 226–7; Eximbank loan, 227–8, 235, 236–7; *caisse noire*, 229–33, 238, 240, 242, 247–9, 253; 'Boeing Affair', 230–54; campaign against Asad Nasr, 237; inermediaries, 243–4; considers buying Airbus A310s, 251–3, 254
Middle East Airlines – Air Liban, 95
Middle East Institution, 133–4
Mideast Aircraft Service Company (Masco), 53, 55, 56, 57, 61, 62–3, 68, 74, 250
Mitaki, Captain Zouheir, 208
Military Air Transport Services (MATS), 46–8
Ministry of Agriculture, 33
Ministry of Aircraft Production, 38

Palestine, 18–23, 143–4
Palestine Liberation Army, 209
Palestine Liberation Organization
(PLO), 274; Cairo Agreement, 185;
and the hijack threats to MEA, 187;
and the PFLP hijacks, 192; and the
Israeli invasion of Lebanon, 267,
268–9; evacuation from Beirut, 270
'Palestine Revolution', 185–7
Palestinians: attack El-Al aircraft in
Athens, 177, 191; hijack threats to
MEA, 185–8; hijack aircraft, 190–4,
196–7; guerrilla campaign against
Israel, 194, 202; Israeli raids on
refugee camps in Lebanon, 195;
resistance movement in Lebanon,
197–9, 256; in Lebanese civil war,
203–4, 257–8; and the Israeli
invasion of Lebanon, 267–71
Palmyra, 1
Pan-Am, 35, 172, 250, 254;
involvement in MEA, 39, 40, 41;
deteriorating relations with MEA,
45–6, 48–53; insurance claims, 174;
aircraft hijacked, 191, 197
Paris, 86–7, 135, 136, 141, 173, 198,
209, 210–11
Parker, Paul, 137, 139
Parliament, 124, 125, 153–5, 262–3
Paul VI, Pope, 221
Payne Field, 39
'Peace for Galilee', 267, 268
Peace Keeping Force, 270, 271, 272,
273–4
Pentagon, 270
Penzel, Horst, 41
Pérol, Gilbert, 238, 241–2, 247
Perth, 110
Phalangists, 203, 271
Picot, François, 15
Piquet, Jules, 159
Point-Four Aid Programme, 33–4, 115
Popular Front for the Liberation of
Palestine (PFLP), 188, 191–4, 197
Porath, Professor Yehoshua, 268–9
Port Authority, 115
Port Company, 143
Price Waterhouse, 148–9, 153, 158

Protein Company, 203
Protter, David, 196
Prussia, 260
Punch, 213
Putna, Jonas, 208

Qatar, 141, 152, 159, 160
Qaysi Druzes, 1–2, 3
Qaysouma, 206
Queen Elizabeth, 49, 50

Rababy, Sami, 80
Rabbath, Dr Edmond, 249
Radio Orient, 143
Ramat David military airport, 188
Reading University, 28
Reagan, Ronald, 2, 235, 257, 270, 273
Reform Law, 124–6, 129, 274
Resora, 231, 238, 246
Révue Trimestrielle de Droit Commercial,
168–9
Rolls-Royce, 31
Rome, 56–7, 141, 149, 152, 155, 222,
235
Rothschild, Lord 21–2
Rothschild, Brigadier-General Tat-Aluf
Danny, 268
Round Table Conference on Palestine
(1939), 18–23
Royal Air Maroc, 233
Royal Armament Research and
Development Establishment
(Britain), 207
Royal Navy, 260
Rush, Colonel, 47
Russia (Tsarist) 22, 260; *see also* Soviet
Union

Sa'ad, Charles, 31
Al-Sabah family, 141
Sabena, 233
Sabra camp, 192, 271
Sa'd, Colonel Antoine, 88
Sa'd, Charles, 182
Sa'd, Marouf, 203
Sa'd, Victor, 182
Sadat, Anwar, 194
Sadiq, Pierre, 218